CAESAR'S GALLIC WAR

GAUL

UNELLI

LEX

ESUVII

AU
EB

CURIOSOLITES

OSISMI

AULERCI
GENOMAN

REDONES

VENETI

G A L

NAMNETES

ANDES

LI

PICTONES

C E

SANTONI

Garumna

NI

AQUI-

SONTIATES

Sos

Tou

TANI

PYRENA

B.V. Darbishire, Oxford, 1910.

SCALE 100   50   0

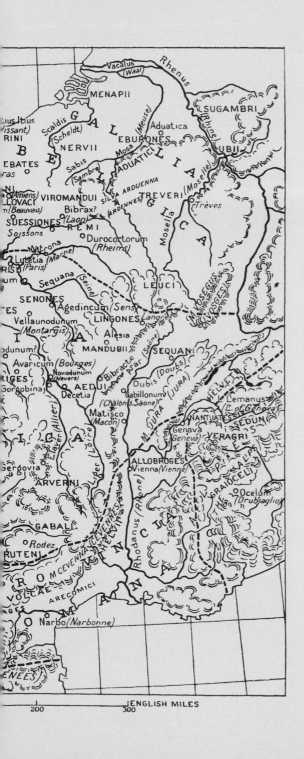

CAESAR'S GALLIC WAR

JULIUS CAESAR

TRANSLATED BY F. P. LONG

1828 Press

**1828
Press**

A Baker & Taylor Business
2810 Coliseum Centre Drive
Suite 300
Charlotte, NC 28217

ISBN: 978-1-970184-19-8

Typeset by: Flipside Digital Content Company
Cover design: Samantha A. Meyer
Printed at: Baker & Taylor Publishing Services, Ashland, Ohio

Contents

BOOK V

BOOK VI

BOOK VII

LIST OF MAPS

TRANSLATOR'S NOTE

APART FROM A FEW PASSAGES, MARKED IN THE NOTES, THE TEXT HERE
followed is Du Pontet's (*Oxford Classical Texts*). In dealing with
ancient geographical terms, my plan has been to give the modern
equivalent, where that exists, or the town or district that forms the
best representative.

To Mr. H. J. Cunningham, Fellow of Worcester College, and other
friends who have kindly helped me in the translation, I gratefully
accord my thanks.

F. P. L.

BOOK I

SECTION I. THE HELVETIAN WAR

THE COUNTRY KNOWN COLLECTIVELY AS GAUL PRESENTS IN REALITY THREE distinct divisions, inhabited respectively by the Belgae, the Aquitani, and a race which, though commonly described by us as Gauls, is known in the vernacular as Celts. Between these three divisions there exist fundamental differences both of language, customs, and political organization. Geographically, the Gauls lie midway between the Aquitani and Belgae, the respective boundaries being the Garumna (*Garonne*) in the south, and the Matrona (*Marne*) and Sequana (*Seine*) in the north. Of the three the Belgae are conspicuously the bravest race, a fact doubtless derived from the peculiarity of their position, which not only keeps them strangers to the civilization and refinement so characteristic of the Province (*Provence*), and protects them against traders and all their attendant evils, but brings them also into closest contact with the Germans beyond the Rhine, between whom and themselves there exists perpetual war. The same cause, it may be noted in passing, produces in the Helvetii those striking martial qualities in which they so far excel all the other Gauls; there being scarcely a day that does not witness some border skirmish with their German neighbors, either in repelling a raid upon themselves, or in making reprisals across the frontier. The middle section of the country, inhabited, as already stated, by the Gauls, begins from the Rhone, and from there extends to the Garonne, the

Outer Ocean, and the Belgae; while on its eastern border, at the territories of the Sequani and Helvetii, it marches with the Rhine. The general trend of the country is northwards. The Belgic division starts from the frontier of the Gauls, and from there stretches to the lower reaches of the Rhine, the country therefore facing north and east; while the Aquitani fill up all the region between the Garonne, the line of the Pyrenees, and the bend of the Bay of Biscay, fronting accordingly northwestward.

Among the Helvetii at the time our narrative opens the most conspicuous figure, both as regards wealth and family descent, was a chieftain named Orgetorix. Three years earlier, in the consulship of M. Messalla and M. Pupius Piso, his restless craving for absolute power had led him to inaugurate a secret movement among the ruling chiefs, by which he persuaded the government to undertake a national migration from their present homes, having as its object (what, according to him, would be an easy result of their military supremacy), the ultimate domination of all Gaul. Such a proposal won the more ready acceptance, from the natural obstacles to expansion by which the Helvetii on all sides found themselves surrounded. Along their northern and eastern frontiers the Rhine forms a barrier which by its formidable depth and width effectually bars all outlet toward the Germans; westward the lofty range of the Jura blocks the way to the Sequani; southward the lake of Geneva and the Rhone cut off all access to the Province (*Provence*). The effect of these obstacles was seriously to impede their freedom of movement, as well as greatly to diminish the opportunities for border warfare; two restrictions which, to a people of born fighters, were peculiarly distasteful. And further, there was the constant feeling among them that their present limited area, embracing as it did no more than 240 miles in length and 180 in breadth, was neither adequate to their dense population, nor worthy of their great military name and fame.

To these predisposing causes for action the appeal of Orgetorix added the required occasion, and the Helvetian authorities at once decided to make the necessary preparations for a general exodus.

Sumpter beasts and wagons were to be bought up wherever procur-
able, all the land possible was to be laid down with corn, in order to
guarantee supplies upon the road, peace and friendship were to be
secured with all neighboring states. For these several measures two
years were deemed to be sufficient; the third, by a solemn resolution
of the tribe, was fixed for the departure. The general supervision of
affairs was entrusted to Orgetorix, and he accordingly undertook as
his special duty the mission to foreign states. The first to be visited
were the Sequani; where, entering into communication with a chief
named Casticus, a son of that Catamantaloedis, who during his long
reign over his people had been honored by the Senate with the coveted title of "Friend of Rome," he urged him to seize upon the scepter
so lately wielded by his father. Proceeding next to the Aedui, he made
similar proposals to a prince called Dumnorix, commending his suit
by bestowing upon him the hand of his daughter in marriage. He was
to rise against his own brother Divitiacus, at that time the acknowledged ruler of the Aeduan country and the trusted representative of
the people. In the case of each, success was to be guaranteed by the
approaching accession of himself to sovereign power at home: and
the military preeminence of the Helvetii being unquestioned throughout Gaul, they were bidden to look to him for the acquisition of their
crown, through the civil and military resources that would then be
his. These allurements succeeded in their aim, and the three conspirators, having pledged one another to mutual loyalty, looked forward,
when once established on their thrones, to climbing, through a coalition of the three most powerful and resolute tribes in the country, to
the consolidated empire of a united Gaul.

But their secret was ill kept: their plot was betrayed, and fully
reported to the Helvetian authorities. In accordance with tribal usage
Orgetorix was summoned to stand his trial in chains; conviction was
to be followed by being publicly burned at the stake. On the appointed
day the accused surrendered to his judges; but he came at the head of
ten thousand serfs, who had been specially drafted from his wide
estates, and with countless numbers of retainers and poor debtors
also impressed for the occasion, and, thus surrounded, successfully

defied the court. Justly incensed at so gross an outrage, the Helvetian authorities prepared to uphold the civil arm by an appeal to the sword; and steps had already been taken to call out the tribal levies, when suddenly Orgetorix died; nor is there wanting the suspicion, strongly held by the Helvetii, that his death was self-inflicted.

It was not, however, allowed to affect their decision as to migration. When to the best of their judgment every arrangement had been perfected, under a strong impulse to take an irrevocable step that should more easily reconcile them to whatever dangers fortune might have in store, they deliberately burned down every one of their twelve fortified towns, four hundred open villages, and every private residence throughout the land. At the same time all stocks of corn not destined to be carried with them on the march were indiscriminately committed to the flames; the only provisions permitted to remain being three months' supplies of ground grain for each head of the population. Three of their nearest neighbors, the Rauraci, Tulingi, and Latovici, were also induced to follow their example of burning their towns and villages, and to throw in their lot with the migratory movement; while another people, the Boii, whose home had been formerly beyond the Rhine, but who had since invaded Norican territory and there laid siege to Noreia (*Neumarkt* in *Styria*), were invited to join them and received into close alliance.

Two routes, and two only, presented themselves as practicable for their purpose. They might either pass through the country of the Sequani, by a narrow and difficult defile running between Mount Jura and the Rhone;—so narrow that even a single line of carts could hardly pass, and so completely dominated by the frowning heights, that even a slender force could easily bar it in their face—or they might go through the Roman Province, a far easier and less complicated route, where, just across the upper Rhone, which here forms the boundary, lay the friendly district of the Allobroges.[1] This people had been only lately reduced to obedience, and numerous

---

[1] *Savoy:* capital *Vienne.* Conquered as early as 121 BC (see 1–45), but quelled after an insurrection in 61.

fords were also available in their country. The actual point of contact of the two tribes is the city of Geneva, which lies at the easternmost end of the Allobroges, and communicates by a bridge with the Helvetii on the opposite side. Either then, they argued, they would peacefully persuade the Allobroges, who hardly yet seemed reconciled to Roman rule, to grant them a passage through their borders, or else they would compel them by armed force. Everything being ready for the start, a date was fixed on which the entire nation was to assemble along the northern bank of the Rhone; this date being the twenty-eighth of March, in the consulship of Lucius Piso and Aulus Gabinius (58 BC).

The news that the Helvetii were contemplating a movement across the Province reached Caesar while still in Rome. Upon its receipt, he hastily quitted the capital, and traveling through post-haste to Further Gaul, quickly reached Geneva. Arrived here, he issued orders to raise the military forces of the Province to their utmost limit (the whole of Further Gaul, it should be mentioned, was at the time garrisoned by a single legion only), and to cut down the bridge at Geneva. His arrival had not escaped the notice of the Helvetian leaders, and a deputation of their chief notables, headed by the two chiefs Nammeius and Verucloetius, presently appeared to lay their case before the Roman governor. These informed him that their sole intention was to march through the Province without causing any disturbance of the peace, and only for the reason that no other route lay open to them, and that for this they humbly solicited his leave. In considering his answer, Caesar found it impossible to forget that these same Helvetii had not so many years before[2] first routed a Roman army and afterward forced it under the yoke, while causing the death also of its commander, the consul Lucius Cassius. This fact alone precluded a favorable reply; but apart altogether from this, it was difficult to believe that a people, who harbored no very friendly feelings toward Rome, would repress their natural instincts of plunder and pillage, if once allowed the chance of marching through the

[2] 107 BC.

Province. On the other hand, it was essential to temporize till the concentration of the new levies was completed; and he therefore replied to the envoys that he should require to think over the matter, and that if they had anything further to urge they might return on April 13.

Meanwhile he proceeded to strengthen his own defenses. The distance between the western end of Lake Geneva, where it passes into the Rhone, and a point lower down the stream where the Jura range (the barrier between the Helvetian and Sequanian lands) descends upon the river, is between eighteen and nineteen miles. Along this stretch of water he constructed, with the single legion of his original command and the various drafts since arrived from the Province, a fortified embankment, sixteen feet high, protected by a ditch, which when completed was strengthened by a line of forts garrisoned by detachments. These measures, he hoped, would successfully frustrate any attempt on the part of the enemy to force a passage against his will. The Helvetian envoys, on the day appointed, again presented themselves in camp. Here they were plainly told that the settled policy of the Roman government was never to allow anyone a passage through its southern Province, and any attempt at violence on their side would be instantly resisted. Disappointed in this expectation, the Helvetii next turned to the desperate expedient of forcing the Roman lines. For this operation every device was exhausted. Pontoon bridges, rafts improvised by the score, the fords of the Rhone where the river was shallowest, were all tried in turn: sometimes by day, though more often at night, until, finding themselves always and everywhere rolled back before the solid strength of the obstructions, the rapid mobility of the defense, and the ceaseless discharge of spears, they finally abandoned the attempt.

There remained the single route through the Sequani; a route that, owing to the narrow gorge through which it leads, it was impossible to take should the Sequani prove unfriendly. Failing therefore to obtain the necessary consent by direct negotiations of their own, the Helvetian authorities dispatched a deputation to the Aeduan chieftain Dumnorix, conceiving that his advocacy might perhaps enlist for them the sympathy of the Sequanian government. To the task now devolving on him Dumnorix was admirably fitted. Popular manners and a judicious employment of immense wealth had won for him an assured place in the counsels of the Sequani; while his marriage with a Helvetian princess, a daughter of the late chief Orgetorix, cemented his friendship with that people. He cherished, moreover, certain dynastic ambitions of his own, and with that object was secretly plotting the overthrow of the present Aeduan régime; it was therefore to his interest to lay under obligation all the surrounding nations that he could. Most willingly, therefore, did he now listen to the preferred appeal for help; and at his request the Sequani agreed to grant the Helvetii the desired passage, each party giving pledges to the other, the Sequani, that they would not oppose the march of the Helvetii, and the latter, that they would commit neither robbery nor violence on their road.

These intrigues were duly reported to the Roman governor, who now learned that the present Helvetian design was to march by way of the Sequani and Aedui to the distant settlements of the Santones, in Southwestern Gaul. As the lands of this tribe are situated not far from the territory of Tolosa (*Toulouse*), and Tolosa, as need scarcely be added, is an important center of the Roman Province, the new movement, if consummated, was fraught with grave danger to the Empire; for it could not fail to bring upon the flank of the rich corn plains of this district a race of turbulent tribesmen, openly and avowedly hostile to Rome. In the face of such a menace one course alone was possible. Deputing his chief of staff, Titus Labienus, to hold the recently erected line of works, the Roman commander by rapid stages hastened back to Italy; where, besides embodying two new legions, he summoned from their winter cantonments round Aquileia (*Aquileja*) the three that formed his original establishment in these quarters. At the head of these five he then selected the nearest route across the Alps and started back for Gaul. A certain amount of trouble was encountered from the hill tribes of the Ceutrones, Graioceli, and Caturiges, who gathered on their mountain fastnesses to obstruct his passage; but though frequent actions were necessary to dislodge them, the army accomplished the march from Ocelum, the last town on the Italian side, to the Vocontii in the Further or Western Province, in just under a week. From thence the advance was continued to the Allobroges, and from the Allobroges to the Segusiavi, who, as the first people beyond the Rhone, lie outside the Roman Province.

The Helvetii were found to have already passed the gorge of the Jura, and to have crossed the country of the Sequani. They had now appeared among the Aedui (district of *Lyon*), whose cultivated lands they were plundering on all sides. Unable to protect either themselves or their property from such a scourge, the Aedui dispatched an urgent appeal for help to Caesar, reminding him of their unswerving devotion in the past to Rome, which, as they put it, had surely deserved a kinder fate than, virtually beneath the eyes of a Roman army, to see their fields ravaged, their children swept into slavery, and their cities carried by the sword. Along with this appeal there came a similar message from the Ambarrian Aedui (politically and racially connected with the parent stock) announcing that the enemy had already licked up all the countryside, and only with the greatest difficulty were kept out from the towns. The same story was repeated by a body of Allobroges, who came flying from their settlements beyond the Rhone, bearing the pitiful tale that, beyond the bare surface of the soil, they had nothing left to call their own. Reports like these admitted of but one solution. To look on quietly while the Helvetii slowly made their way across Gaul to their goal among the Santoni, amid the wreckage and ruin of prosperous Roman allies, was a course of conduct wholly indefensible in the eyes of a responsible Roman governor.

Between the territories of the Aedui and Sequani there flows a tributary of the Rhone, called the Arar (*Saône*), so extraordinarily sluggish in its movement that the eye can scarcely discern the direction of the current. This river the Helvetii were now engaged in crossing by means of rafts and temporary pontoons; and according to the reports of scouts had already transported three-fourths of their number to the western bank, leaving about a quarter still remaining. Shortly after midnight, therefore, a force of three legions quietly left camp under the personal leadership of Caesar, and coming up with that section of the enemy which had not yet passed the stream, fell upon them without warning. Disorganized by their passage, large numbers were destroyed, and the rest only escaped by seeking refuge in the woods. The particular division thus accounted for proved to be that of the Tigurini, one of the four principal cantons into which the Helvetian race is subdivided. It was this division which, in the memory of those still alive, had by itself issued from its homes, and after destroying a Roman consul, Lucius Cassius, on the field of battle, had forced the survivors to pass under the yoke. Fortuitously, therefore, or providentially, that particular section of the Helvetian people which had inflicted this signal disaster upon Roman arms was now the first to pay the penalty. An interesting circumstance of the event that may perhaps be mentioned was that Caesar was able to avenge not only a national but also a private quarrel; for among those who fell that day with Cassius before the swords of the Tigurini was one of his generals, Lucius Piso, grandfather to the present bearer of that name, whose daughter Caesar had lately married.

After the decision of this battle, there remained the further task of overtaking the rest of the Helvetian force. For this purpose it was necessary to bridge the Arar; and this having been done, the army was transported to the farther side. Such a rapid advance on the part of their opponent took the Helvetian leaders completely by surprise. That an operation like the passage of this river, which had taxed all their ingenuity to accomplish within three weeks, should be safely conducted by their pursuers in twenty-four hours, was a feat that filled them with amazement, and their immediate answer was an offer to negotiate. Their spokesman on this occasion was the old chieftain Divico, famous as having led the Helvetian army in its memorable campaign against Cassius. He now put forward the following proposals. "As the price of peace, the Helvetii were prepared to retire to any part of the country that Caesar might enjoin, and to settle anywhere that he might wish. Any further attempt to goad them into war would be answered as they had already answered it by that first reverse inflicted on Roman arms, and as became a nation of their spirit. True, Caesar had surprised an isolated detachment, where circumstances rendered it impossible for those who had first crossed the river to go to the assistance of their kinsmen: yet he would be a bold man if he exaggerated the importance of this achievement, or made the fatal mistake of underestimating his opponent's strength. If there was one thing which the Helvetii had inherited as a tradition from their fathers, it was to fight in the open like men, and not to rely on trickery or ambuscade. The Roman commander therefore would be wise to pause ere hazarding a step, the result of which could only be to associate the name of the place on which they stood with a terrible disaster to the Roman race, and the annihilation of a Roman army."

To such language there could be but one reply. Any difficulty, he told them, he might otherwise have felt in coming to a decision, had been dispelled by his own vivid recollection of the events they had been good enough to mention; events which only stirred his deeper resentment, because so utterly unmerited by his own nation. Had Rome been conscious of any act of past injustice committed on her side, she could, by being forewarned, have been forearmed; in point of fact she had been betrayed by her own conscious innocence of any grounds for fear, and by her refusal to entertain fears that seemed groundless. Assuming, however, on his part a willingness to forget their truculent attitude in the past, it was quite impossible to rid his mind of their more recent deeds of violence—their attempt to force a passage through the Province in defiance of his orders, and their pillaging of the Aedui, Ambarri, and Allobroges. Their presumptuous boasting of their earlier victory, and their wonder at the dispensation of Providence which had allowed them to go so long unpunished, was, he told them, but one more indication of their impending doom. When Heaven was preparing vengeance for past crime, she not unfrequently gave the guilty a longer lease of prosperity and impunity, simply to deepen the remorse raised by a contrast with their previous lot. In spite of all, however, one way still lay open. If the Helvetii would give hostages as a guarantee of their desire

THE HELVETIAN WAR ◄ 11

loyally to abide by their compact, then, provided they also indemnified the Aeduans for the damage done to them and their allies, and similarly reimbursed the Allobroges, Rome would also, on her side, conclude a lasting peace. To these terms of Caesar's Divico replied that it was a tradition of the Helvetians, and one always observed by them, never to give hostages, but only to take them; and in proof of that statement he haughtily referred him to the experience of Rome herself. This ended the conference.

The next day the enemy broke up their encampment, and was followed in so doing by Caesar. To ascertain the precise route taken by the Gauls, the native cavalry, 4,000 strong, were all ordered to the front: they were a mixed body of horse, recently raised in the Roman Province and from the Aedui and their allies. With an ardor all too impetuous, these now pressed the enemy's rear so closely, that soon they became engaged with the Helvetian horse on ground that was much to their disadvantage. The consequence was that a few of their number fell in the encounter. Greatly elated by this action, the Helvetian leaders, finding that their slender force of cavalry, not exceeding 500 sabers, had completely routed the large number of mounted troops opposed to them, now began more boldly to halt their column, and with their rear guard threaten the advancing Romans. Caesar, however, declined to be drawn into a conflict, and for the present was contented to repress the enemy's acts of brigandage, to bar them from forage, and prevent the wholesale plundering of the country. Under these conditions both sides continued marching for above a fortnight, the distance between the rearmost portion of the Helvetii and the advanced guard of the Romans never exceeding five or six miles.

Throughout this period the Aedui were continually pressed by Caesar to deliver the corn publicly promised him by their government. Such supplies were all the more necessary to him since, owing to the rigorous climate of Central Gaul, due, as explained above, to its high northern latitude, not only were there no crops yet ripe in the fields, but even fresh grass was still exceedingly scarce. And though corn had been brought up the Arar (Saône) by barges, its use was rendered very difficult by the fact that the Helvetii had lately left the neighborhood of the river, and Caesar naturally was most loath to relinquish his pursuit. Day after day the Aedui procrastinated: now the corn, the story went, was being collected, now the convoy had actually started, now it was just arriving. Perceiving at last that he was being trifled with, and knowing the day to be all but due when rations must next be distributed to the army, he called a meeting of their chiefs. These were present in large numbers in his camp, and included both Divitiacus and Liscus, the latter being the holder of the principal Aeduan magistracy, known as the "Vergobret,"[3] an annual office with capital jurisdiction over all classes. Upon their assembling, Caesar delivered a very sharp reprimand for their failure to support him at so critical a time, when, being in the near neighborhood of the enemy, it was impossible for him either to buy in the open market, or to live upon the country as he went. Reminding them that the campaign had to a large extent been undertaken in deference to their own appeal, he expressed in still stronger language the indignation that he felt at so base a desertion by their leaders.

Such a reproof wrung from Liscus a full and frank confession on a matter he had hitherto studiously avoided mentioning. The truth was, he explained to Caesar, that there existed in his nation certain individuals of immense influence with the people, whose private authority more than outweighed the collective powers of the government. These individuals were at that very moment engaged in a seditious and unscrupulous propaganda among the uneducated classes of the people, and were so terrorizing over them that they dared not deliver the corn demanded. The argument used by these agitators was that, if the Aedui, as they must, had now to abandon their old supremacy in the country, then at least Gallic rule was preferable to Roman; for, they added, it should be clearly understood that the destruction of the Helvetian power by Rome would be quickly followed by the loss of Aeduan independence, and would open the way to the universal subjugation of Gaul. Moreover,

[3] Reading "praeerat."

continued Liscus, these men were at that moment playing the part of spies; and there was not a plan formed or an incident that passed in the Roman lines which was not instantly reported to the enemy. These intrigues he as a magistrate felt himself powerless to thwart, and in speaking out as he did from sheer necessity, he was well aware that he carried his life in his hand, and for that reason had kept silent as long as possible.

It was not difficult to identify the subject of these insinuations, and to see that Dumnorix, brother of Divitiacus, was meant. Being, however, averse to a public discussion of such topics before a large audience, Caesar hastily dismissed the assembly, but detaining Liscus with him, pressed for an explanation of his language at the meeting. Thus urged, Liscus spoke with greater confidence and without his former reticence; and the other chieftains being next admitted to audience in turn, all were closely cross-examined by Caesar. From this it appeared that the charges were substantially true, and that Dumnorix was the real author of all the mischief. A man of boundless ambition, he had used his great popularity with the masses, acquired by princely liberality, to further his own private schemes for a *coup d'état*. For many years past, it seemed, he had been allowed to buy up the tolls and other sources of public revenue at a ridiculously low price, for the simple reason that, when he was a candidate, no one else dared to bid against him. With the monopoly so gained he had largely increased his private fortune, besides providing himself with ample means of corruption; and a powerful cavalry force maintained at his own charges was always about his person. Nor was his ascendancy confined merely to his own country; it extended abroad among many of the surrounding nations. To foster it, he had contrived various matrimonial alliances. His widowed mother he had bestowed upon a chieftain of the Bituriges (*Bourges*), a prince of noble blood and assured position; his own consort had been selected from the Helvetii; while for a half-sister on his mother's side, as well as for several other near kinswomen, he had procured husbands from equally powerful states. His alliance with a Helvetian house had naturally identified him with the interests of that people, though apart from that he had his own reasons for disliking Caesar and the Romans; for their arrival had not only checked his own aggrandizement, but had also restored to his former position and influence his brother Divitiacus. Should disaster befall the Romans, his prospects of seizing the scepter through the help of his Helvetian friends were of the brightest; on the other hand, were Rome now to take over the country, he might bid goodbye not merely to his chances of a crown, but even to that measure of personal popularity which he then enjoyed. In further investigation it came out that, in the unsuccessful cavalry engagement a few days earlier, the Roman repulse had in the first instance been due to Dumnorix and his troopers. The command of the mounted contingent furnished by the Aeduan authorities to Caesar had been given to him; and apparently it was their flight which created the subsequent panic in the rest of the force.

The story thus unfolded threw grave suspicions on the conduct of Dumnorix; suspicions which were only too strikingly confirmed by the incontestable facts already known. There was the part he had played in bringing the Helvetii through Aeduan territory; his arrangements for an interchange of hostages; the general air of secrecy he had given the affair, in acting not merely without the permission, but even without the knowledge of Caesar and the Aedui; and last, but not least, there was the damning fact that he was now impeached by his own chief magistrate. So serious a list of charges seemed to warrant either direct proceedings against the accused by Caesar in person, or an order to the native authorities to take such for him. The sole consideration which yet stayed his hand was the eminent position and lofty character enjoyed by his brother Divitiacus; for in this prince he had discovered an unwavering attachment to the cause of Rome, a genuine devotion to himself, and a sense of honor, an uprightness, and a dignified self-restraint that were alike remarkable. To wound the feelings of such an ally, were it necessary now to proceed against the brother, was a contingency not lightly to be faced; and prior therefore to moving in the matter, he determined to call Divitiacus before him. Dismissing the regular interpreters, he conducted the interview through a personal friend of his own, Caius Valerius Procillus, a distinguished native from the southern Province, implicitly trusted by himself on all matters of importance. After reminding Divitiacus of the language used about his brother in his own hearing before the assembled Gauls, Caesar informed him of the private communications subsequently made by each, and finished by a strong appeal to allow him, without straining their sense of mutual regard, either to try the case himself, and so settle the man's punishment, or else to hand him over to the Aeduan authorities.

At these words Divitiacus completely broke down, and falling at Caesar's knees pleaded passionately for mercy to be extended to his brother. The substantial truth of the charges made against him he fully admitted, and dwelt upon the peculiar mortification that they had caused himself. Dumnorix, it seemed, had risen to power by simply trading on his brother's name; for at the time when the position of Divitiacus stood unrivaled, both with the outside Gallic world and in his own country, that of Dumnorix, owing to his youth, was still insignificant. The considerable resources thus acquired by the younger man were now being turned against the elder, who found himself threatened, not merely with loss of prestige, but even with actual political extinction. He had no wish, however, to appear insensible either to the claims of brotherly affection, or to the public opinion of his tribe; and he assured Caesar that any severe penalty now visited on his brother would, from his intimate relations with the Roman governor, be universally regarded as having his approval, and as a consequence he would most certainly lose the sympathies of every man in Gaul. This appeal he continued to urge with steady persistence and even with tears, until at last Caesar, taking him by the hand, begged him to calm his fears and to say no more, assuring him that the high value he attached to his good opinion would, after this earnest expression of his wishes, lead him to forget both the slight put upon his government and his own just resentment at it. After this Dumnorix was summoned to his presence, and was then informed before his brother of the indictment against him, including both those incriminating facts that were known to Caesar and the further complaints of the Aeduan authorities. A caution to avoid for the future all grounds for suspicion was then administered; but this time he was told, out of respect for his brother Divitiacus, the past would be overlooked. By Caesar's orders the man was afterward cut under surveillance, and a constant report was made both of the way he spent his time and of the company he kept.

On the day of this incident the scouts reported that the enemy had bivouacked at the foot of some hills eight miles distant from the Roman camp. A careful reconnaissance having been made of the heights, and of the possibility of turning them in flank, the operation was found to present no difficulties. Shortly after midnight, therefore, T. Labienus, a general of division holding praetorian rank, was directed to take two legions with those who had reconnoitered the road as guides, and to scale the summit from the rear; the general scheme of operations being first carefully detailed. Some two hours later the main body under Caesar, preceded by the cavalry in full force, rapidly advanced on the Helvetian camp by the same road as the enemy had traversed earlier in the day. With the advanced scouts was sent an officer of some considerable reputation as a soldier of experience, viz. Publius Considius, who had served in the army of Lucius Sulla, and later under Marcus Crassus.

At dawn the position revealed was as follows. The mountain ridge had been safely occupied by Labienus; the bulk of the Roman army under Caesar was within one and a half miles of the enemy's encampment; and, as shown by the subsequent evidence of prisoners, the approach of neither force had as yet been detected. At that moment was seen furiously galloping toward the Roman commander a single horseman, who turned out to be Cansidius, bearing the tidings that the hills, whose seizure by Labienus had formed part of Caesar's design, were actually in possession of the enemy. Of this fact he had made sure from the Gallic arms and banners seen upon the heights. Upon this announcement Caesar at once moved up toward the nearest high ground, and there made all dispositions for battle. In the meanwhile Labienus, acting upon his instructions not to begin an engagement until he saw the principal Roman column within striking distance of the enemy's laager, so that the combined attack might be delivered simultaneously, after successfully occupying the summit, was now anxiously awaiting his chief's arrival, without venturing to offer battle. Late in the day the true position of affairs was reported by the scouts; and the Roman commander then learned that not only was the hill in the hands of his own detachment, but that the Helvetii had since struck camp and moved on, and that Considius had been betrayed by nervousness to report as a fact what only existed in his own imagination. Once more, on the afternoon of the same day, the pursuit was taken up with the usual distance between the two parties, and that night the Romans camped three miles from the Helvetian position.

A period of only two days had now to run before the next issue of rations to the army would be due. At this critical stage of the operations, the Roman force found itself within eighteen miles of the important town of Bibracte,[4] by far the largest and wealthiest of those belonging to the Aedui. So favorable a conjuncture of circumstances for securing his supplies could not, in Caesar's opinion, be safely disregarded; and accordingly, on the morrow of the incident just narrated, the immediate pursuit of the Helvetii was broken off, and the march turned in the direction of that city. The new movement was at once reported to the enemy, through some runaway slaves in the service of Lucius Aemilius, a squadron leader in the Gallic horse, and quickly produced a change of plans among the Helvetian leaders. In their minds this sudden deflection of the Roman force was probably mistaken for an admission of fear; a view which would naturally be confirmed by Caesar's strange neglect on the previous day to give decisive battle after successfully occupying the higher ground; on the other hand, it is quite possible that they felt themselves strong enough to dispute the way with the Romans toward a place that must replenish their supplies. Be that as it may, their strategy was now completely changed, and wheeling round, they began to follow up the Roman column by hanging on its rear, thus openly challenging a combat.

[4] Probably a town on *Mt. Beuvray*, subsequently superseded by *Autun*.

Perceiving their intentions, Caesar withdrew from the lower ground, and while moving with all his infantry to the nearest hills, threw forward his cavalry to check for the moment the enemy's hostile advance, in order to form for battle. The formation adopted was as follows. Midway up the hill in three parallel lines were posted the four veteran legions. In rear of these, and resting on the extreme summit, came the two recently raised in Italy, along with the auxiliaries; and the whole of the hill being by these measures closely occupied with men, the marching kits of the troops were piled on a single corner of the ground, which was then hastily entrenched by those stationed in the topmost line. Meanwhile the Helvetii had been steadily advancing, still accompanied by their train of wagons; but as soon as they had deposited these and all their heavy baggage on a separate part of the field, their fighting men, after brushing aside the weak resistance of the cavalry, rapidly formed into battle squares, and in deep serried ranks swept on toward the slope where the first line of Roman infantry stood awaiting them.

To reduce all ranks to the same level as regards risk, and to banish once and for good the thought of flight, Caesar first sent his own charger to the rear and then those of his officers; after that, having briefly addressed his men, he gave the signal to engage. The legionaries had little difficulty with the advantage of position that they held in breaking up the solid phalanx of the enemy by the swift and deadly discharge of their heavy spears; and the main formation once shattered, they quickly drew their swords and charged. In the hand-to-hand conflict which followed, the Gauls were sorely handicapped by a curious result of this first volley. In many instances single Roman javelins had cut their way through two or more Helvetian bucklers, locking them together; and as the soft iron heads had bent before the blow, the Gauls could neither wrench them out, nor fight with any freedom with the left hand so impeded. Eventually many of them, after vainly trying to shake their arms clear, had no alternative but to fling away their shields and to fight with the body exposed. Under the rapid exhaustion caused by wounds the enemy's line at last gave way, and fell back toward the protection of some hills about a mile distant from the field of battle. This object they successfully attained, but on the Romans once more advancing to dislodge them, there suddenly appeared upon the scene a new division altogether, consisting of some fifteen thousand Boii and Tulingi, who closed the enemy's column when on march and regularly acted as its rear guard, and now arrived in time to fall upon the exposed flank of the legions and to threaten them in the rear. Perceiving this, the Helvetii who had retreated to the hill once more descended to the attack, and a fresh battle ensued. Rapidly changing front, the Romans broke into two divisions; and while their first and second lines advanced to meet those who had already once been defeated and driven from the field, the third turned to receive the new assailants.

Along both fronts a long and fiercely disputed battle then raged. When at last Roman determination had beaten down all further resistance, the main division once more retreated to the hills, while the other drew off in the direction of the wagons; for though fighting had lasted uninterruptedly from one in the afternoon until sunset, no one that day ever saw the back of an enemy. At the baggage trains the struggle was extended far into the night. The Gauls had pushed out their carts all round to serve as a rampart, and from this post of vantage poured in their volleys of spears upon the Romans as they came up; while in many cases pikes and javelins were thrust up at the men from beneath the wheels and wagons, inflicting serious wounds. A long sustained conflict ended at last with the capture of both camp and convoy, among the prisoners here taken being a daughter and son of the late chief Orgetorix. Through the rest of the night the survivors, still numbering about a hundred and thirty thousand souls, pursued their unbroken flight, and aided by this uninterrupted marching, succeeded in reaching, on the third day after the battle, the country of the Lingones (*Langres*). On the Roman side pursuit had been impossible, since the care of the wounded and the burial of the dead had necessitated a delay of three days. Caesar, however, had sent on at once to the ruling authorities of the Lingones an imperative order to give no assistance, either by food or other means, to the fugitives; such action, he warned them, would render them liable to precisely the same treatment as that meted out to the Helvetii. Three days thus having elapsed, the entire Roman army once more took up the pursuit.

Meanwhile the retreating host had reached a state of such utter destitution that envoys to arrange for its capitulation soon appeared. These met the Roman army while still in full pursuit, and after prostrating themselves at Caesar's feet, in the attitude and tones of suppliants begged him to grant them peace. His answer was a command to await his arrival at the place where they were then encamped, a command they faithfully obeyed; and the army having arrived here, he demanded of them hostages for their future good conduct, the surrender of all arms, and the restoration of all slaves who had deserted from the Roman camp. During the work of collecting and delivering these, night fell upon the scene; whereupon under cover of darkness some six thousand of the prisoners of the canton known as the Verbigenus, secretly left camp and made off for the Rhine and the distant German territories. They apparently calculated that in so vast a crowd of captives their surreptitious flight could either be hushed up or else escape notice altogether: it is also possible they had genuine fears lest the surrender of their arms might be only the prelude to some horrible act of vengeance from their captors.

On hearing of this treachery, Caesar at once sent peremptory orders to those tribes that lay along the route that if they wished to be acquitted of complicity they must immediately hunt down the fugitives and fetch them back to camp. On their reappearance, they suffered the legitimate penalty of enemies; though all the rest, who had surrendered at discretion, after hostages, arms, and deserters had been delivered, had their rights respected to the full. There remained the question of their future. The Helvetii, Tulingi, and Latovici were ordered to return to the districts which they had vacated; and the wanton destruction of the season's crops having left them without resources against famine, Caesar directed that the Allobroges should provide them with a market, while they themselves bent all their energies to the task of rebuilding the towns and villages burned on the eve of their migration. On behalf of the Boii, who had given in the recent encounter such signal proofs of martial qualities, the Aedui requested that they might settle in their country; a course which Caesar approved. Accordingly lands were found for them, and in future the Boii were admitted to equal rights and privileges with the Aedui.

In the camp of the Helvetii certain documents were discovered, which on being brought to Caesar were found to contain in Greek characters detailed lists, first of the grand total of emigrants, with the proportion of those capable of bearing arms, and secondly in another column the figures for the old men, women, and children. From these it appeared that the Helvetii numbered 263,000, the Tulingi 36,000, the Latovici 14,000, the Raurici 23,000, and the Boii 32,000, the total fighting force being 92,000 men. The figures for all classes had thus originally stood at 368,000; but on a census being taken by Caesar's orders, the number of those who returned to their homes amounted to only 110,000 souls.

Section II. Ariovistus and the Germans

The successful termination of the Helvetian war was welcomed by almost every state in Central Gaul, whose leading chiefs now waited upon Caesar to offer their congratulations. After stating that they fully realized that it was the old offences of the Helvetii that had brought down upon them the avenging sword of Rome, they went on to declare that this event was of not less happy augury to Gaul than to Rome; for the object which the Helvetii had proposed to themselves in thus vacating their homes when at the very height of their national strength, was nothing less than warfare and empire throughout Gaul. To secure this they had intended first carefully to select some central point in the whole country that offered the greatest strategical and agricultural advantages, and then from this to hold all other tribes as tributary. Continuing, the envoys requested Caesar formally to sanction a general Diet of the states of Celtic Gaul, on a date to be arranged, since there were certain matters of grave importance on which they desired to appeal for his assistance, with all the weight attaching to a public resolution. The required leave having been granted, a date was fixed for the Assembly, and all present then bound themselves by oath not to divulge anything of its proceedings, excepting those who were specially empowered to do so.

In due course this Diet met and dissolved, whereupon the same chieftains who had previously waited upon Caesar once more returned to solicit a secret discussion on certain vital questions of public policy. On his ready consent, they all humbly prostrated themselves to the ground and then proceeded to explain with surprising passion that what really concerned and exercised them, even more than the gratification of their suit, was that the proceedings should be conducted in strictest privacy; since any disclosure must involve them, they well knew, in the most dreadful retribution. On behalf of his colleagues, the Aeduan chief Divitiacus then formally opened the discussion. He began by explaining that there existed in Gaul two rival political factions, under the respective hegemony of the Aedui and Arverni. Between these there had raged for many years an internecine struggle for supremacy, until at last the Arvernian and Sequanian party had agreed to invite the paid aid of the Germans, who coming over at first some 15,000 strong, had subsequently (under the charm exerted on a rude and savage people by the civilization, prosperity, and agricultural wealth of Gaul) crossed the Rhine in larger and larger numbers, until now there were as many as 120,000 in the land. Again and again the Aedui and their allies had encountered these invaders upon the field of battle, but always to be defeated, and indeed had suffered such irretrievable disaster, that they had lost in the struggle the whole of their nobility, knighthood, and tribal senate. Broken by these contests, and crushed beneath the weight of such calamities, they who had once been the proud possessors of the premiership of Gaul, not less by their own strong arm than by the honored friendship they enjoyed with Rome, had been forced to yield their noblest sons as hostages to the Sequani, and solemnly to bind their government never to ask them back, nor appeal to Rome for aid, but humbly to acquiesce in a state of permanent dependence upon their rivals. Alone of all the Aedui he, the speaker, had steadily refused this oath, and for this reason being forced to quit the country, had used the freedom which his own exemption from oath and hostage permitted to go to Rome and there to lay his country's cause before the Senate. But the policy of the Sequani had recoiled upon its authors, and though victorious, their lot was now even worse than that of the conquered Aedui. Ariovistus, the German king, had permanently settled in their country, exacting as his payment a full third of all their land (which was the very best in Gaul), and was at the present moment actually demanding their withdrawal from another third; for in the last few months a swarm of 24,000 roving Harudes had joined him, for whom he had to find new lands and homes. A few more years of such a process, and the whole of Gaul must inevitably be denuded of its present population, and the German migration across the Rhine would be complete; for just as there was no comparison between the German and Gallic soil, so the standards of living enjoyed by the two peoples differed absolutely. Coming next to the actual rule of Ariovistus, which he had exercised since the day on which he overthrew the Gallic confederacy in a great battle fought at Admagetobriga, the speaker described it as cruel and insolent to a degree. The young sons of all their noblest families were constantly demanded as hostages; and on these, should anything occur to cross his humor, he would inflict every outrage that fiendish ingenuity could devise. The man was an untutored savage, of a capricious and ungovernable temper, and it was impossible to endure his domination further. If help of some kind were not forthcoming from Caesar and the Romans, every Gaul would have to follow the example lately set them by the Helvetii, and leaving their ancestral settlements, take fortune in both hands and seek out new homes in new lands, far removed from the German terror. Once more they begged Caesar to understand that should a word of this come to the tyrant's ear, the hostages now in his hands would beyond a doubt suffer terribly; and concluded by saying that in him alone lay their hope; since he, either by his personal influence and that of his army, or by the moral effect of his recent victory, or by the magic name of Rome, could now stop the further influx of the German tribes, as well as make himself the common champion of Gaul against the tyrannous oppression of Ariovistus.

On the conclusion of this speech, all present burst into tears, and implored Caesar to come to their aid. The latter observed that hitherto the representatives of the Sequani had adopted an attitude in striking contrast to that of all the other chiefs, and with head bowed and eyes riveted on the ground, had remained throughout in deepest gloom. At a loss to account for such strange behavior, Caesar turned for an explanation to the delegates themselves. But the Sequani still continued speechless, with no change of expression on their mute, unhappy faces; and it was only after repeated questionings had failed to elicit any reply, that Divitiacus the Aeduan again undertook to answer for them. The condition of the Sequani, he explained, was one of peculiar pathos and hardship. Unlike their fellow sufferers, they dared not, even in the secrecy of the audience chamber, utter a syllable either of complaint or of appeal, for even in his absence the cruel menace of Ariovistus was always before their eyes. Others at least had the remedy of flight; the wretched Sequani, having opened their arms to the invader and allowed him to seize upon all their towns, were now exposed to every horror that cruelty could inflict.

With this important information before him, Caesar first made it his business to restore the drooping spirits of the Gauls, and assured them that the matter should certainly have his best attention, though he was glad to think that Ariovistus, both from motives of gratitude and policy, would soon cease from his aggressions. With this he dismissed the assembly. Following on their withdrawal, various reasons suggested themselves to his mind why, in the highest interests of Rome, the situation thus revealed should be met by a policy at once clearly defined and vigorously executed. First and foremost was the picture of the Aedui in helpless bondage to German suzerainty—those same Aedui who had so often been distinguished by the Roman Senate with the honored title of "Brothers and Kinsmen." Hostages from this people, he now learned, were actually at the present moment in the custody of Ariovistus and the Sequani; and such a state of things, under a great empire like that of Rome, was a deep disgrace both to himself and the country he represented. Secondly, it was perfectly clear that for the Germans to be allowed to pass the Rhine as a matter of course, till large bodies of that people were settled in Gaul, must eventually create an imperial danger of the greatest magnitude. It was highly improbable, again, that a nation of their wild and lawless instincts would so curb their natural inclinations as to rest content merely with the acquisition of Gaul. Like the Cimbri and Teutoni of an earlier date, they would most assuredly overflow into the Province, and from there press on into Italy; especially as the only barrier between the Sequani and the Province was the river Rhone. And apart from all other considerations, he could not help feeling sensible that the insolent pretensions of Ariovistus had now become intolerable.

Deciding therefore to dispatch commissioners to the king, he invited him to select some spot midway between their two camps for the purpose of a conference, as it was, he declared, his earnest desire to discuss certain important matters of state of deep interest to them both. To this embassy Ariovistus replied as follows: "Tell Caesar that if I had wanted anything from him, I should have come to him for it. In the same way I expect that any requests he may have to make of me may be made in person. Besides, in that part of Gaul which is now occupied by your master I dare not trust myself without an army, and an army is a costly and complicated thing to mobilize. I must, however, be allowed to express my wonder at what business either Caesar or the Roman Government can possibly have in my part of Gaul, which I hold by the right of the sword."

On receipt of this answer, Caesar again sent his delegates to the German monarch, this time with his clear demands. After a reference to the king's great obligation both to himself and the Roman Government, which during his administration had, through the Senate, formally recognized his title and added that of "Friend to the Republic"; he went on to state that, since the only acknowledgment he had made was to decline on the score of excessive trouble Caesar's invitation to meet him in a conference, and since he considered it superfluous either to give or to receive information on matters touching their common interests, Caesar must insist upon the following stipulations. In the first place, Ariovistus must bring no more Germans across the Rhine into Gaul; secondly he must restore to the Aedui their hostages, and likewise allow the Sequani to restore all they held themselves; and lastly, he must abstain from all unprovoked attacks on the Aeduan people, and from all hostilities against either them or their allies. So long as these conditions were observed, cordial relations might still continue without interruption between the king and Rome: in the event of their rejection, Caesar had ample authority to carry the matter further. Three years ago, in the consulship of Messala and Piso, the Senate had empowered the Governor of Gaul for the time being, so far as might be consistent with Imperial interests, to protect the Aedui and any other people friendly to Rome; and on those instructions he was prepared now to act.

To these proposals Ariovistus rejoined that by the rights and usages of war the treatment of conquered peoples rested entirely with the conqueror. In accordance with this principle, Rome had always administered her dependencies, not at the dictation of an outside Power, but solely by what she conceived to be her own interests. If he did not dream of prescribing to Rome the terms on which she should exercise a right which was undoubtedly her own, then, in common fairness, Rome ought not to interpose between him and his prerogative. The Aedui had appealed to the arbitrament of war; they had met on the tented field, and had there been overthrown: by natural consequence, they now paid tribute as his vassals. Indeed, he might justly complain that by his presence in the country Caesar was materially diminishing the value of his revenues. Therefore, to the demand that he should restore his hostages, he returned an emphatic negative. As to making wanton attacks upon them or their allies, they were perfectly safe as long as they observed their compact, and annually paid the tribute. Should they, however, fail in this, then the vaunted title of "Brothers to the Roman People" would prove but a broken reed. With regard to Caesar's threat not to overlook any so-called outrages against the Aedui, nobody, he might remind the Roman general, had ever met himself on the field without going to his own destruction. Caesar had only to name a day for the encounter, and he would quickly learn the true mettle of those Germans who had never tasted defeat, who had been trained from infancy to arms, and who for fourteen years had never slept beneath a roof.

Side by side with the delivery of this answer, there appeared in the Roman camp two separate bodies of delegates from the Aedui and the Treveri (*Trèves*) respectively. Of these the Aedui came to complain that the new swarm of immigrants were engaged in plundering their lands, so that they had failed to secure peace from Ariovistus even at the price of the hostages surrendered. The Treveri, on the other hand, brought the alarming intelligence that the hundred cantons of the Suebi had just camped at the banks of the Rhine, which they were then endeavoring to pass, under the two brothers Nasua and Cimberius. These two reports, taken in conjunction, caused Caesar the liveliest alarm, and it was now clear to his mind that nothing but the swiftest action could save the situation. Should this fresh band of Suebi be allowed to form a junction with the existing forces under Ariovistus, the difficulty of coping with the invaders would be increased fourfold. Rapidly organizing his supplies, therefore, with all the speed of which he was capable, he began his march in the direction of Ariovistus.

At the end of three days he was met by the news that the German monarch, at the head of all his forces, was moving rapidly upon the town of Vesontio (*Besançon*), the capital of the Sequani, with the intention of making it his base, and was already three days advanced from his own territory. Such a *coup* was one to be prevented at all hazards. Not only was the place richly supplied with all kinds of munitions of war, but by the peculiar strength of its position it afforded admirable facilities for prolonging a campaign; for with the exception of one tiny gap, the entire circumference of the town is, as though drawn with a pair of compasses, surrounded by the river Dubis (*Doubs*); and even this section that is left by the break in the river (no more than 500 yards across), is completely dominated by a lofty hill, so placed that on either side its spurs descend straight to the river banks. Girt by a fortified wall, this hill is virtually transformed into a citadel, and is itself connected with the main defenses of the town. Toward this stronghold Caesar now pushed rapidly forward, making long marches day and night alike, until having secured possession, he had placed it in the hands of a sufficient garrison.

A few days' halt outside Vesontio, required for the better organization of supplies, was the occasion of a remarkable incident in the
Roman army. Inquiries were naturally made in course of conversation as to the character of the enemy about to be engaged, and no
less naturally the Gauls and resident traders had much to say upon
the matter. The Germans were depicted as men of gigantic stature,
whose courage was something more than human, and who used
their weapons as no other soldiers could; and though often encountering, them on the field of battle, they always found it impossible
not to quail before their fierce flashing eyes. The effect of listening
to such idle tales was quickly apparent. A palsied fear crept over the
entire army, paralyzing to a strange degree the energy and courage
of all ranks. The mischief began with the young commissioned officers lately gazetted to their regiments, the attaches, and various
members of the suite, who for reasons of personal friendship had
accompanied Caesar from the Capital to his province, and whose
military experience was not therefore large. One by one, each of
these now discovered some urgent reason for his departure, and
came to Caesar requesting leave of absence. A few, from motives of
shame, and to avoid the imputation of cowardice, decided to stay
on. These last, failing to look the part, and unable at times even to
refrain from tears, gradually withdrew to the privacy of their tents;
where in gloomy solitude, or in the company of friends, they either
brooded over their own fate or bewailed the danger impending over
all. In every part of the camp wills were being freely signed. The language used by these under the influence of their fears gradually
infected even old and tried campaigners;—viz. the rank and file of
the legions, the noncommissioned officers, and the commanders of
irregular horse. Those who were anxious still to preserve some
shreds of self-respect, now declared that it was not the enemy they
were afraid of, but the difficulties of the road and the vast forests
lying between themselves and Ariovistus; or else they were concerned about the question of supplies, and feared the transport
would break down under the heavy strain imposed upon it. A few,
indeed, even ventured to predict that the troops would refuse to

obey orders, when commanded to strike camp and resume the march, and that in their present state of demoralization they would flatly decline to advance.

Resolved to arrest such a state of things before it proceeded further, Caesar summoned a council of war, admitting to it the noncommissioned officers of every company throughout the army. In tones of sharp reprimand, he sternly rebuked their presumption in daring to question or discuss either the scene or plan of any operations they might be called upon to carry out in the field. With regard specially to Ariovistus, only as late as the preceding year, he told them, during his own consular administration, that monarch had gone out of his way to solicit Roman friendship, and it was therefore unreasonable to suppose he would lightly repudiate the obligations he then incurred. Indeed, his own conviction in the matter was that the German king had only to understand the true nature of the demands addressed to him, and the inherent fairness of the conditions proposed, and he would cease to contemplate the dissolution of that friendship which he had so recently contracted with himself and the Roman government. In the event, however, of his proving such a fool and madman as to issue a declaration of war, what, he asked his officers, was there so very terrible in all that, or why should it lead them to lose both their own courage and their belief in the ability of their general. It was not the first time that Romans had encountered these redoubtable warriors. Many were still alive who could recall the day when Marius broke the power of the Cimbri and Teutoni;[1] and that great fight, as he went on to remind them, was as much a soldiers' victory as it was due to the genius of the man who led them. Quite recently again, at the last great rising of their slaves,[2] they had fought the same foe on Italian soil; though on that occasion these had been in no small degree aided by the science and discipline adopted from their masters. Than this last rebellion, no better example of the value of cool self-possession in the hour of danger could be

[1] 102, 101 BC.
[2] 73–71 BC.

imagined; for, beginning with unreasoning dread of bands of unarmed insurgents, it had ended with the complete overthrow of formidable armies after these had been flushed with the tide of victory. And finally, the enemy now before them, he pointed out, had been constantly encountered by the Helvetii, both on Helvetian and on German soil, and almost as constantly defeated; yet the Helvetii, as they well knew, had proved no match for Roman troops. Then turning to those who professed to be much impressed by the disasters incurred by the Gauls, and by their flight before the invader, he showed the hollowness of all such fears. Examination would prove that the true reason for the Gauls' defeat was weariness at the interminable length of the war; and that having long lost hope of obtaining a pitched battle, as month after month went by and Ariovistus still clung to his camp and marshes, they had allowed their forces to become scattered, and so exposed themselves to a sudden attack from their adversary, who had snatched a victory that was far more due to clever artifice than to any merit of his own. But a trick that might be played upon levies of raw natives, not even the German king could expect would succeed against the disciplined armies of Rome. So much then for honest doubts, for which he had some respect. But, he continued, there were others of his audience who endeavored to conceal their faintheartedness under the cloak of pretended anxiety for the commissariat, or the obstacles attending the advance. Such conduct, he told them, was nothing less than impertinent, for it implied that the commander in chief did not know his business, and that it was their duty to teach him it. These matters were, as a fact, then engaging his attention. Corn would be provided during the campaign by the Sequani, the Leuci, and the Lingones (*Langres*), and in addition there were the crops already ripe in the fields: while as to the route, they should quickly have an opportunity of testing the wisdom of his methods for themselves. One last word on the rumor that the men would refuse obedience when ordered to advance. Such a rumor, he declared, left him perfectly unmoved. In all cases of mutiny recorded of an army, the true explanation, as he read history, had invariably been either the want

of success that attends on incapacity, or the detection of such misconduct in a general as showed evidence of personal greed: and that
his own hands were clean was attested by the whole of his career;
while that he knew how to command success was proved by the
Helvetian campaign. Resting, therefore, on that assurance, he would
now proceed to do what it had been his intention for a time to defer;
and on that very night, somewhere between the last watch and the
dawn, the order would be given to strike camp. That at least would
enable him to learn the worst; whether honor and the sense of duty
still weighed with them most, or the base promptings of fear. If no
one else were found to follow, then he would go with the Tenth
legion alone; for at least he was sure of their loyalty, and they should
act as his bodyguard.

This regiment, it should be explained, was a special favorite
of Caesar's, and owing to its fine soldierlike qualities he trusted
it implicitly.

The speech produced an extraordinary revulsion of feeling, and
in all ranks alike there was now an eager desire to proceed to the
front. The lead was taken by the Tenth legion, who expressed
through their officers their deep sense of gratitude to Caesar for the
high compliment he had paid them, and assured him that they were
ready for action at a moment's notice. The other regiments quickly
followed suit, and the men, going to their officers and senior ser-
geants, requested them publicly to apologize to Caesar, and to
explain to him that they had never harbored either doubts or fears,
or imagined that it lay with themselves, rather than with their commander, to decide on the conduct of a campaign. This apology
Caesar graciously accepted, and then consulted with Divitiacus,
whose sincerity he could trust more than that of all others, as to the
best line of advance. Upon his advice, he decided to make a detour of
fully fifty miles in order to take the army through open country,
and in the last watch of the night, as he had already stated, he struck
camp. At the end of a week's continuous marching, the scouts
reported that Ariovistus and the Germans were twenty-four miles
from the Roman force.

This rapid advance on the part of his opponent drew a message from the king, in which he explained that having now brought his own position nearer, there were no longer the obstacles there had originally been to the conference desired by Caesar, and that therefore he thought he might now safely grant it without risk to himself. This somewhat tardy concession Caesar took no exception to, but gladly welcomed it as a sign of returning saneness in the monarch. For when the king was found spontaneously to offer what formerly he had refused to do upon request, there was good ground for believing that further acquaintance with the tenor of the Roman demands, when fortified by the sense of his own obligations to Caesar and the Roman Government, might lead to some abatement of his present uncompromising attitude. Accordingly a meeting was arranged— the date fixed being four days hence. In the meanwhile the diplomatic agents of both parties passed freely to and fro, and it was in the course of these preliminaries that Ariovistus suddenly raised the demand that Caesar should on no account bring infantry with him to the conference; the reason alleged being his fear of finding himself trapped or ambushed. Both, he declared, must come with cavalry alone; on no other terms would he consent to appear. This new turn to the negotiations raised a serious difficulty. Though unwilling to sacrifice the projected meeting to a petty obstacle of this nature, Caesar yet felt that to trust himself solely to the protection of his Gallic horse would be to incur a very grave risk; and he had therefore to contrive some other expedient that would best meet the case. He decided to dismount all his native irregulars, and to put up in their places the men of the Tenth legion, knowing well that on these he could rely: should any emergency then arise, he would have round him an absolutely devoted bodyguard. While the transformation was being effected, one of the privates of the Tenth remarked, not without a touch of humor, that Caesar was proving better than his word. "He had promised to make the regiment a corps of Footguards: in future they would appear on the roll of the Knights."

A wide open plain separated the two camps, broken at one point by a hill of soft material, which formed a conspicuous landmark.

This spot was nearly equidistant from the positions occupied by Caesar and Ariovistus, and to it both, as previously arranged, now proceeded to the interview. Arrived on the ground, Caesar stationed the legion, which had so recently been converted into mounted infantry, at a point three or four hundred yards in the rear of the hill, while Ariovistus's cavalry likewise drew up at a similar distance. The German leader then asked that the conversation should be conducted from the saddle, and that the escort accompanying either should be limited to ten troopers. At last the two being face-to-face, Caesar opened the discussion by enumerating the various distinctions which at his instance had been conferred on Ariovistus by the Roman Government. His title of king had been publicly recognized by the Senate, the friendship of Rome had been formally extended to him, and the gifts of the Republic had been conveyed to his court with all the ceremony proper to such occasions. Few indeed, he reminded him, had been honored by such great compliments, which were generally reserved as a reward for eminent services rendered by their recipients. In the case of the king, there had been nothing either to suggest or to warrant even a claim to such distinctions: if they had been bestowed, it was solely by Caesar's kind intervention on his behalf, and by the goodwill of the government which he represented. He next proceeded to explain how ancient and indisputable were the ties uniting Rome with the people of the Aedui. The Senate's numerous resolutions in their favor and the honorable nature of their contents were severally recounted, and Ariovistus was reminded that, even before the Aedui appealed to Roman friendship, they had from long antiquity enjoyed an undisputed ascendancy over Central Gaul. Rome, the king must understand, whenever she bestowed on a people her friendship or alliance, not only saw that these were not losers by the bargain, but endeavored to promote, as far as in her lay, the prestige, dignity, and respect paid to her protégés. That she should permit any of these actually to be despoiled of what they had originally brought into the alliance, was a contingency that could not be contemplated for a moment. In conclusion, the conditions were reaffirmed which had been originally conveyed by Caesar's envoys, viz. that hostilities must cease against both the Aedui and their allies; that that people's hostages must be restored them; and that, even if it proved impracticable to send back any portion of the Germans already settled on Gallic soil, yet at least no further bands should be permitted to cross the Rhine.

To these demands, Ariovistus's reply contained little that was relevant or satisfactory, but dilated at large on the subject of his own admirable virtues.

He had crossed the Rhine, it seemed, not at all in self-interest, but solely on the urgent summons of the Gauls; and it was only the great expectations held out to him, and the considerable sums paid him by way of installment, that had induced him to leave his ancestral home and to part from kith and kindred. In strict accordance with these terms, his new home in his adopted country had been provided by the Gauls themselves, with whose free consent also the hostages had been given; while, as to the tribute, he levied that by right of conquest, as the recognized burden always laid by the victor on the vanquished. In common fairness it should be remembered that it was not he who began hostilities with the Gauls, but they with him. They had gathered in their thousands, with the avowed object of crushing him and his people, every state in Celtic Gaul contributing its share of warriors; they had proudly planted their camp right over against his own as a direct challenge to combat; and in a single battle the whole mighty host had been shattered and driven from the field. If they wanted to repeat the experiment, he was ready to abide by the result of a second encounter: if they wished to continue living in peace, then it was unreasonable to raise difficulties about the tribute, which up to that moment they had regularly and ungrudgingly paid.

A reference had been made to his own request for Roman friendship. It was true he had taken some pains to acquire that gift, but it was under the impression that such a tie would materially enhance his reputation and increase his safety, not,

as was now proving the case, seriously damage both. If the loss
of his tribute and surrender of his prisoners were made a condition of its retention, then he would as gladly decline the
preferred friendship of Imperial Rome as formerly he had
sought it. With regard to Caesar's third demand, he admitted
he was still bringing Germans across the Rhine, but it was
solely to safeguard his own position, not for the purpose of
raiding Gaul. That this was his true motive was clear from
what had already been explained, viz. that his presence in the
country at the first had been wholly unsolicited, and that
the hostilities which had ensued had been, on his part, purely
defensive. Yet he had a better claim than Rome to decide the
destinies of Gaul, for it rested on priority of tenure, and Rome
found him already in possession. Indeed, this was the first time
in history that a Roman force had crossed the boundary of her
southern Province. He was therefore entitled to ask for an
explanation of its presence in his preserves, for this part of Gaul
was as much a province of his kingdom, as the other was of the
Republic. Just, then, as he would not be tolerated, were he to
lead a hostile invasion into Roman territory, so the Romans
were clearly in the wrong in interfering with his established
rights. It might please Caesar to describe the Aedui as the
adopted brothers of his own countrymen, but he was not such
a rude savage, or so entirely ignorant of affairs, as not to be
aware that neither in the recent war of the Romans against
the Allobroges had any help been given by the Aedui to their
newly found relatives, nor in the numerous struggles of the
Aedui with himself and the Sequani had they ever received
one atom of support from Rome. He was therefore driven to
the conclusion that, under the veil of pretended friendship,
Caesar's presence in the country did but conceal a fixed intention to compass his destruction; and unless he at once retired,
and withdrew his military forces from the district they then
occupied, he would be compelled to treat him, not as a friend,
but as an open and avowed enemy. Should Caesar fall by his

sword, it would be welcome news to many of the first nobility in Rome,—so much he had learned from their own lips, communicated through their agents; and he was well aware that, at the price of Caesar's head, he could purchase the interest and friendship of the entire oligarchical party. On the other hand, Caesar had only to retire, and to leave him in undisturbed possession of Celtic Gaul, and he would find a rich compensation for his compliance; while any further wars he might desire to carry out he might safely leave to him and his Germans, without risk or trouble to himself.

In reply to this, many arguments were adduced by Caesar to show how impossible it was for him to recede from the position he had already taken up. In the first place, to abandon allies whose loyalty had stood the test of time, was to be false both to his own character and to the best traditions of his race. And on the wider issue, he did not admit the claims of Ariovistus to the country to be superior to those of Rome. Rome, too, he reminded his hearer, could point to a verdict given by arms. Many years ago,[3] Quintus Fabius Maximus had reduced the Arverni (*Auvergne*) and the Ruteni (*Rodez*); though afterward the Roman Government of the day had generously refrained from forming them into a province, or imposing a tribute. But that argument he need not pursue further. If they must scrutinize the records of ancient history, it was obvious that the position of Rome in Gaul rested on a firm basis of justice: if, on the contrary, the decision of the Senate was to be upheld, then Gaul had every right to be free; for, after being fairly conquered, she had been allowed by her conqueror to retain her independence.

In the midst of the discussion, word was sent to Caesar that Ariovistus's horsemen were advancing nearer to the hill and threatening the Roman escort, whom indeed they were already attacking with stones and spears. At once terminating his speech, Caesar galloped back to his men and ordered them on no account to return the fire;

---

[3] 121 BC.

for though he had no misgiving as to the result of a contest between his own picked regiment of footguards and the cavalry of the enemy, yet it was undesirable to take any step which could afterward be interpreted by the beaten party as a betrayal of confidence or an abuse of the rights of parley. On returning to camp, the news quickly spread among the men of the studied insolence the German king had shown throughout the interview, and how he had even warned the Romans off the whole of Central Gaul; and when to this was added the treacherous attack made by his horsemen, and the consequent interruption of the negotiations, a most remarkable increase of enthusiasm and desire to engage the enemy was perceptible in all ranks.

Forty-eight hours after this incident representatives from Ariovistus again appeared in the Roman camp, bringing with them a message from the king to the effect that, wishing to continue the discussion of those matters which had been broached between them but not yet definitely settled, he would be obliged to Caesar if he would either appoint a day for a second interview, or, if adverse to that, would send some member of his staff. The first of these proposals, viz. that for an interview, Caesar now held to be superfluous, especially as on the previous day it had been impossible to restrain the Germans from firing on his troops. On the other hand, to send one of his higher officers was to run a very grave risk, as it would be placing him at the mercy of a lot of savages. The most satisfactory solution appeared to be to employ the services of a young Gallic nobleman named Caius Valerius Procillus, a son of that Caius Valerius Caburus, who had received Roman citizenship under the governor, Caius Valerius Flaccus.[4] Of gallant and courteous bearing, he combined with undoubted trustworthiness the further advantage of speaking the Gallic tongue, with which Ariovistus from long habit was tolerably familiar; while in his case there could scarcely be the same temptation to treachery on the part of the Germans. He was accompanied by Marcus Mettius, a man who enjoyed rights of hospitality with Ariovistus. Their instructions were to listen to any

---

[4] Circ. 83 BC.

further statement the German had to make, and to bring back word to Caesar. As soon as his eyes fell upon these visitors to his camp, the German monarch, with all his army standing by and looking on, fiercely exclaimed, "What is your business here? To play the spy, I suppose"; and on their attempting to explain, brutally cut them short and ordered them off to prison.

The same day he moved a little nearer to Caesar and encamped at the foot of a hill six miles from the Roman position. On the day following he made a further movement across the flank of his opponent and established himself at a point well beyond Caesar's entrenchments, with the object of cutting the latter's communications with the Sequani and Aedui, from whom the army drew its provisions and stores. For five successive days after this Caesar regularly showed himself in the open, and marshaling his line immediately in front of camp gave Ariovistus the opportunity of either accepting or declining battle. His answer on all occasions was to confine the bulk of his army to camp, but to engage in daily skirmishes with his cavalry.

The German method of fighting with this arm, which by long training they had brought to perfection, merits some description. Their cavalry proper numbered six thousand sabres; but with these there was combined an equal force of infantry, all of them picked men, taken from the whole army for their exceptional strength and stamina. Each trooper was then associated with a single footman, to whom he looked for personal assistance, and in battle the two forces always acted together. As occasion demanded, these runners could form a retiring support for the mounted men, or could concentrate rapidly upon any point of special danger: they would rally round a wounded comrade who had been unhorsed, and should the progress of the action require either a lengthened advance or a quick retreat, so surprising was the pace developed in them by constant practice, that merely by holding on to the horses' manes, they could keep their places in the movement.

Ariovistus now clearly intending to shelter behind his laager, in order to restore his own threatened communications, Caesar selected a spot suitable for his purpose, a thousand yards or more beyond the German camp, and marshaled in three embattled lines, advanced toward the place; his first and second lines then stood to arms, while the third proceeded to entrench a camp. As already stated, the position chosen lay about a thousand yards distant from the enemy, and to it Ariovistus now dispatched some 16,000 of his lighter infantry, supported by his entire division of cavalry; with the evident intention of so menacing the Romans at their work as to prevent the fortification of their lines. His action did not affect the dispositions of Caesar, who simply continued his orders that the first and second lines were to repel the enemy, while the third and rearmost went on with the work. The new camp was at length rendered secure, whereupon a force of two legions, with a section of auxiliaries, was left in garrison, while the remaining four returned to the old site.

The next day Caesar repeated his previous tactics, and the Roman forces, emerging simultaneously from both camps and taking up a position in line a little advanced from the larger of the two, gave Ariovistus his chance of fighting. Even this elicited no responsive movement from the enemy, and the recall had been sounded and the men were back in quarters, when suddenly, about the hour of noon, Ariovistus detached a portion of his forces for an assault upon the smaller of the two camps, where a fierce action, obstinately contested on either side, lasted till evening. At sunset the German leader called off his troops, both sides having suffered heavily. On inquiring from prisoners why Ariovistus showed such a marked reluctance to hazard a decisive combat, Caesar received the answer that by German custom their women first investigated, by means of incantations and lots, the amount of success likely to attend any pitched battle; and that these now reported that no victory could be expected if they fought before the new moon.

The accuracy of this statement Caesar resolved to test, and leaving a sufficient force behind him in either camp, and massing in front of the smaller the whole of his native auxiliaries, forming a conspicuous object to the enemy,—a device by which he compensated for his relative weakness in legionary troops when compared with the large numbers of the Germans—with his main body drawn up in three parallel lines he marched boldly up to the laager. The enemy had now nothing left but to fight, and issuing in force, they formed for battle, ranged in order of tribes, with regular intervals separating each. There were Harudes and Marcomani, Triboces and Vangiones, Nemetes, Sedusii, and Suebi. The whole line rested on a huge semi-circle of wagons and carts which had been dragged into position so as to preclude all thought of flight, and were now filled with masses of wildly excited women, who, as their fighting men moved out to battle, waved their arms in passionate entreaty that they might be saved from Roman slavery.

In order that every man might realize that his conduct on that day was under observation from a responsible officer, Caesar first appointed his staff officers and paymaster to the command of his separate legions; then noticing that the enemy's line was weakest on his own right, he opened the battle at that point. The Roman infantry, on receiving the signal, charged with impetuous fury; but finding themselves encountered by an equally swift advance on the part of the enemy, they had no means of using their javelins, and so throwing these away, they at once went to work with the sword. With a lightning-like movement, of which long experience had made them masters, the Germans threw themselves into solid squares, and with shields thrust out like a wall, caught the descending swords of the Romans. To break up this formation, many of the troops did not hesitate to leap boldly on the living mass, where, tearing the interlocked shields aside with their hands, they drove their swords downward. Before long the Roman right was plainly victorious; the enemy had been routed, and was now in full retreat. On the other hand, upon the left, the superior numbers of the Germans had borne down all before them, and the Roman line at this moment was in course of giving way. Observing the critical nature of the position, P. Crassus, the young officer commanding the cavalry brigade, who was better placed than those actually engaged in the fighting line to give the necessary orders, at once assumed the responsibility of sending up the third line to reinforce the threatened wing.

This action restored the battle, and the Germans from one end of the line to the other now turned and fled, their flight continuing uninterruptedly till they reached the Rhine, some five miles distant from the field. There just a handful who trusted to their powers of swimming plunged into the water, or finding a few small rowing boats, pulled out into safety. Among these last was Ariovistus, who, lighting upon a little vessel that was tied up to the shore, made good his escape by its means. The rest were all ridden down and killed by the cavalry. Of Ariovistus's two wives both perished in the pursuit, the one a Suebian, who had accompanied him on his leaving home, the other a Norican princess, a sister to King Voccio, who had been sent by her brother to the German king and married to him while in Gaul. Of his daughters one was killed and one captured. Most remarkable was the fate that overtook the young Gallic nobleman C. Valerius Procillus. In the midst of the pursuit, as he was being dragged along by his keepers heavily manacled in three chains, he stumbled right upon Caesar himself, who was riding with the cavalry. His unlooked-for reappearance brought no less pleasure to the Roman commander-in-chief than the victory itself; and the sight of this distinguished chieftain so unexpectedly rescued from the enemy and safely restored to himself (a man who not only belonged to one of the most aristocratic families in the Province, but was an intimate friend of his own, whose hospitality he had often shared), did but complete the satisfaction proper to the occasion, by the knowledge that Fortune had not tinged it with any cloud of regret for the loss of such a comrade. He used afterward to tell the story that on three separate occasions in his own presence lots were cast to determine whether he should be forthwith burned to death or held over for a future date, and that he owed his life to the lucky throw of the lots. His companion, M. Mettius, was discovered under similar circumstances and brought back to Caesar.

The news of this battle quickly made its way on the farther side of the Rhine, and the Suebi, who had camped at the river, at once broke up and started to return home. They were closely followed by the Ubii, a neighboring people whose lands lie along the banks, and in their state of trepidation suffered severely. Thus in a single summer Caesar had completed two campaigns of more than ordinary importance, and though the season of the year did not necessitate it, he yet determined to send his army into winter quarters without further delay, choosing for this purpose the country of the Sequani. The command of the various camps was entrusted to Labienus, after which he himself left Gaul to return to Northern Italy, there to conduct the civil administration of the courts.

BOOK II

THE CONQUEST OF THE BELGAE

IN THE MIDST OF THESE OCCUPATIONS SOUTH OF THE ALPS, TIDINGS reached the Roman governor of fresh disturbances in Further Gaul. At first nothing more than vague rumors, the unwelcome news was presently confirmed by a dispatch received from Labienus, reporting that the entire Belgic confederacy, or in other words one of the three principal divisions of Gaul, was combining in a hostile movement against Rome, and that to ensure mutual loyalty hostages were already being freely interchanged. The rising was due to various contributory causes, chief among which was the fear lest the advance of Roman arms should not be stayed with the recently effected pacification of Central Gaul, but would next be made to embrace the northern divisions of the country. These misgivings were, moreover, sedulously fostered and exploited by interested agitators from without. Appeals were made to the Belgae from three classes of disappointed Celts. Many of these, though glad enough to see an end put to the long residence of the German invader in the land, were now chafing on the other hand at the sight of the Roman army wintering in their midst, to all appearances in permanent occupation of the country. Others again, with the easygoing lightheartedness of their race, were for trying any change of masters, provided only it were a change; while with others the motive was frankly selfish. In the Gaul of those days kingdoms and thrones were as often as not the prize of any more prominent chief who could afford to gather round him a large mercenary force; and this practice, it was felt, under Roman rule, would be considerably curtailed.

Such news was too serious to be ignored, and as a first precaution Caesar determined to increase his military establishment by raising two new legions in his Italian province. About the time of the spring equinox these were sent over the Alps under a staff officer, Q. Pedius, and as soon as there was grass enough to make military operations practicable, he himself rejoined his army. The Senones (*Sens*) and other tribes skirting the Belgic frontier were made responsible for discovering the real state of things within the suspected area, and for reporting this at once to the commander in chief. In every case the answer was the same: the tribal levies were massing, and the confederate army was rapidly being gathered. Satisfied at length with the nature of the evidence, Caesar no longer hesitated about an armed invasion of their land, but waiting only till his supplies were properly organized, he broke up from winter quarters, and within a fortnight was upon the Belgic border.

Such a movement, in itself quite unexpected, had by the rapidity of its execution overthrown all calculations. As a consequence the Remi (*Rheims*), the nearest tribe of all to Central Gaul, hastened to send in a deputation to the Roman general, consisting of their two leading chieftains, Iccius and Andecomborius. These, speaking on behalf of their government, announced their unconditional surrender to the Roman people, whose supremacy they acknowledged, and whose protection they craved. They further declared that from the first beginning the Remi had held aloof from the other Belgic states, and were innocent of all complicity in the movement against Rome. To support this contention, they assured the Roman commander of their willingness to deliver hostages, to execute any orders he might impose, to open their gates to his army, and to furnish it with corn and anything else in their power. Continuing their information, they declared that the rest of the Belgic states were, to a man, in arms, and were aided and abetted by the German tribes settled west of the Rhine. To give some idea of the wave of

fanaticism then sweeping the country, the envoys cited the case of
the Suessiones (*Soissons*). This people was of the same stock and lin-
eage as themselves, enjoyed community both of public and private
rights, and owned the same legislative and executive authority: yet
every effort on their part to restrain them from joining the national
cause had been consistently rebuffed.

Inquiry by Caesar into the nature, number, and military efficiency
of the tribes who had taken the field elicited the following information. The vast majority of the Belgic people were of German origin,
having crossed the Rhine in very early ages, through the allurement
exercised by the rich lands on its western bank; where, after first
expelling the existing Gallic occupants, they had permanently settled. More recently, at the great irruption of Cimbric and Teutonic
hordes, a time which many living could still remember, while the
rest of Gaul lay prostrate before the invaders, they alone had pre-
served the inviolability of their frontiers. Of this feat of arms they
were inordinately proud, and on it founded a claim to exceptional
authority among their neighbors. With regard to numbers, the
Remian representatives, owing to their geographical and racial affin-
ity with the tribes concerned, professed to have most accurate
information, based on the exact figures promised by each confederate at the general assembly called to discuss the war. From this it
appeared that the most formidable were beyond doubt the Bellovaci
(*Beauvais*), regarded from the point of view of their fine military qualities, the great influence they exercised over others, or the density of
their population. Able to put 100,000 men into the field, with a promise of a picked contingent of 60,000 they had coupled a demand for
the exclusive conduct of the war. Next in order came the Suessiones
(*Soissons*), those neighbors of the Remi who have been already mentioned, whose country, the envoys declared, both for fertility and
extent, to be superior to all. Only a few years ago this tribe had produced a king who stood unrivaled among the princes of Gaul, and
whose dominions included not only most of the neighboring territories, but even parts of Britain. Their present ruler was a king named
Galba, whose disinterested and farsighted character had procured for

him by common consent the supreme direction of the war. They possessed twelve regular towns, and had engaged to furnish 50,000 fighting men. The same contribution was made by the Nervii, who were generally regarded as the fiercest of the tribesmen, and lived at the greatest distance. Then followed a long list of smaller contingents; 15,000 from the Atrebates (*Arras*), 10,000 from the Ambiani (*Amiens*), 25,000 from the Morini (*Boulogne-Calais*), 7,000 from the Menapii (*Maas* and *Scheldt*), 10,000 from the Caleti, 10,000 also from the combined Veliocasses and Viromandui, 19,000 from the Aduatici; and lastly, as far as the Remian ambassadors could estimate, another 40,000 supplied from the Condrusi, Eburones, Caeroesi, and Paemani, tribes collectively known as Germans.

This concluded the information of the envoys, who after a courteous reception by Caesar and an assurance of his warmest sympathy, were dismissed with the message that their tribal council must appear in person, bringing with them as hostages the sons of their leading chiefs. This order they punctually and scrupulously obeyed, and meanwhile he himself once more took into his confidence the Aeduan prince Divitiacus. Addressing to him an earnest appeal for cooperation and support, he pointed out how much it would conduce from a military point of view to the ultimate success of the campaign, if they could first break up the various combinations of the enemy, and so avoid the necessity of fighting with such dense masses of tribesmen at once. This object, he explained, the Aeduan government now had it in its power to secure, by ordering its military forces to invade the country of the Bellovaci, and to begin devastating that country. Thus instructed, the Aeduan chieftain took his departure. It soon became evident that the enemy had succeeded in their concentration, and were already marching to the attack; and accordingly very soon afterward their near approach was reported to headquarters, both by the Remi and by the Roman scouts. On receipt of this intelligence, Caesar hastened to transfer his army to the right bank of the Axona (*Aisne*), which here forms the northern boundary of the Remi, and to take up an entrenched position on its farther side. Three advantages accrued from this movement. In the first place, it gave him the natural defense of a riverbank for one side of his camp; in the second it effectually secured all the country in his rear; and in the third, it enabled supplies to be transported by the Remi and other friendly tribes without fear of molestation to the convoys. The river itself being spanned by a bridge, a detachment was posted at the northern end to command the approach, while on the southern side a force of six battalions was left in a strong position under the divisional officer, Q. Titurius Sabinus. The camp itself by Caesar's orders had a rampart twelve feet high, and a ditch fully eighteen feet in width.

Eight miles north of the Roman position lay a town called Bibrax. A desperate attempt to capture this on the march was made by the united Belgae in their movement southward; so fierce indeed was the attack, that on the day it took place the garrison barely held its own. The Belgian method of assaulting walled towns, it may here be explained, differs in nowise from that commonly followed by the Gauls. The enemy's defenses are first surrounded by force of over-powering numbers, whose object is by a devastating fire of stones to sweep the battlements bare of defenders; this done, locking their shields, above their heads, and so forming a tortoise, they advance to fire the gates and to breach the walls. Such a method on the present occasion was peculiarly easy of execution, for in face of the deadly discharge of stones and spears from so numerous a foe, not a man among the defenders could keep his footing on the walls. Night at length brought a respite to the assault, and an urgent summons for help was at once sent off by the garrison commander to Caesar. The former was a distinguished and highly influential chief of the Remi named Iccius, being in fact one of the two envoys who had lately come to Caesar to ask for peace with their own people, and the message he sent was that, unless reinforced, he could not possibly hold out longer.

Though it was now past midnight, Caesar at once, in answer to this summons, dispatched to the relief of the townspeople, under the guidance of Iccius's messengers, a force of Numidian and Cretan archers with some Balearic slingers. Their timely arrival infused

THE CONQUEST OF THE BELGAE ◀ 49

fresh life into the defense, as the prospects of saving the town
improved, while in the assailants it created a corresponding depression, as they saw their hopes of capture now finally vanish. After a
short stay, therefore, in the environs of the town, which they spent
in plundering and wasting the lands, and in burning every village
and homestead anywhere within range, they once more swept on
in undiminished volume toward the Roman camp, halting for the
night within two miles of the position. Their bivouac, as estimated
by the smoke and flare of their campfires, covered a front of more
than eight miles.

Dangerously outnumbered as he was, and that, too, by an enemy
whose reputation for fighting was quite remarkable, Caesar at first
resolved to defer decisive action. The interval he employed in testing,
by means of daily cavalry skirmishes, the real quality of their mettle,
as well as the amount of resistance that might be expected from his
own men; until, on discovering that these were in no sense inferior
to their redoubtable opponents, he hastened his preparations for the
final conflict. The ground immediately in front of camp was from
its natural conformation admirably adapted for a line of battle. The
Roman position lay on a hill but slightly raised above the level of
the surrounding plain, presenting a front just wide enough to
accommodate the army when fully extended for battle; and though
its flanks fell away in sharp lateral slopes, on the side facing the
enemy the inclination was gentle and ran down by a uniform descent
to the plain. The sole danger of such a position was the chance that
during the battle it might be turned in flank by a numerically superior foe; and to prevent this, a ditch, 700 yards long, was now run out
at right angles at either end of the hill, terminated by redoubts armed
with artillery. These preparations completed, the two legions lately
raised in Italy were left to hold the camp and to form a reserve wherever needed, while the other six took up their position in line before
the camp. In the meanwhile the enemy also had moved out of the
laager and were now in battle order.

The two hostile lines were parted by a fair-sized swamp, which
the enemy waited for the Romans to cross; while they, on the other

hand, stood steadily to arms, ready to attack their opponents directly they became disorganized, should they be the first to attempt the crossing. During this period of waiting the mounted forces on either side were hotly engaged. When at last it became evident that neither side would risk the passage, Caesar, satisfied with the successful issue to the cavalry engagement, withdrew to camp. This was at once the signal for the enemy to turn aside toward the Axona (*Aisne*), which flowed, it will be remembered, in the rear of the Roman lines. Finding the fords, they endeavored to pass a portion of their force across to the opposite bank, their main object being to storm the blockhouse there held by Q. Titurius, and afterward to cut the bridge; or, failing that, to devastate the country belonging to the Remi, which was so invaluable to the Romans in their prosecution of the war, and the loss of which would sever their communications.

The movement was at once reported by Titurius to Caesar, who immediately took the whole of his cavalry, with a force of Numidians, archers, and slingers from the light-armed contingent, and hastened across the bridge. On the opposite bank a fierce struggle ensued. The Roman sharpshooters came up with the enemy while these were still in the stream, battling with the water, and were thus enabled to inflict upon them heavy slaughter. With a magnificent contempt for death, however, others quickly took their places, and strove to fight their way across over the bodies of the slain; but before the withering volleys from the shore they too were forced to beat a retreat, and their overthrow was finally completed when those who at first had succeeded in crossing were hunted down and cut to pieces by the cavalry. Thus the attack upon the town of Bibrax and the attempt to cross the Axona had equally ended in disappointment. The enemy's hopes of fighting a big battle were daily growing fainter before the obvious determination of the Romans not to engage upon unfavorable ground; while to crown their discomfiture, their supplies of food already showed signs of running out. A council of war was summoned, and it was resolved that their best course was for each contingent now to return home;

there they could wait and see which of their territories the Romans selected for the theater of war, and could then renew their concentration for its defense. Such strategy, they argued, would allow them to fight the final battle on friendly instead of on hostile soil, and would also put at their disposal the home supplies of corn. Among the causes contributing to this decision, not the least potent had been the news that Divitiacus with the Aedui was approaching the borders of the Bellovaci. Nothing would now persuade that people to remain out any longer with the allies, instead of hurrying back to defend their homes.

The decision once taken, no time was lost in carrying it out. Toward midnight a loud and confused murmur was heard proceeding from their camp, showing that its evacuation by the unwieldy host had begun. But their departure, destitute alike of orderly arrangement or central control, with each tribe bent on securing for itself the leading place in the column and on reaching home as fast as possible, gave the impression of nothing but a wild stampede. His spies at once reported the movement to Caesar, but, unable at the time to account for so precipitate a retreat, the natural fear of ambush forced him for the moment to keep both infantry and cavalry strictly to camp. Dawn having enabled his scouts to confirm the truth of the midnight report, the cavalry in force was at once dispatched to the front under two generals of division, Quintus Pedius and Lucius Aurunculeius Cotta, with orders to harass the rear guard: a force of three legions, under Titus Labienus, another leading staff officer, was to follow immediately behind. Delivering a joint attack on the rearmost portion of the column, the pursuers kept in close attendance on it over many miles of country, killing as they went large numbers of the fugitives. The Belgic leaders made no real attempt to stay this process. The rear guard, indeed, finding itself always the special object of attack, would from time to time wheel and boldly face the advancing Romans, but it was left to fight alone. The van and intervening ranks, feeling themselves secure from all immediate peril, and under no obligation to fight either from the necessities of their own position or from allegiance to any superior orders, heeded the shout of battle in their rear just enough to lose whatever formation they still possessed, and to strain every nerve to outdistance their pursuers. Under such circumstances the work of slaughter was restricted only by the length of daylight available for the troops; and when sunset at last put an end to the carnage, the Romans were able according to previous instructions, to return to camp, without having encountered any appreciable risk or danger.

Resolved to follow up this initial blow before the enemy could recover from the severe mauling just received, Caesar on the next day crossed the frontiers of the Suessiones (*Soissons*), and marched rapidly upon the town of Noviodunum. As this was reported to be without a garrison, the Roman commander hoped to capture it without checking his advance. In this he was disappointed, since a ditch of great width and a wall of imposing height, even when manned by nothing more than a skeleton force, proved quite sufficient to defy all attempts to carry it by assault. A camp had therefore to be entrenched before the place, battery sheds to be carried up, and every preparation made for regular siege. During the night the town was entered by the whole rabble of defeated tribesmen, coming hot from their flight. The Roman works made rapid progress, and the inhabitants soon saw rising before their eyes the great siege mound with its crown of artillery towers. Such works and such rapidity of execution surpassed anything in their experience: in their alarm they decided to capitulate, and, aided by the intercession of the Remi, obtained the grant of their lives and liberties.

Caesar's terms included the surrender of all the national leaders as hostages (among them two sons of King Galba himself), and the production of all arms contained within the town; and these orders being complied with, he once more set out against the Bellovaci. That people had collected all its movable property and retreated in a body to a stronghold called Bratuspantium (*Beauvais?*); but as soon as the Roman army was within five miles of this city, it was met on the march by all the graybeards belonging to the tribe, who with hands uplifted in token of submission, began to express to Caesar their wish to throw themselves unreservedly on his mercy, without any thought of measuring themselves against the might of Rome. A similar incident occurred a little later, on his actual arrival before the town and the laying out of the Roman camp, when from the walls there could be seen the helpless women and children stretching out their hands to the Romans in mute appeal for quarter.

They found a spokesman in the Aeduan leader Divitiacus, who, having sent home his own tribal levies after the successful dispersal of the confederate host, had now rejoined headquarters. The Bellovaci, he declared, had from time immemorial been staunch friends and allies of the Aeduan people, though lately they had become the dupes of unprincipled mischief-mongers. Their own chiefs had betrayed them into revolt from the Aeduan alliance, and into open war with Rome, by the monstrous lie that the Aedui had been enslaved by Caesar, and were now the objects of every sort of indignity and insult. These men had at last realized the depth of ruin to which by their fatuous policy they had brought their country, and had now fled to the neighboring island of Britain. Under such circumstances he begged to add to the prayers of the Bellovaci the powerful intercession of the Aedui, and to plead for a lenient and merciful treatment of their case. Should Caesar decide on such a policy he would greatly extend Aeduan influence throughout all the area of the Belgae; and it was to Belgic allies and to Belgic resources that they had to look in whatever wars they found themselves engaged.

In delivering judgment, Caesar announced that though he was willing, out of esteem for Divitiacus and the Aedui, to accept the proffered allegiance of the Bellovaci and to preserve their national existence, yet, on the other hand, so great was the position occupied by this tribe in the eyes of the other Belgae, and so populous their state, that he must make a demand for at least six hundred hostages. As soon as these were delivered and all arms in the town had been received, he resumed his march into the country of the Ambiani (*Amiens*), who at once made unconditional surrender.

There remained only the Nervii, whose territories lay adjacent. Inquiry by Caesar into the national characteristics of this people

produced some interesting details. No foreign trader was allowed to
enter their country; and the importation of wine and other luxuries
was strictly prohibited, under the idea that the use of such was a certain prelude to national effeminacy and decay. A wild and primitive
race and brave to a degree, they bitterly resented the action of the
other Belgae in their unworthy betrayal of the spirit of their ancestors by such a weak surrender to Rome; for themselves, they wished
to make it known that they would never send an envoy to a foreign
foe, or accept terms of peace at his hands.

After three days' march through their territories, some prisoners reported that ten miles from the point at present occupied by
Caesar lay the river Sabis (*Sambre*), across which the entire body of
Nervii, now reinforced by their neighbors the Atrebates and Viromandui, who had been persuaded to join in this appeal to the sword,
were awaiting the arrival of the Romans. They added that a further
contingent was expected from the Aduatuci and was, indeed, already
on the march; and that all their womenfolk and noncombatants
had been removed to a fen district that was wholly inaccessible to a
regular army.

Upon this information Caesar sent forward some mounted
patrols and centurions, with orders to select a good position for his
next camp. During the night an act of treachery, which was only discovered afterward from the disclosures made by prisoners, took place
on the Roman side. The army being at the time accompanied by
numerous native Gauls,—some of them surrendered Belgae, others
members of other Gallic tribes, and all alike in professed allegiance to
Caesar—a number of these men, having previously made a careful
study of the dispositions observed by the Roman force throughout
the preceding days, under cover of darkness slipped across to the
Nervian lines to report the result of their observations. The legions,
they declared, were severed from each other in the column by large
blocks of intervening baggage: all therefore that the Nervii had to do,
was to wait quietly till the leading regiment had arrived on its camp-
ing ground, and as the others would be still a long way in the rear, to
attack it before the men had disencumbered themselves from their

marching kits. Once this was routed and its baggage plundered, the other regiments, they would find, would offer little or no resistance. To the plan thus outlined by their informants there was added a further strong recommendation in a certain peculiar feature of the Nervian country. Being decidedly weak in cavalry (a military defect which has continued to this day, and is only compensated for by an admirable body of infantry), they had, in order to guard against raids on the part of neighbors, from very early times hit upon a device that was as simple as it was effective. Young forest trees at appropriate intervals are first notched partly through and then laid over horizontally; and the thick lateral shoots which they send out, intermingled with a dense undergrowth of briers and brambles, produce in time a system of hedgerows which is little inferior for defensive purposes to a solid wall, and which is as impenetrable to the eye as it is by the body of an enemy. Calculating, therefore, on the obstruction that would be caused to the Roman advance by such a series of entanglements, the Nervian leaders resolved that the plan suggested should have a trial.

The site selected by the Roman officers for the camp was of the following description. A hill, connected by a uniform slope with the Sambre below (the river already mentioned), stood faced on the opposite side by another height, which rose at a similar inclination. The lower courses of this second hill for the first three or four hundred yards up were open ground: the higher parts were so thickly wooded that the eye could hardly penetrate them. Within these woods the main body of the enemy was known to be in hiding: all, however, that could be made out were a few horsemen patrolling the open space along the stream, the depth of which was about three feet.

Toward this position the Roman army was now approaching, the cavalry thrown well forward in advance; but its order of march differed widely from the description given of it to the Nervii by the Belgae. Following his invariable practice when nearing an enemy, Caesar had six of his legions massed in one division, with every man accoutered solely for battle. Behind these came the baggage trains of the army, followed again by the two corps recently raised, who now closed the column, and acted as escort to the convoy. Arrived upon the ground, the cavalry, supported by slingers and bowmen, at once crossed the stream, and was soon hotly engaged with the mounted portion of the enemy. The action, however, was rendered futile by the constant recurrence of the enemy's perplexing tactics. At one moment they would fall back hastily to their supports within the wood; only at the next, however, suddenly to reemerge and deliver a spirited charge upon the Roman horse, who on their side never dared to press their pursuit beyond the limits of the open ground. These indecisive skirmishes were still in progress when the six regiments of infantry forming the head of the Roman column proceeded to their task of cutting the trenches for the camp, each on its allotted length. A few moments later, and the eyes of those waiting in the opposite woods were rewarded by the sight of the Roman baggage trains slowly laboring toward camp. This was the signal agreed upon for battle. Forming their line behind the trees, and completing there all their dispositions, after briefly rallying one another to the work before them, they suddenly swept out from cover, and at full strength charged down upon the Roman horse. These they scattered like chaff, and then with lightning speed raced on toward the river, in so impetuous a torrent that to a spectator it seemed that at one and the same moment they were up in the wood, down in the riverbed, and actually exchanging blows with our men. Maintaining the same furious pace, they next breasted the hill in front of them on the Roman side of the stream, and making for the camp, dashed at the infantry while these were still busily engaged upon the work of fortification.

The Roman commander in chief had to take all his measures at once. The flag, which was the usual signal for action, had to be unfurled; the bugle call to be sounded, the men to be summoned from the trenches, and a warning to return sent after those who in quest of entrenching material had strayed farther afield; the line had to be formed, the troops to be addressed, the signal to commence action to be given. Many of these orders, from the little time available and from the rapid onrush of the enemy, were necessarily left imperfectly executed. But, critical as the position was, two circumstances combined to mitigate its appalling difficulties. The first was the splendid power of initiative shown by the troops themselves, who, from the training they had acquired in previous battles, knew instinctively how to meet such a crisis just as well as their officers could direct them: the second lay in the instructions previously issued to his divisional commanders by Caesar, not to leave their respective legions and that portion of the entrenchments for which each was responsible, until the fortifications of the camp were complete. Perceiving, therefore, how near the enemy already were and how rapidly they were coming on, these no longer waited for orders to arrive from Caesar, but at once took upon themselves the responsibility of making the necessary preparations for battle.

Caesar himself in the meanwhile had merely paused to give such directions as the occasion rendered absolutely necessary, and then hurrying down the hill to rally the troops for the approaching struggle, found himself, as chance would have it, in the midst of the Tenth legion. The time was barely enough to exhort the men to remain true to the ancient traditions of their corps, to keep a cool head and hand, and to stand firm against the enemy's rush; and then seeing they were now within javelin's throw, without more ado he gave the signal to engage. Hastening on with similar object to another quarter of the field, he found the action already briskly proceeding. So short, indeed, had been the warning, and so determined was the fighting spirit shown by the foe, that not only was there no time for fastening on military badges and distinctions, but the Romans had even to go helmetless into action, with their shields still inside their leather coverings. As the troops came pouring down from the trenches, each man, without looking for his own company, at once formed up round whatever standard first caught his eye, eager to lose no time before plunging into the fight.

The Roman line of battle was thus to a large extent dependent upon the special circumstances of the moment: in other words, the peculiar features of the ground, the steep slope of the hill, and

above all, the lack of time had far more to do with its formation
than any system of military rules or science. The legions were drawn
up on several fronts and fought in detached groups, parceled out
over a wide field of action. Another grave disadvantage was that,
owing to the dense hedgerows which everywhere, as previously
described, broke the line of vision, from no single point was it possible to obtain a comprehensive view of the operations; for which
reason no regular reserves could be posted, nor provision be made
for the various exigencies of the battle as they arose, nor could the
action be directed and controlled by a single mind. Accordingly,
where circumstances differed so widely, results also showed similar
fluctuations of fortune.

To begin with the extreme left of the line, where the Ninth and
Tenth legions were in position. The particular division of the enemy
opposed to these was that of the Atrebates, who, arriving breathless
and exhausted with their charge, had to meet the galling delivery of
the two regiments' heavy spears, which still further added to their
confusion, and were then driven headlong down the slope into the
river. This they tried to cross, but in their crippled state suffered
heavily at the hands of their pursuers, who were now freely using
their swords. Indeed the two corps did not hesitate to ford the stream,
and though the enemy again turned at bay, with the ground now in
their favor, the legions yet once more engaged them and finally
drove them from the field. Success no less decisive had likewise
crowned the center of the Roman line, where the Eleventh and
Eighth legions on a somewhat different front had encountered the
forces of the Viromandui, and after rolling back their attack, had carried the tide of battle right down to the banks of the river, taking full
advantage of the ground. But the inevitable result of this double success was to expose to a most dangerous degree almost the entire front
and left flank of the Roman camp; a situation of which the Nervii,
who formed the third and last division of the enemy, were not slow
to avail themselves. The Roman right was held by the Twelfth and,
separated from it by a slight interval, by the Seventh legion. Toward
this point the entire Nervian contingent in dense serried ranks now

advanced under Boduognatus, the acting commander for the day; until, breaking into two divisions, one half turned off to outflank the infantry on their unshielded side, and the other passed on to seize the summit of the hill and camp.

At this particular moment the Roman cavalry and light-armed skirmishers, after being routed in the manner described at the opening of the engagement, were making their way back to camp, and coming now full upon the advancing Nervii, once more bolted in the opposite direction. A second and similar stampede was caused by the camp followers. Watching the fortunes of the fight from a position near the postern gate and crest of the hill, they had witnessed the victorious passage of the Sambre by the Roman infantry, and emboldened by this result, had sallied out from camp in quest of plunder; but, on looking now behind them, they saw to their dismay that the camp was in the hands of the enemy, and at the astounding sight fled precipitately. To complete the scene of wild confusion reigning at the moment, the air was rent with the shouts of the mule drivers coming up with the convoy, whose helpless state of panic carried them to every quarter of the field. Upon one portion of the Roman auxiliaries this bewildering succession of disasters told with fatal effect. No branch of the Gallic race has a higher name for courage than the Treveri, a corps of whose famous cavalry had been sent by their local government in support of Caesar: yet on perceiving that the camp was now swarming with the enemy, that the legions were struggling to hold their own and were all but mastered in the masses of enclosing tribesmen, that camp followers, cavalrymen, slingers, and Numidians were all broken and shattered and flying in every quarter, these gave up the day as lost beyond retrieve, and rode off the field to their home. There they reported that the Roman army had been routed and hopelessly beaten, and that camp and baggage had alike fallen into the hands of the enemy.

Meanwhile Caesar had passed, after rallying the men of the Tenth, to the extreme right of the line, where the peril was now most urgent. There the Twelfth legion had been driven in upon itself, and with the standards of its different companies all crowded together, had lost so much of its formation that the men were hampering one another in the free play of their weapons. One battalion, the Fourth, had lost all its six centurions; a standard-bearer had been killed and his standard lost; in the others a large majority had been either killed or wounded. Among these was a very gallant soldier named Publius Sextius Baculus, one of the first centurions of the legion, who, wounded severely in several places, was now so exhausted that he could no longer keep his feet. Disheartened by this loss of officers, the rank and file already showed signs of wavering, and there were even cases in the rear of men leaving the ranks in their efforts to avoid the hail of spears. And all the while the attack never weakened; but round the center thick masses of the enemy were still surging upward from the lower slopes, and on either wing the pressure was constantly maintained. It was the moment of supreme crisis: for of reserves that might have been pushed up to the front there were none. Snatching a shield from one of those in the rear (having come up himself without one) Caesar hurried forward into the fighting line, where calling on his officers by name, with cheering words to the rest, he ordered the whole regiment to advance, and at the same time to extend, so that the men might use their swords with more effect. The sight of their commander in chief inspired the weary troops with fresh hopes, and revived their drooping courage; desperate as their situation might be, each man was now determined to surpass himself, and soon there was a perceptible lull in the attack.

In close proximity to the Twelfth the Seventh legion was being equally hard pressed, and as some alleviation therefore to the difficulties of the position, Caesar directed the tribunes of both corps gradually to maneuver toward a junction between the two till they were locked back to back, when a combined advance, front and rear, was to be made against the enemy. This movement was successfully carried out; and the men, no longer in dread of being surrounded on their defenseless rear, where mutual protection was now assured, began to offer a more spirited resistance to the attack and to fight with better heart. Meanwhile from two opposite directions help was rapidly approaching. From the far end of the Roman column the two regiments of recruits escorting the convoy had by this time received news of the fighting, and breaking into a double, could already be discerned by the enemy coming over the hill. From beyond the river also Titus Labienus, after capturing the enemy's laager, had seen from his elevated position the state of things on the opposite side of the valley, and at once sent back the Tenth as reinforcements. As the regiment passed on its way, it learned the true position of affairs from the flying rabble of native horse and sutlers which it everywhere encountered; and, realizing the deadly nature of the peril in which the legions and their commander must be placed, they strained, it need scarcely be added, every nerve to reach the scene of action in time.

The arrival of these twin succors caused a complete revolution in the fortunes of the day. Men who had sunk to the ground in sheer exhaustion from their wounds, now raised themselves upon their shields to strike another blow. The crowd of followers, seeing the panic everywhere pervading the enemy, now flung themselves upon the opposing ranks, all heedless of the fact that these were armed and they were not. Last, but not least, the cavalry, eager to atone for their earlier disgrace by deeds of present valor, could now be seen offering battle to the enemy in every quarter of the field, bent on surpassing in courage their comrades of the legions. But the enemy's resistance was not yet broken. Though all hope of saving the day had gone, they yet continued to fight on with a spirit worthy of all admiration. When their first ranks were mown down, their second line mounting on their prostrate bodies fought from thence: when these in their turn had been swept away, leaving great heaps of slain to mark where they had stood, the survivors, standing defiant on what was now a hillock of human flesh, drove their spears down upon their assailants, and catching the Roman javelins on their shields, sent them back at their owners. In presence of a courage so exalted, we may hesitate to condemn the special tactics they had adopted for the battle. To cross an exceptionally broad stream in face of an enemy, to scale banks of peculiar steepness, and to advance up ground than which none could have been more trying, are doubtless operations of the very greatest military difficulty: yet all these were made to appear easy before the intrepid spirit they had displayed.

The result of this battle was the virtual extermination of the Nervii and the temporary disappearance of even the very name.[1] When the news reached the elders of the tribe, gathered together, it will be remembered, with their women and children in the low flats of the river estuaries, a council of war was summoned to discuss the situation. Nothing, it was there felt, could now stay the further advance of the victors, just as nothing could disclose any door of safety to the vanquished; and by the universal consent of the survivors, delegates were sent to Caesar and formal submission made. In describing the extent of the disaster that had overwhelmed their people, they declared that their governing council had been reduced from 600 members to 3, and that out of a total fighting population of 60,000, barely 500 remained alive. Their surrender afforded Caesar a welcome opportunity for publicly showing his sympathy toward a prostrate and a suppliant foe. Every care was taken to protect them; their territory and their fortified towns were restored to them intact, and strict injunctions laid on neighboring tribes to refrain from all acts of violence or depredation at their expense, and to see that their vassals did the same.

With regard to the Aduatuci who, as will be remembered, were at the time marching to support the Nervii in full military strength, on hearing of the issue to the decisive battle, they had turned back homewards, and after evacuating all towns and villages, had thrown themselves with all their belongings into a single stronghold of their country, of extraordinary natural strength. On all sides it looked down on sheer rock and sharp precipices, broken only at one point by a gently inclined plane some seventy yards in width. This too had been strongly fortified by a doubly scarped wall of great height, on the summit of which the garrison were now engaged in placing large stone projectiles and in fixing a ring of bristling stakes. The tribe itself

[1] They afterward reappear (v. 38).

was descended from the famous Cimbri and Teutoni in the following manner. At the time of the great migration of these peoples into Provence and Italy, all movables which they could not either carry or drive with them had been left behind on the western bank of the Rhine under an armed escort of six thousand of their number, specially detached for that purpose. On the overthrow of the invaders, this body had for years continued living in a state of constant warfare with their Gallic neighbors, until, finally, all parties consenting to make peace, they had been allowed to choose their present territories as their permanent abode.

Arrived before the town, the Roman army had at first to meet a number of sallies from the garrison, and numerous petty skirmishes were fought with the troops; but as soon as the besiegers' lines (nearly three miles in circumference and intersected by frequent redoubts) were completed, the townsmen showed a preference for the shelter of their walls. From these they could watch the sappers' huts being dragged into position, and could see a beginning made to the great siege mound, already terminated by its lofty artillery tower, though as yet very far from its final objective: and the sight at first provoking their merriment, plentiful was the satire lavished on the legionaries for raising so pretentious an edifice at so absurd a distance. Where, they asked, were the hands, and where the muscles which would enable anyone, let alone such little dwarf men as they, to plant a tower of that magnitude against their city walls? (The Gauls, it should be explained, are usually highly contemptuous of the diminutive stature of the Romans compared with their own large bulk.)

But when they saw it moving, and slowly bearing down upon their ramparts, the strange and unprecedented sight so filled them with amazement, that, sending out envoys to Caesar, they begged him to grant them peace. The powers of heaven must indeed, said they, be on the side of the Romans, if these could move engines of that weight at so astonishing a pace, and no alternative was left them but to surrender unconditionally to so wonderful a people. Yet they had heard of the kindly heart possessed by Caesar, and that encouraged them now to proffer one petition. Should his generous nature lead him to grant them their lives and liberties, they begged he would not insist on their disarmament. Powerful and hostile tribes surrounded them, jealous of their military preeminence, and disarmament would leave them wholly at their mercy. Indeed, were this the fate in store for them, they would far sooner accept any degree of humiliation at the hands of their Roman conquerors, than be tortured to death by those whose acknowledged sovereigns they had long continued.

To these representations Caesar's reply was that, provided they made submission before the Roman battering ram actually touched the walls, they would be allowed to retain their independence; though it was more as an act of grace on his own part than any concession to their merits. On the question of arms he was obdurate; and any fears they might entertain about their neighbors, might, he assured them, be dismissed, since what he had done in the case of the Nervii, he would also do in theirs, i.e. solemnly warn them against offering any violence to those who had formally surrendered to Rome. With this answer the envoys departed, but soon afterward returned to announce the acceptance by their people of the terms imposed. Accordingly the arms of the garrison began to be thrown over the ramparts into the ditch below; and though the heaps rose almost to the level of the battlements and the adjacent siege embankment, yet, as was discovered afterward, not less than a third were artfully kept behind and concealed within the town. After this the gates were thrown open, and throughout the remainder of that day the privileges of peace were openly enjoyed by the inhabitants.

Toward evening, with the object of sparing the townspeople any ill treatment during the night at the hands of the soldiery, by order of Caesar the gates were closed, and the troops withdrawn from the town. What followed is inexplicable, except on the hypothesis of preconcerted design. They had, it would seem, calculated that on their surrender the Roman military posts would either be withdrawn altogether or else maintained with diminished vigilance. Bringing out of hiding, therefore, the arms which they had treacherously retained and secreted, and replenishing these by shields rapidly improvised from bark or wattlework woven with skins, they chose a point where the scaling of the Roman lines seemed to offer fewest difficulties, and a little after midnight suddenly dashed from the town. In conformity with the previously issued orders of Caesar, the alarm was quickly conveyed by a line of fire signals, and soon from all the nearest redoubts troops were hurrying up to the threatened quarter. The assailants fought as desperately as their cause was desperate. It was a case of brave men making their last effort, where all the advantages of position were against them, where from the security of fortified entrenchments their enemy could pour down volleys of spears, and where nothing but naked courage stood between them and certain destruction. After 4,000 had fallen at the trenches, the rest were hurled back upon the town; and with the morning the legionaries, having smashed in the gates without encountering the least show of resistance, once more entered the place, which by Caesar's orders was then put up to auction, with all that it contained, and sold. The returns made by the purchasers showed a total population of 53,000 souls.

Contemporaneously with these events, the expeditionary force of one legion under Publius Crassus among the tribes of the Atlantic seaboard had been completely successful; and its commander was now able to report that the Veneti, Venelli, Osismi, Curiosolitae, Esubii, Aulerci, and Redones had all tendered their submission and accepted the suzerainty of Rome.

From one end to the other Gaul was now quiet. The military operations of this summer had made a profound impression upon the native mind, the effects of which reached even beyond the Rhine. From various German tribes envoys now appeared in the Roman camp with offers to give hostages to Caesar and to accept his authority. Anxious as he was, however, to proceed to Northern Italy and Illyricum, the other districts of his government, he contented himself for the moment with directing his visitors to return at the opening of the next spring; and having stationed the troops for

the winter among the Carnutes, Andes, and Turones, with others
that lay nearest to the scene of the recent operations, he set out for
Italy. When the dispatches reporting these various victories reached
Rome, a public thanksgiving of fifteen days was formally declared
by the Senate, surpassing in extent anything ever yet voted to a
successful general.

BOOK III

Section I. Chastisement of Alpine Tribes

On leaving for Italy, Caesar had been detained with a matter of much difficulty and annoyance which had grown up in the southeastern corner of his Transalpine Province. The Nantuates, Veragri, and Seduni are three mountain tribes inhabiting the district stretching southward from the Allobroges and the line formed by Lake Geneva and the Rhone valley, to the highest summits of the Italian Alps. Through their territories runs an important trade route, upon which merchants had for long been subjected to grave personal risks, as well as the most extortionate tolls, and which therefore Caesar was now determined to have cleared. An expedition for the purpose was accordingly fitted out, consisting of one legion (the Twelfth) and a section of native cavalry, all under command of Servius Galba, who was given full discretion about wintering in the district. Galba, after fighting a number of successful actions, and storming and capturing many of their mountain fastnesses, succeeded in winning the submission of the entire neighborhood; hostages were given, and peace concluded. He then decided to stay through the winter, and with this object detached two of his battalions to hold the Nantuates, while with the remaining eight he took up his position in the principal village of the Veragri, named Octodurus (*Martigny*). This place lies in a sheltered valley, which after broadening out into a moderate plain, is then completely shut in by masses of towering rock. A river cuts it in two halves, one of which Galba made over for their own use to the native population, the other he occupied with his infantry, entrenched behind lines of ditch and palisade.

Life in winter quarters was proceeding satisfactorily, and requisitions for corn had been issued to the neighborhood, when one morning the scouts reported to the commandant that during the night the natives had completely evacuated their section of the village, and that the overhanging heights were now thronged with dense masses of Seduni and Veragri. The truth was that the Gauls had suddenly determined to renew the war and to make a bold attempt to crush the legion. Of the several causes underlying this resolve, the chief of all was the self-evident weakness of the Roman force, which, originally but a single legion, had permanently parted with two out of its ten battalions; while the subsequent dispatch of various units on commissariat duty had still further depreciated it in the eyes of the inhabitants. But besides mere numerical inequality, they trusted much to the marked difference of natural position occupied by themselves and their opponents, and imagined that, by an impetuous descent from the heights under cover of a cloud of spears, they could render their opening charge perfectly irresistible. And apart altogether from military considerations, there was the passionate resentment at the violent removal of their children under the title of hostages; and lastly there was the widespread belief that in this occupation of the Alps the Romans were seeking, not only the adequate protection of the roads, but a permanent footing in their country, and its incorporation in the southern Province.

Upon Galba the rising came with crushing surprise. It found his fortifications and defenses still to a large extent unfinished, and the winter stocks of corn and other stores dangerously inadequate; for the enemy's submission and delivery of hostages had removed all fear of further complications from his mind. A council of war was hastily summoned, and at this the officers were asked for their opinions. That they were confronted with a situation perilous in the extreme, without either warning or suspicion, was evident; it was also evident, as they looked out on the line of heights, almost all of them now bristling with armed men, that their communications with the outside world were cut, and that no help could be expected either of reinforcements or supplies. Under the circumstances, which were felt to be well-nigh desperate, more than one voice was raised in favor of abandoning stores and baggage, and of cutting their way out, sword in hand, by the roads along which they had come. To the majority, this plan commended itself only as a last resort; and meanwhile, they were of the opinion that they should await events, and continue to hold the camp.

A brief interval followed, barely sufficient for the making of the needful dispositions consequent on this decision, and then the attack opened. On the given signal, the enemy on every side dropped from the heights, and soon all four faces of the camp were lashed by a withering fire of stones and the light Gallic spears of the country. The assault, however, was gallantly met, and fighting with coolness and precision the garrison, as long as their strength lasted, with the advantage of position on their side, made every stroke tell: gaps in the line were instantly filled, and the pressure on weakened points at once relieved. But as the engagement wore on, the unequalness of the combat became painfully apparent. On the side of the assailants fresh men were constantly ready to step into the place of those temporarily exhausted: within the Roman camp, the slender numbers of the defense made all such expedients impracticable. Not only was it impossible for tired men to withdraw for a while from the fighting line, but even the wounded could not leave their places on the wall and seek shelter in the rear.

Amid such incessant fighting six hours and more had now passed. The men's strength had begun to fail, and even the reserves of ammunition threatened to give out. The fierceness of the attack showed no signs of waning, and the assailants, perceiving the resistance to be weakening, had already begun to tear down the stockade and to fill up the trenches. A little more, and the fate of the garrison must be decided, when the promptitude and foresight of two of the

Roman officers found a way of escape. Publius Sextius Baculus, the senior centurion of the Twelfth legion, has already come before us as desperately wounded in the great battle with the Nervii. He, together with Caius Volusenus, a man whose coolness of judgment was only equaled by his intrepid courage, approached the Roman commander and submitted to him that the only chance now left the Roman force was to cut its way out and to risk everything on one supreme effort. Upon this, Galba hastily summoned his centurions, and through them the troops were rapidly informed of the line of action to be pursued. By slightly relaxing their efforts, and by merely parrying the blows of their opponents, they were quietly to husband their strength until, on the given signal, a combined sortie would be made, after which every man's safety must depend on his own right arm.

These instructions the men carefully observed, and when, a few minutes later, all four gates of the camp were suddenly flung open, the Romans burst upon their astonished foe with a charge that carried everything before it and never allowed them to recover their presence of mind. A more complete reversal of the conditions it is difficult to conceive; and those who a moment before had imagined themselves on the brink of capturing a Roman camp, now saw themselves hemmed in and cut down on all sides by the very garrison they had been so lately beleaguering. Fully a third of the 30,000 men and more, known to have gathered for the assault, soon lay lifeless on the field; while the rest, driven before the victorious legionaries, dared not even rally on reaching the surrounding heights. No vestige of the enemy anywhere remained, and the troops, after stripping the dead of their arms, returned at their leisure to the fortifications of camp. But to tempt fortune too often was not the desire of Galba. The contrast between his original motives for wintering in the district and the present actual results of that policy was sufficiently glaring; moreover, and this weighed with him most, his magazines and stores were now dangerously depleted. On the morrow of this battle, therefore, he first burned all the buildings of the place, and then set out to make a rapid march back to the Province. No opposition was encountered from the enemy on the march, and the country of the Nantuates having been safely reached, the now united legion continued its way on to the Allobroges, and there passed the remainder of the winter.

Section II. Naval War
with the Veneti

THESE OPERATIONS SUCCESSFULLY CONCLUDED, CAESAR HAD GOOD REASON to regard the pacification of Gaul as complete. The power of the Belgae had been broken, the German invaders expelled, and even on the Alps Roman arms had been carried to victory over the Seduni. At the beginning of winter he had felt justified in extending his visits to Illyricum,[1] from a natural desire to inspect that portion of his government, when suddenly war once more broke out in Gaul. The causes of this were as follows. In making his military distributions for the winter, Caesar had stationed the Seventh legion, under Publius Crassus, a comparatively young officer, in the country of the Andes (*Angers*), nearest of all therefore to the Atlantic. The local supplies of corn here proving inadequate, its commander had dispatched to the neighboring tribes several of his officers to arrange for the improvement of the commissariat. Among these T. Terrasidius had gone to the Esubii (Sees), M. Trebius Gallus to the Curiosolitae (west of *Dinan*), and Q. Velanius, with T. Silius, to the Veneti (*L'Orient* to the *Vilaine*).

Of these three peoples, the last named exercise an unchallenged supremacy along all the seaboard of this corner of Gaul. Not only

---

[1] Between the Adriatic and Middle Danube.

72

have they very strong mercantile fleets, with which they commonly trade with Britain, but in practical seamanship and knowledge of naval warfare they far surpass their rivals. The whole coast is here wild and storm-beaten; and as it is intersected with few harbors, all of which are in their hands, they have succeeded in bringing under them as tributaries the large majority of tribes who sail the seas in these quarters. Such was the people who now headed the movement against Rome, by seizing the persons of Silius and Velanius, under the impression that this would regain them their own hostages, lately given to Crassus, by forcing an exchange. Where the Veneti led the way other tribes were not slow to follow; and it being natural with Gauls to act without forethought or deliberation, it was not long before Trebius and Terrasidius were likewise seized. The three tribes then rapidly communicated with each other, and represented by their leading chiefs, swore to observe a common policy, and that, come what might, they would stand or fall together. Then widening their appeal to more distant tribes, they implored these to hold fast by that liberty which formed the precious heritage of their fathers, and not tamely to acquiesce in a state of servitude to Rome. With extraordinary quickness the entire seaboard was won to their cause, and an embassy representing the confederates was then dispatched to Crassus, informing him that, if he wanted to get back his officers, he must first surrender them their hostages.

The dispatch reporting these events reached Caesar many hundreds of miles from the scene of the disturbance: all he could do therefore for the present was to order a fleet of warships to be built on the Liger (*Loire*), which flows into the Ocean, galley crews to be trained in the southern Province, and sailors and helmsmen to be held in readiness. These preparations were pushed forward rapidly, and as soon as the season of the year allowed, he himself rejoined the army. His arrival did but deepen the apprehensions of the Veneti and their accomplices, which a just appreciation of the heinousness of their offence had already excited. Knowing that with all nations alike the name of envoy has always been regarded as sacred and inviolable, and that they had rudely seized and thrown such into prison, what, they asked themselves, could they possibly do under the circumstances but prepare for war on a scale commensurate with their danger? For such a war their principal reliance lay in their fleet, and every measure tending to the more perfect equipment of this weapon was now eagerly embraced. They were the more sanguine of success because of the great confidence reposed in the natural strength of their position. The land routes of their country were constantly intercepted by the sea, the navigation of its waters was, in the absence of local knowledge, most perilous, and on either element they felt tolerably certain that want of proper supplies would make any long campaign impossible for the Roman armies; while should all these expectations fail, there still remained their fleet, and the undoubted superiority which this afforded. The Romans, on the contrary, could hardly be said to possess a fleet, and knew nothing of the real factors that must determine any military operations in that country, viz. the shoals, harbors, and islands; and they would quickly learn that sailing on the boundless waste of the Atlantic was a very different thing from what it was on the landlocked Mediterranean. Relying on these expectations, they proceeded to strengthen their towns, and to provision them from the country; at the same time as large a naval force as possible assembled off Venetia, this being the point at which Caesar would admittedly open the campaign. For the struggle now impending alliance was made with the Osismi, Lexovii, Namnetes, Ambiliati. Morini, Diablintes, and Menapii, and even from the opposite coast of Britain assistance was summoned.

The difficulties confronting military operations in such a country have been sufficiently set forth above; yet from many points of view the campaign appeared to Caesar advisable. The provocation offered by the arrest of distinguished Romans; the treacherous renewal of hostilities after the conclusion of peace, and rebellion after the surrender of hostages; the formidable coalition of so many hostile tribes that was now gathering—each of these reasons, though in itself adequate, was strengthened fourfold by the fear that to shrink from dealing with the present situation would encourage others in the belief that a similar license was allowed themselves. The peculiar characteristics of the Gallic temperament were only too well known to Caesar—their restlessness and love of change, their quick susceptibility to any appeal to arms—and when to this was added the universal instinct of mankind, which makes them love liberty and loathe slavery, it seemed to him advisable, in order to prevent the further spread of the movement, to make a more general distribution of the Roman forces.

To this end a division of cavalry was dispatched to the Treveri[2] (*Trèves*) and the Rhine border, under Titus Labienus, with orders to maintain a strict watch on the Remi and other Belgic tribes, and to keep them to their allegiance; and, there being current a report that the Germans were being invited into the country by the Belgae, to stop any attempt by that people to force the passage of the river. Similarly, to hold the country of the south, a force of twelve battalions with strong cavalry supports was sent into Aquitania under P. Crassus; since the importance of preventing the dispatch of auxiliaries from those regions to Central Gaul, and the formation of a coalition between these two powerful groups of tribes, could hardly be overestimated. Lastly, three legions were sent northward under Titurius Sabinus, to overawe the Venelli, Curiosolitae, and Lexovii, and to isolate all that section from the main area of disturbance. The newly built fleet, reinforced by such vessels as the Pictones, Santoni, and other friendly tribes had, on receiving Caesar's commands, been able to contribute, was entrusted to D. Brutus, one of the younger officers; whose orders were to sail for the Venetian coasts as soon as ever circumstances made it possible. After that Caesar, with the land forces for the campaign, started for the same objective.

The enemy's towns were for the most part situated on sites almost inaccessible, such as the extreme points of long spits of land, or jutting promontories. On the landward side therefore, it was impossible to approach when once the flood tide was in from the deep, a flow that takes place twice a day at twelve hours' interval; while to advance by ship was equally ineffective, because, on the succeeding ebb, the

---

[2] Famous for their cavalry. Cf. ii. 24.

vessels were bound to be knocked to pieces on the shoals. Their investment therefore was on either element seriously retarded. Occasionally the Roman engineering works would so far triumph as to shut out the surrounding sea by gigantic moles and breakwaters, carried to the level of the town walls, making the garrison doubtful about maintaining their position. But in all such cases a large fleet of vessels stood ready to take off all that was of any value, and as their maritime resources were practically inexhaustible, it was easy to sail away to the adjoining towns, and there to avail themselves once more of the same admirable system of defense. In repeating these tactics for the greater part of the summer, they were largely aided by the prolonged absence of the Roman fleet, due to bad weather;[3] nor must it be forgotten that navigation in such a waste of open waters, where the tide runs like a millstream, and where harbors are few and far between, is beset with no ordinary difficulties.

On the other hand, their own ships had been specially designed and equipped to suit the conditions of the coast. Slightly flatter at the keel than those of the Romans, so as to take the shoals and falling tide with greater ease, they rose at their stem and stern sheer from the waterline, and were thus admirably adapted to withstand the heavy seas of stormy weather; and being built throughout of solid oak, their hulls were proof against any amount of strain or buffeting by the elements. Inboard, the timbers athwartships were fully a foot deep, and were bolted home by iron rivets as stout as a man's thumb: the anchors were held by chain cables in place of hawsers, and their sails were raw hides or roughly tanned skins. This last device was possibly due to their want of flax, and consequent ignorance of how to work it, or (what is far more probable), to their conviction that, for riding out the heavy gales of the Atlantic, with its violent squalls of wind, as well as for steering vessels carrying so

---

[3] It is somewhat difficult to discover the part played by the fleet in the operations, owing chiefly to Caesar's method of description, and its transition from the general to the particular. It seems clear he had ships before his main fleet arrived, and these may have been the Gallic vessels of ch. 2, manned by trained crews.

much deadweight, canvas is not the best material. In fighting ships of such a type, the Roman fleet possessed one and only one tactical advantage, viz. that of speed, produced by the powerful stroke of their oars: from every other point of view, the peculiar nature of the local conditions, as well as the constant heavy weather, told strongly in favor of their opponents. The effective employment of the ram was precluded by the massive nature of their timbers, and to throw a spear on to their decks was, owing to their immense height, a feat of no ordinary skill; while a similar difficulty affected every attempt to hook them by the grappling irons. Nor did even this close the list of inequalities. In case of a sudden freshening of the wind, when they turned to run before the gale, the Venetian vessels not only made lighter of the storm, but could afterward bring up in shoal water; and when left high and dry by the tide, were haunted by no fears of sunken reefs and rocks; all of which were a constant source of anxiety to their opponents.

That his present resources were inadequate for coping with so elusive an enemy was now clear to Caesar. Town after town had been carried by assault; yet as long as it was impossible to cut off retreat at the moment of capture, all these efforts were so much wasted labor, nor could any real damage be inflicted on the defense. Under such circumstances the only course was to await the arrival of the fleet. This at last made its appearance, and was no sooner sighted by the natives, than putting out to meet it with some two hundred and twenty sail, they took up their position, all ready for instant action and all armed to the teeth. What tactics to adopt under these conditions was to Brutus and his officers (the tribunes and centurions in charge of separate ships) a matter of much perplexity. The use of the ram had proved quite ineffective, and the other chief method of attack, the movable turret, was hardly less so, for these when raised were still overtopped by the high poops of the Venetians, which not only made it difficult for the Romans to fire at so high an angle, but also caused the missiles of the Gauls to fall with greater impact on the decks. One device there was on the Roman side, specially designed beforehand, which proved of signal service. This was a kind of pointed hook let into the end of a long pole, much like the common weapon used in siege warfare to loosen the enemy's walls. With these the halyards connecting the yards and masts of the Venetian vessels were skillfully caught and drawn in; upon which the Roman galley was quickly put under way, thereby snapping the halyards with the sudden impetus of her movement. The halyards cut, the yards of necessity fell in a heap to the deck, and as the enemy relied almost exclusively on the sails and rigging of their ships, the loss of these at once left them helpless and disabled. The rest resolved itself into a hand to hand encounter, and here the Romans quickly asserted their superiority; for the action being fought out under the eyes of Caesar and all his army, who were posted on every hilltop and coign of vantage that offered a good view of the sea, no act of more than ordinary daring could pass unnoticed.

Having torn away the yards in the manner described, the Roman galleys by twos and threes closed in upon single Venetian ships, and the troops, with a fierce rush, poured over their sides. The new tactics carried dismay into the heart of the enemy. Ship after ship was carried by storm, and all efforts to stop the progress of their opponents seemed futile. At length they turned and fled, the whole of the vast flotilla scudding before the wind. But at this moment the breeze suddenly died away, leaving such a dead calm behind it that the ships remained motionless on the water. Nothing could have been more opportune for completing the work of victory. One by one they were rowed down, boarded, and captured; and it was only the friendly intervention of night that allowed a few survivors to make the shore, after a fight that had raged from nine in the morning till sunset.

This battle was decisive of the campaign against the Veneti and the rest of the maritime tribes. On board the fleet had been not only the flower of their manhood, but practically everyone of riper years whose ability or rank constituted him a natural leader of the nation. The fleet itself likewise represented the full measure of their naval capacity, and its loss was thus irreparable. Left to themselves, the survivors found no further means either of retreat or of defense, and accordingly decided to surrender. In apportioning their punishment, Caesar was determined to teach the natives to respect in future the sacred rights of envoys, and having had the whole of their tribal council publicly beheaded, sold the rest of the inhabitants as slaves.

Section III. Three Subsidiary Campaigns

Contemporaneously with these events among the Veneti, the Roman force sent to operate in the north under Q. Titurius Sabinus had arrived at its destination among the Venelli. The ruling chief of this people, a man named Viridovix, had been appointed generalissimo of all the insurgents of the district, and had now succeeded in raising a powerful army from the separate contingents furnished by each tribe. Within the last few days he had been joined by other allies, viz. the Eburovican Aulerci and the Lexovii, who after massacring their councils, because these refused to countenance the war, had shut their gates against the Roman general, and declared themselves on the side of Viridovix. There also flocked to his standard all the desperadoes and freelances throughout Gaul, whom lust of plunder and a passion for fighting had drawn from their farms and other occupations. Sabinus, after choosing a site for his camp in every respect admirable, sat down to await events. Two miles on his front lay the rebel leader encamped, and morning after morning he moved out in force to challenge his antagonist to a contest. But the latter adhered closely to his lines, incurring thereby not only the contempt of his barbarian foe, but even some hostile criticism from his own men; and so strong did the impression of his timidity grow, that the enemy actually had the effrontery to march straight up to the

Roman lines. Sabinus's reason for this conduct was a deep sense of responsibility; for where the numerical preponderance of the enemy was so overwhelming, it did not seem to him, in the absence of the commander in chief, to be the duty of a subordinate to fight a pitched battle unless the conditions were favorable or some unusually happy chance presented itself.

Having waited, however, till the belief in his cowardice was firmly rooted, he proceeded to turn it to advantage. Choosing for his purpose a crafty Gaul from among his auxiliaries, and explaining to him the object that he had in view, he induced him by the offer of a handsome bribe to make his way to the enemy. Welcomed there as a deserter, the Gaul proceeded to give a telling picture of the trembling Romans sheltering behind their earthworks, and also of the tremendous difficulties encountered by Caesar in his struggle with the Veneti. That very night, he asserted, Sabinus intended secretly to evacuate his camp, in order to march to the relief of his Chief. Loud cheers greeted this statement, and on all sides the opinion was expressed that so golden an opportunity should not be let slip, but that an immediate advance must be made to the camp. This resolve was in reality the effect of several coincident causes. The previous vacillation of Sabinus, now confirmed by the report of the supposed deserter; their increasing shortness of supplies due to defective foresight, the expectations raised by the Venetian war—all these had their weight, but above all was the common weakness of human nature which readily believes what accords with its hopes. Fired by these incentives, they now resolutely declined to let Viridovix and the other leaders quit the council before leave had been granted to arm for an assault upon the Roman camp; and having secured their point, as if victory were an accomplished fact, they rapidly collected bundles of faggots and brushwood with which to fill up the Roman trenches, and then, wild with elation, set off in the direction of the camp.

Situated on lofty ground, this could only be reached by a long and gradual ascent of something like a mile. Up this they charged in hot haste, anxious to give the Romans as little time as possible for recovering from their surprise, and for seizing their arms, and on arriving at the top were consequently much distressed. As Sabinus's men were only too eager for the fray, after brief exhortation he gave the signal to engage. Finding that the enemy were much hampered by the loads they were carrying, he suddenly ordered two of the gates to be flung open and a charge to be delivered. The result surpassed all expectation. So irresistible was the combined effect produced by the strong position of the assailants, the unreadiness and physical exhaustion of the enemy, the disciplined courage of the legionaries schooled by the experience of past encounters, that even before they closed the Gauls broke and fled. Disorganized and bewildered, they continued to be pressed with undiminished strength by the victors till large numbers had fallen, and the cavalry then taking up the pursuit left but a tiny handful finally to make good their escape. Thus Caesar and Sabinus each had the satisfaction of hearing of the other's victory at one and the same moment; the immediate result of both being the total collapse of the rebellion, and a general surrender to Titurius of all the revolted tribes. For high-spirited as the Gauls may be and ready to rush into war, yet experience shows that their mettle is of the softer kind, and if tried by the furnace of affliction offers but a very weak resistance.

Concurrently, or nearly so, with these events, the Roman expedition to the south under P. Crassus, which formed part of the same general scheme of operations, had made consistent progress. Aquitania, whether regarded from the point of view of area or of population, may, as already stated, be considered one of the three chief divisions of Gaul. In its past history, as it now occurred to Crassus, there was contained more than one disaster to Roman arms. A few years ago it had seen the rout of a Roman army and the fall in battle of its commander Lucius Valerius Praeconinus; while earlier still the Proconsul L. Mallius had been forced to abandon his baggage, and to fly with his defeated troops. With such precedents to warn him, Crassus saw plainly that no ordinary circumspection on his part would be required. Great pains were therefore taken to safeguard his supplies; auxiliary foot were raised and his cavalry strengthened; while from Tolosa (*Toulouse*) and from Narbo (*Narbonne*), both districts of the neighboring Roman province, large numbers of the colonial reserve, the finest troops imaginable, were expressly summoned for the campaign. His preparations completed, he crossed the frontier at some point in the territories of the Sontiates (*Sos*), who, on hearing of the approaching expedition, had collected strong military forces, principally cavalry, for which they were specially famous; and as the Roman column advanced through their country, fell upon it while on the march. The first attack was delivered by the cavalry only, and was easily repulsed; afterward, on the Romans taking up the pursuit, their infantry divisions, till now cunningly concealed in a glen, stood suddenly disclosed, and rising to attack their scattered opponents once more restored the battle.

A long and stubborn action followed, under circumstances that were well calculated to bring out the highest qualities of either combatant. The Sontiates were inspired by memories of bygone victories, as well as by the knowledge that on their gallantry that day rested the hopes of all Aquitania: the Romans on their side were no less eager to show the world what they could accomplish under their brilliant young leader, far away from their commander in chief and the other legions. Crippled by wounds, the enemy at last turned and fled, and in the pursuit that followed lost heavily. Endeavoring after this to capture their principal town upon his march, Crassus was obliged, owing to the stout resistance offered, to halt and proceed by regular siege. The garrison fought most bravely, sortie and mining being both tried on various occasions (the latter with a skill peculiar to the Aquitanians, owing to the numerous copper workings in their country); but Roman vigilance foiled every stratagem, and feeling the hopelessness of the struggle, the Sontiates at length sent out word to Crassus begging to be allowed to surrender. This was granted, and in compliance with the terms dictated the delivery of arms forthwith proceeded.

Suddenly, while everybody's attention was diverted by this business, from another quarter of the town a treacherous attempt at escape was made by the enemy. Among the Sontiates there exists a sort of military order, known as Soldurii, whose members live under

vows of perpetual friendship. Each pair of friends shares in common
all the material goods of life, and should either of such companions
come to a violent end, the other is bound either to incur the same
fate by his side, or afterward to perish by his own hand; nor is any case
on record where the survivor has refused to die when he, to whose
friendship he had been solemnly dedicated, has been killed. With six
hundred of this band, the commander of the town, named Adiatunnus, now attempted to force his way out; but the alarm being quickly
given, troops were hurried up to the threatened point, and after desperate fighting, the whole party was flung back again upon the town.
Notwithstanding this act of treachery, Adiatunnus was allowed to
surrender on precisely the same terms by Crassus.

The disarmament effected and the hostages in safe custody,
Crassus next advanced upon the Vocates and Tarusates. Such rapid
advance came with startling alarm upon the natives. That within a
few days of his arrival before the place the Roman general should
have captured a stronghold, whose natural defenses were not more
conspicuous than those of art, was a feat that filled them with dismay. Far and wide throughout the country the call was sent to rally
to the national cause, and tribe after tribe began to give and to take
hostages and to assemble its armed bands. Envoys even traveled
beyond the Pyrenees, to the Spanish tribes bordering on Aquitania,
begging the loan of auxiliaries and trained leaders for the war; upon
whose arrival, with not merely large additions to their forces, but
with what was even more, the prestige that attaches to great names,
they prepared for a regular campaign against the Romans. For their
generals they elected those who had served under Q. Sertorius during all those years of his residence among them, and who in
consequence enjoyed a reputation for ripe military experience.
Adopting Roman methods, these at once began to seize all the strate-
gic points of the country, to fortify their camps, and to cut the
communications of their opponents. Such methods were not slow to
win success, and Crassus soon found that while his own meager
forces rendered any further subdivision difficult, the enemy roamed
at will about the country, lay astride the roads, always left in camp a

sufficient garrison, seriously menaced his convoys of provisions and stores, and to crown all, were daily receiving fresh accessions of strength. The position calling for decisive measures, without further delay he laid the matter before his officers, and finding their support unanimous, settled on the morrow to give decisive battle.

At dawn he moved out in force and, formed in two lines, with his auxiliaries massed at the center, stood waiting the intentions of the enemy. These, though they had no misgivings about a contest, and felt assured that superiority of numbers and ancient pride in noble deeds of arms would give them the victory over the weak forces of their opponents, yet thought that they saw a still surer road to success. To block the roads and cut the communications of the Romans would bring about a bloodless victory; or if through lack of provisions the enemy decided to evacuate the country, they could then attack while the legionaries were in heavy order of march, weighted down with their haversacks, and with little stomach for a fight. This policy being endorsed by their Spanish generals, the only answer made to the Roman challenge was to keep strictly behind their lines. Crassus was not slow to seize on the full significance of this decision. The vacillation of purpose which it disclosed reacted on its authors, and the enemy's confidence in their own prowess was shaken just in proportion as the fighting spirit of the Romans rose. On all sides was heard the opinion that the proper course was now to assume the offensive without delay, and to march upon the camp. Accordingly, with a few words of encouragement to his men, who were but too eager for the fray, Crassus set his army in motion straight for the hostile camp.

Arrived before it, some of the legionaries quickly began filling up the trenches, while others with a raking fire of hand missiles endeavored to sweep the defenders from their place on the rampart and fortifications. In this work the auxiliaries played a useful part. Not trusting them much for purposes of actual fighting, Crassus had assigned them the duty of carrying ammunition and of bringing up sods for the ditches to the regulars; and in this way they succeeded in giving both the appearance and the impression of combatants.

The enemy, however, were worthy foemen and betrayed no sign of flinching, while their spears coming from the higher position fell with deadly effect upon the assailants. The battle was still undecided when news of a possible diversion in the rear reached the ears of the Roman general. His cavalry, having by this time ridden round the camp, returned with the report that in the neighborhood of the postern gate the defenses were not quite so elaborate, and might be easily approached.

On this Crassus called round him his various squadron leaders, and after carefully explaining his intention, urged each to excite the daring of his troopers by the promise of handsome rewards. Acting on these instructions, they then first returned to the Roman camp, where they picked up the garrison battalions whose strength was still unimpaired by the toil of battle; and then making a wide detour, so as to avoid detection from the camp opposite, reached the weak spot in the enemy's defenses, alluded to above, while the eyes and attention of all were still riveted on the struggle raging at the front. There, tearing away the stockade before any indication of their approach had been noted by the enemy, or these had awakened to the full measure of their peril, they quickly established themselves on the inner side. A few moments later, and the roar of battle coming from that quarter fell on the expectant ears of the stormers at the front; and at the sound, as so often happens where victory is in sight, strength and dash were renewed, and the attack pressed home with fiercer energy. Surrounded on all sides, the enemy now gave up the day as lost, and in a wild rush for life began leaping over the defenses. But across the perfectly level plains the cavalry pursued with deadly effect; and when at last the men rode back to camp far on in the night, they had left alive barely one fourth of the 50,000 tribesmen known to have assembled from Aquitania and the country of the Cantabri (*Northwest Spain*).

The tidings of this disastrous battle was at once followed by the surrender of the vast majority of tribes; and hostages from the Tarbelli, Bigerriones, Ptianii, Vocates, Tarusates, Elusates, Gates, Ausci, Garumni, Sibuzates, and Cocosates were now given up to Crassus.

The sole exceptions were a few tribes from the outlying portions of the country, who considered that the near approach of winter made it safe to refuse compliance.

The whole of Gaul was now quiet, the only tribes still in the field being the Morini and Menapii,[4] neither of whom had as yet shown any disposition to accept terms of peace from the Roman governor. Although therefore the season was almost over, Caesar determined to make yet one more expedition this year, under the belief that a campaign against these two tribes could be rapidly carried through. On entering their country, however, with the Roman forces, he found that they had adopted a method of warfare wholly at variance with the previous practice of the Gauls. Perceiving that the attempt to fight the Romans in the open had invariably brought disaster upon even the strongest tribes, they had decided to make full use of their natural advantages; and with this object had buried themselves and all their belongings in the heart of those immense tracts of forest and fen that characterize this district. The Roman army had arrived on the outskirts of these forests, and had begun entrenching for the night, no sign being yet anywhere seen of the enemy, when just as the men had scattered for their work, suddenly from all sides of the wood a furious charge was made upon the astonished troops. The latter flew to arms, and, the attack having been beaten off, drove them back into the wood with heavy loss; though in attempting to follow them into the intricacies of the forest, they suffered certain casualties of their own.

The next few days were spent in cutting a wedge through this dense woodland. To protect his men from being suddenly assailed in flank, when for the time the sword had been laid aside for the ax, Caesar directed that the timber, as fast as it was felled, should be stacked in two parallel rows facing the enemy, thus forming a steep rampart on either side. The work proceeded with amazing rapidity, and in a few days a sufficient avenue had been cleared to enable the

---

[4] They had joined not only the Veneti this year, but also the Belgic confederacy of the year before (II. 4).

troops to seize some of the enemy's cattle and the hindmost portion of the baggage, though they themselves ever receded toward the thicker parts of the bush. At this stage operations had to be suspended, bad weather and continual rain making it impossible to keep the troops any longer under canvas. Having therefore wasted all the cultivated lands and burned every village and homestead within reach, Caesar returned with the army, which was then distributed for the winter among the Aulerci, Lexovii, and other tribes lately in rebellion.

BOOK IV

SECTION I. THE USIPETES AND TENCTERI

IN THE WINTER WHICH FOLLOWED, SOME TIME AFTER THE CONSULS FOR THE New Year (C. Cn. Pompeius and M. Crassus) had taken office, Gaul was once more afflicted with an irruption of German tribes. Two of these, the Usipetes and Tencteri, crossed the Rhine with an immense following at a point a little above its junction with the sea. The invasion was caused by pressure from behind, the two tribes having for a long period been subjected to a galling persecution at the hands of the Suebi, who made the tillage of their lands impossible. In territorial extent, as well as in natural aptitude for war, the Suebi are among the first of German tribes. Common report credits them with the possession of 100 cantons, each of which furnishes an annual contingent of 1,000 armed warriors. Year by year these cross the frontiers for war, while the rest of their manhood stays at home in order to raise the necessary food both for themselves and their comrades abroad, until they in their turn go forth to battle, and the others return to civil life. In this way they contrive to maintain unimpaired both the cultivation of their lands and also the adequate training of the nation for war. Yet there is a curious want of permanence in all their relations to the soil. Not only is private ownership unknown among them, but even in their communal holdings they are forbidden to remain longer than a single year in the same district. On the other hand, they are not greatly dependent on the raising of corn, their staple food consisting of milk and the flesh of herds, while hunting also is a very favorite pursuit. Indeed their wonderful physique is mainly attributable to this pastime, as it necessitates a rough diet, constant hard exercise, and an untrammeled freedom of life (from boyhood they are taught no habits of obedience, and never think of practicing the least degree of self-restraint) resulting in that immense bodily strength and proportion of limb and muscle that are truly astounding. So hardy is their condition, that though the climate is one of the most rigorous, they are accustomed to wear nothing but a few skins, the scanty covering of which leaves a large part of the body exposed, and they habitually bathe in their rivers.

As to their intercourse with the outside world, traders are admitted among them more to provide a market for the disposal of the spoils of war, than for any need they feel for the use of foreign wares. Even the excellent horses of the Gauls, which form their special pride, and on the rearing of which they will spend enormous sums, the Germans do not take the trouble to import, but prefer their own small, coarse, country-bred animals, which by constant usage they can render capable of the hardest work. In cavalry engagements they will often suddenly dismount and fight on foot, and during this time the animals are trained to stand perfectly still, until at the right moment their riders rapidly rejoin them. Nothing in their code of honor is a deeper disgrace, or a more certain sign of sloth, than the use of a saddle; and against cavalry so mounted they will not hesitate to charge, whatever be the disparity of numbers. Another import strictly forbidden by them is wine. This, they consider, saps the vigor and energies of a man, and ultimately destroys his manhood.

On the political side of their character we find a similar spirit of exclusiveness and love of isolation. To have a vast desert of unpopulated lands lying round their frontiers is to them a subject of much complacency, since in it they discern a striking tribute to their own invincibility from a large number of defeated rivals. On one side of the Suebi, indeed, there is said to exist a tract of not less than 600 miles of untenanted lands. Along the opposite side, however, the

Ubii march with their frontiers. Time was when this people formed, according to the German standard, a strong and prosperous community, and they have attained to a civilization that is in some respects superior, not only to that commonly found in a similar state of society, but even to others outside it. This is explained by their nearness to the Rhine, and their consequent easy intercourse with traders, and by the fact that through having the Gauls for their neighbors they have succeeded in assimilating much of the Gallic refinement. At the point we have now reached persistent efforts had been made by the Suebi to dispossess this troublesome neighbor of their lands, and war after war had been waged between them; but though they had failed in their principal object, owing to the strength and vitality exhibited by their opponents, they had yet succeeded in imposing on them a tribute, and in leaving them shorn of much of their original power and greatness.

A similar treatment had been meted out to the Usipetes and Tencteri, the two tribes mentioned at the beginning of this section. For many years they had offered a stout resistance to their persecutors, but in the end their eviction had been accomplished; and after wandering homeless about Germany for a space of three years, they had finally reached the Rhine. The particular point of the river which they struck was occupied by the Menapii, whose settlements, with cultivated lands, homesteads, and villages, lay on either bank. The approach of so formidable a host naturally produced grave alarm among these inhabitants, and, evacuating their homes on the farther side, they fell back to the western bank of the river, which they then closely picketed in hope of stopping the passage of the Germans. To accomplish this end the emigrants tried every conceivable device. The attempt to cross by force failed for want of boats; every endeavor to snatch a surreptitious crossing was foiled by the watchful Menapian posts, until, nothing being left to them but artifice, they pretended to have abandoned their migratory movement and to be returning home, and took a three days' march into the interior. Then, suddenly wheeling round, they covered the whole of that distance on horseback in a single night, and falling on the hapless

Menapii, who, when informed by their scouts of their departure, had confidently returned to their settlements across the Rhine, they slaughtered these without resistance, and then seized upon their boats. Quickly making the passage before word could be brought to the main body of the Menapii on the western bank, they dispossessed these of their houses and then supported themselves at their expense for the remainder of the winter.

On receipt of this news Caesar at once recognized the real measure of its gravity. He had learned by experience to distrust the restless spirit of the Gauls; and in dealing with a people who are only too ready for adventure, and as a rule only too anxious to upset the established order of things, he was determined to take no risks. Most characteristic of this weakness is their habit of stopping travelers on the road, and, in spite of protest, of closely questioning them on any facts or rumors concerning any event of passing interest each may have gathered on the way. The same thing is done to traders on reaching a town; the crowd surrounding them and compelling them to give a clear and full account, both of the district they have come from and of the news they found current in it. On the strength of this intelligence, or rather hearsay, they will frequently take decisions of the highest moment; decisions that, in the very nature of things, are bound to be regretted almost as soon as taken, since not only do they make themselves the victims of idle gossip, but their informants usually shape their answers to the known wishes of their questioners.

Remembering this national propensity of the Gauls, Caesar felt the supreme importance of at once forestalling any possible extension of the disturbance; and for this purpose anticipated slightly his usual time for returning to the army. There he found his fears corroborated: certain Gallic tribes were already in communication with the Germans, inviting them to leave the neighborhood of the Rhine, and guaranteeing in advance any demands or stipulations they might make. The expectations raised by these overtures had led the immigrants to enlarge the area of their depredations, and they had now reached the country of the Eburones and Condrusi, both states dependent on the Treveri (*Trèves*). Summoning the leading chiefs of Gaul to meet him at his camp, Caesar purposely disclaimed all knowledge of the facts discovered, and strove instead to recall them to a sense of calm and confidence; and having ordered fresh contingents of cavalry, he prepared for war with the invaders.

Arrangements for supplies being completed, and a picked body of Gallic horse having been selected, he started for the district commonly reported to be the whereabouts of the Germans. Within a few days' march of their encampment, envoys arrived bearing a formal declaration of policy. After denying that they were in this case the aggressors, they expressed themselves as perfectly ready to accept war with Rome, if driven to that alternative; for it was, they said, a point of honor among Germans, resting on long tradition, to take up at once any challenge offered them without a thought of compromise. But though that was the case, they would like to make one remark. Their presence in the country was quite unintentional, as they had been driven from their proper homes; but they might still prove useful allies to Rome, if Rome desired their friendship; and to gain that, she had only to give them lands or allow them to remain on those already won for themselves by the sword. The only superiors they acknowledged were the Suebi, with whom, as they naively put it, not even the gods in heaven could hope to contend. Any other race of mortals would find them invincible.

To these remarks Caesar made what seemed an appropriate rejoinder, and finished by a clear statement of the terms on which alone friendship could be recognized with Rome. At all costs they were told they must quit the country, for, as he reminded them, it was scarcely consistent that those who had failed to guard their own possessions should now keep those of others: and as to untenanted lands, there was nothing in Gaul, in any way adequate for such a host, that could be assigned them without inflicting grave injustice. But they might, if they liked, he added, settle among the Ubii, whose ambassadors then happened to be in camp, having come to complain of Suebian violence and to petition Roman aid, to whom therefore he would give the necessary orders.

The German delegates promised to report his terms to their people, and to return with answer in three days' time: meanwhile they begged Caesar not to advance any farther with his army. Caesar replied that this request also he was obliged to decline. The fact was, he had discovered that a large proportion of their cavalry had a few days before been sent across the Mosa (*Meuse*) to plunder and seek provisions from the Ambivariti; and he more than suspected that their desire to procrastinate did but conceal their anxiety to await the return of this force.

This river Mosa (*Meuse*) takes its rise in that part of the Vosges which falls within the dominion of the Lingones (*Langres*). It is subsequently joined by an offshoot of the Rhine called the Vacalus, with which it forms the island of the Batavi, after which it rejoins the Rhine not more than eighty miles from the ocean. The Rhine, on the other hand, rises among the Lepontii, an Alpine tribe. Embracing in its course a wide stretch of country, it sweeps with turbulent current past the Nantuates, Helvetii, Sequani, Mediomatrices, Triboci, and Treveri (*Trèves*). On nearing the ocean, it branches into several distinct streams, forming many large islands, a number of which are inhabited by people not far removed from savagery, including some who are popularly supposed to live upon fish and the eggs of birds, and it finally empties itself into the Ocean by a number of detached mouths.

Not more than a dozen miles separated the Roman army from the enemy when, in accordance with the agreement, the German representatives again made their appearance, and meeting Caesar actually upon the march, implored him once more not to proceed farther. On failing to secure their point, they next begged him to send on an order to the cavalry that preceded the column, not to engage in a battle, and at the same time to allow themselves to send a mission of their own to the Ubii. Provided that people would, through its Senate and chiefs, give a solemn assurance of good faith, they were perfectly ready, they said, to accept the arrangement proposed by the Roman governor. To carry out these measures they requested an armistice of three days. Though firmly convinced that in all this their real object was, as before, simply to gain time, and by a three days' respite secure the return of their absent horsemen, Caesar yet gave them a promise not to advance farther that day than another four miles, required for reaching water, and bade them meet him on the morrow at that point in as numerous a body as possible, when he would be able to learn the nature of their proposals. Meanwhile dispatch riders were sent on to the Roman officers in command of the cavalry, the full strength of which had preceded the column, ordering them on no account to provoke hostilities, but if attacked, to remain on the defensive until Caesar himself arrived nearer with the main army.

No sooner, however, did the enemy see the Roman cavalry approaching than thoughts of treachery began to stir their minds. It was a force numbering fully 5,000, while theirs, owing to the continued absence of the raiding party across the Meuse, was barely above 800. On the other hand, the Romans were not in the least expecting any attack. They had seen the German envoys lately take their departure, and that day, as they knew, was one of armistice, specially concluded at their own desire. Suddenly, without warning, their 800 men fell upon the Roman brigade, and quickly threw it into confusion. Meeting with resistance, they leaped to the ground in their usual manner, and after hamstringing the horses and throwing many of their riders to the ground, they drove the rest before them in such a wild tumult of terror, that it was only arrested on coming into view of the main column of march. Seventy-four troopers fell in this engagement, including that brave soldier Piso the Aquitanian, a scion of a noble house, grandson of a chief who had once borne a kingly tide, and by the Roman Senate had been honored with the name of "Friend." In going to the assistance of a brother whose retreat had been cut off by the enemy, he had, after rescuing him, had his own horse wounded, which had brought him to the ground: when, fighting with the utmost gallantry as long as he had strength, he had at last become surrounded, and finally fell beneath the exhaustion of his numerous wounds. Meanwhile his brother had escaped from the action and was some distance on ahead, when seeing what had happened, he set spurs to his horse, and hurling himself upon the enemy's ranks, so met his end.

After fighting of this kind, there could be no further reception of ambassadors or talk of terms: those who could practice such base deception as first to ask for peace and then openly commence war, had certainly put themselves outside the pale of negotiations. On the other hand, to delay to strike until the enemy's forces had grown in strength by the return of the absent horsemen, was assuredly the height of folly; while there was always the instability of Gallic temperament to be reckoned with, and the moral certainty that by this one action alone the Germans had enormously enhanced their reputation in the eyes of the Gauls. To give them time to hatch new schemes of disaffection would of all possible proceedings be the most impolitic; and with his mind made up, Caesar laid the matter before his general officers and paymaster. But at this point the march of events most opportunely intervened to prevent any delay in bringing on the decisive battle. Early on the morrow there appeared in the Roman lines a crowded deputation from the Germans, embracing every one of their chiefs and elder men, once more bent on trying their favorite arts of duplicity and cunning. They had come in the first place to apologize, as they put it, for the regrettable incident of the day before, when, in violation of the arrangements entered into at their own request, they had started hostilities; and secondly, by means of lies, to extort any concession which they could on the matter of an armistice. With no small gratification that his enemies had thus put themselves in his power, Caesar gave the order for their arrest, and then moved out from camp. The cavalry, which it seemed probable would still be much shaken by their recent encounter, was ordered to follow instead of preceding the column.

In three lines, the army rapidly covered a distance of eight miles, and the German laager was reached before any suspicion of the truth had flashed across their minds. The consternation produced was complete. The swift advance of the Romans, and their own leaders' absence, by removing all chance either of formulating a plan of action or of arming for battle, left them hopelessly bewildered as to the best course to adopt, whether to sally out and meet the enemy, or to stay and defend the camp, or to abandon themselves to flight. Their panic soon betrayed itself to those outside by the noise and confusion heard within, and maddened by the recollection of the preceding day's treachery, the Roman legionaries burst over the entrenchments. Here the few who were able to rush to arms offered a short resistance among the wagons and baggage trains; but the great mass of women and children (the migration and passage of the Rhine having been a national one) fled in all directions, followed by the cavalry hot in pursuit. Hearing the cries in their rear and seeing the slaughter of their people, those who were still fighting now threw down their arms, and, abandoning ensigns and standards, rushed madly out of camp. On reaching the confluence of the Meuse and Rhine the fugitives gave up all hope of escape; and large numbers having already been killed, the survivors, flinging themselves into the river, quickly disappeared beneath the waters, some from terror, others from exhaustion, and the rest from the strength of the current. On the Roman side not a man was killed and but very few wounded, and when they returned to camp it was with conscious relief from the dread of a great war with an enemy not less than 430,000 strong. The arrested leaders, though offered the opportunity by Caesar to go their way, were too much afraid of the terrible vengeance awaiting them from those Gauls whose lands they had ravaged to take it, and preferred to stay where they were. These were given their personal liberty.

This fresh German war over, the conviction forced itself upon Caesar's mind that for various reasons, political and military, he was now bound to undertake the passage of the Rhine. Of these reasons the most unimpeachable was the present lighthearted manner in which the Germans were continually invading Gaul, and the consequent need there was of reminding them that their own possessions did not enjoy any special immunity from attack, but that on occasion a Roman army could and would cross the great river. In the second place, complications had arisen with one of the Transrhenane tribes, viz. the Sugambri. It will be remembered that a considerable section of the mounted tribesmen of the Usipetes and Tencteri had been away on a plundering foray for corn across the Meuse, and were not therefore able to take part in the recent battle. On the rout of its comrades, this contingent had recrossed the Rhine, and sought and obtained shelter with the Sugambri; and on Caesar's sending to demand their surrender, on the ground that they had levied war against himself and Gaul, that tribe haughtily replied that Roman dominion ceased with the Rhine, and that if he considered it an unjustifiable act for Germans to invade Gaul, he must also admit that on their side of the Rhine he could claim no authority or power. Lastly, there was the important question of the Ubii, who of all the tribes beyond the Rhine had alone sent delegates to the Roman general, or had expressed a desire for friendship by delivering hostages. At this very moment they were urgently beseeching help against the continued encroachments of the Suebi; or, if the exigencies of public policy rendered that course impracticable, they requested that the Roman army would merely show itself across the Rhine, since that would be sufficient protection and allow them to breathe freely for the future. So profound an impression, they declared, had this army made upon even the most distant German tribes, and so deep was the respect entertained for its twin exploits of the overthrow of Ariovistus and the recent campaign, that their safety was amply assured by the mere knowledge that they possessed the friendship of Rome. These representations were accompanied by a promise to find a large fleet of transports for the army's passage.

But though for the reasons enumerated above he was now resolved to cross the Rhine, Caesar was nevertheless strongly of the opinion that to do this by means of boats would neither be unattended by risk, nor worthy of his own or his country's dignity. The task on the other hand of bridging a river, of the width, depth, and rapidity of the Rhine, was no light one; and yet it must either be successfully grappled with, or else the army not be transported at all. The type of bridge he finally adopted was as follows. First of all, wooden posts, a foot and a half in diameter, sharpened a little from the end, and measured to the depth of the stream, were coupled in pairs at a distance of two feet. These were then placed in position by mechanical contrivance, and driven down into the bed of the river by rams, being set not like ordinary piles, directly perpendicular with the water, but tilted over at an angle in the direction of the current. This done, a similar set of posts, parallel to the first, but sloping against the force and rush of the tide, was carried across the stream forty feet farther down. Across each corresponding pair stout planks were next stretched, which, being of a width of two feet, exactly fitted the space between the separate posts, the whole framework being kept in position by a pair of underbraces running from either side. As these last crossed diagonally, and had free play at the point of section, the strain of the natural forces at work upon the structure proved so nicely adjusted, that the greater the impact of water against the posts the tighter they were clinched and held together. These large planks were then connected by lighter boards running transversely down the bridge, which in turn were overlaid with poles and fascines to form the floor. To protect the bridge when finished, two breastworks were appended. On the side downstream, a row of piles was driven out at an angle from either shore, forming at the center a sort of buttress, which being linked to the main fabric of the bridge, was able to break the force of the current; while on the upper side the same formation was adopted at a little space above the bridge, whereby, in case the natives should launch trunks of trees or boats down the river for the purpose of wrecking the work, a stout buffer was interposed sufficient to break their shock and to prevent any real damage to the bridge.

Within ten days of the time at which the first timber reached their hands, the engineers had finished the work, and the army passed to the farther shore. Strong detachments having been left to guard both ends of the bridge, the main force at once began to advance toward the district of the Sugambri. As it proceeded, delegates came in from numbers of different tribes, asking for peace and friendship, and, being welcomed by Caesar in cordial terms, were bidden to furnish hostages. The Sugambri were found to have made all preparations for flight from the very first commencement of the bridge; and at the instance of the Usipetes and Tencteri, whom they still harbored, they had now evacuated their country, and, carrying with them all their property, had buried themselves in the heart of their vast forests.

It remained, therefore, only to do the work of devastation, and for this a few days were spent in burning the farms and villages and in rooting up the crops. After that, Caesar retreated upon the Ubii, to whom assurances were then given of Roman protection in their unequal struggle with the Suebi. But that people also was found to have departed. On the first intimation of the building of the bridge, conveyed through their scouts, they had summoned one of their usual councils to discuss the situation, and on its decision the order was sent broadcast through their territories to evacuate all towns, to send their women and children and worldly goods to the depths of the forest, and to assemble at an appointed rendezvous all adult males capable of bearing arms. The site they had chosen lay somewhere near the center of the entire Suebic district, and here they were determined to await the Roman advance and to fight a decisive battle. The reception of this news materially modified the plans of Caesar. In spite of their escape, the real objects proposed to himself in the passage of the Rhine had now been attained. The German tribes had been thoroughly frightened, a reckoning had been made with the Sugambri, and the Ubii had been extricated from their state of siege. Eighteen days in all had been spent on the German side of the river, a period sufficient to satisfy the demands both of honor and of policy, and having regained the Gallic shore he broke down the bridge.

Section II. First Expedition to Britain

THOUGH ONLY A LITTLE OF THE SUMMER STILL REMAINED, AND WINTER arrives early in Gaul on account of its northern latitude, yet there was one further expedition this year which Caesar was anxious to make, and that was an invasion of Britain. In nearly all his campaigns so far with the Gauls, that island, he had cause to know, had secretly abetted the enemies of Rome by the dispatch of auxiliaries. Even therefore should the season of the year preclude any extensive hostilities, much might still be gained by a mere visit to the island, such as would allow him to investigate its inhabitants, and to carry out a rough survey of its formation, harbors, and general lines of approach; matters on almost all of which the Gauls were strangely ignorant. This ignorance is accounted for by two reasons. In the first place, what communication there is with the island is, generally speaking, confined to traders; and in the second, even their knowledge is restricted to the coast, and those regions that lie opposite to the two divisions of Gaul. Although, therefore, he summoned to himself most of the traders of the district, Caesar yet found it impossible to discover either the size and extent of the island, the names and characters of the tribes inhabiting it, their military state and organization, or the harbors suitable for the reception of a large fleet of bigger vessels.

To collect such information before embarking on his project, he determined to send one of his own officers in a warship; and as well qualified for the task he selected Caius Volusenus, who was instructed to make his survey and to return immediately it was finished. With all his available forces he then moved northwards toward the district of the Morini, from whose shores lay the shortest passage over to Britain; and at this point of the coast transports were ordered to assemble from all the nearest maritime states, together with the fleet that had been built the year before for service against the Veneti. Meanwhile news of his intentions had got abroad, and by traders had been conveyed to the Britons, causing many of these to send envoys with a promise to give hostages to Caesar and to acknowledge the suzerainty of Rome. After hearing what they had to say, Caesar liberally encouraged and exhorted them to abide by the decision they had arrived at, and then sent them back to their homes. With them was also sent a certain distinguished Gaul named Commius, a chief of the Atrebates (*Artois*), whom after the conquest of that people, Caesar had appointed as their king, and had always found to be a man of high courage and capacity, perfectly loyal, so far as he could judge, to himself, and exercising by his actions very great authority in those quarters of the island. His orders were now to visit whatever states he could, and to impress upon the natives the advisability of trusting Rome, whose general was soon about to appear in person. Meanwhile Volusenus had, as far as circumstances permitted, where he was afraid either to land or to trust himself to the natives, made a careful reconnaissance of the whole district, and on the fifth day returned to Caesar with the results of his observations.

During the delay necessitated in these parts by the work of collecting transports, envoys arrived from the large majority of Morini to explain the attitude of that people throughout the past. Representing themselves as rude and untutored, and strangers to the great qualities of Rome, and as having for that reason lightly taken up arms against her, they declared their present willingness to accept any orders from Caesar's hands. Such voluntary surrender on their part at such a time was more than opportune. Caesar had no desire

to leave a troublesome enemy in his rear; the season disallowed of
any organized campaign against them; and on any ground, trivial
obstacles of this nature were not to be weighed with the far more
important matter of Britain. He therefore imposed upon them a
heavy toll of hostages, and on their delivery the tribe was formally
admitted to the protection of Rome. Some eighty vessels were at
length assembled at the port of embarkation, sufficient, as he calculated, for the transport of two legions: these were accompanied by a
certain number of men-of-war, the command of which was entrusted
to his paymaster, the senior members of his staff, and other officers of
higher rank. Eighteen other transports which had failed to make the
rendezvous, and now lay windbound at a point some eight miles
farther off, were allotted to the cavalry. The residue of the army was
left under the command of the two generals, Q. Titurius Sabinus and
L. Aurunculeius Cotta, with orders to proceed, the one against the
Menapii, and the other against those districts of the Morini which
had not yet sent in hostages. The port was left garrisoned by what
was considered a sufficient force under P. Sulpicius Rufus.

These dispositions completed, as soon as the wind was fair, he set
sail shortly after midnight, leaving instructions that the cavalry should
proceed to the other port farther up channel and there embark and
follow in his wake. In the execution of these orders a certain amount
of delay occurred; whereas Caesar with the first flotilla made the
shores of Britain early the next morning, about nine or ten o'clock, to
find on his approach that the whole line of hills was crowned with the
armed forces of the enemy. The place was one of peculiar strength,
since there was so little space between the sea and the rising wall of
rock, that the shore was easily commanded by any spear thrown
from above. To land in such a position was clearly impossible, and he
therefore anchored, to wait for the arrival of the other transports.
Meanwhile he summoned a meeting of generals and commanding
officers on the flagship, and after placing before them the report of
Volusenus, carefully explained his own instructions. Reminding
them that in all warfare the first duty of an officer was prompt and
ready obedience to orders, he showed the special applicability of this

maxim to operations afloat, where events necessarily followed one another in rapid succession. After this, they withdrew to their respective quarters; and wind and tide now both being favorable, the signal was made to weigh anchor, and the fleet, standing out along the shore, moved forward for a space of about seven miles, until, finding an open expanse of flat coast, it once more brought up.

The Roman plan had been instinctively divined by the natives, and having sent on their horsemen and charioteers (the arm on which they chiefly rely in battle), with the rest of their forces they also followed along the shore, prepared to dispute the landing. This was for many reasons an operation of much difficulty. Their large draft prevented the transports from riding in anything but deep water, so that the troops had to jump overboard without any knowledge of the bottom, with their hands full, and with their heavy accoutrements weighing them down: in this condition they had then to keep their footing in the surf, and at the same time to carry on a battle with the enemy. They, on the other hand, could either keep the dry shore, or else advance a little into the water, and from there, with every limb free, and perfectly familiar with the ground under them, could boldly pour in their raking volleys, and rapidly maneuver their admirably trained horses. In face of such obstacles, and exposed to a form of fighting so bewilderingly new to their experience, the men showed signs of alarm, and the dash and spirit so conspicuous in all their land engagements were now to a large extent lacking.

In this situation, Caesar had recourse to his warships. The long galley was a sight not so familiar to native eyes as was the rounded merchantman, and moreover it could be more easily handled. The order was given to these to draw off a little from the transports, and then by a swift movement under oars, to take up a position on the unshielded flank of the Britons, and from that point to pour in a hot fire of slingstones, arrows, and artillery shot, until the enemy was dislodged and driven from his place of vantage. The diversion proved of great service to the landing parties. The strange appearance of the ships, the imposing motion of the oars, and the wonderful kind of artillery which they carried, so powerfully affected the imagination of the islanders that they first halted, and then for a little space fell back. As the Romans still hesitated, owing chiefly to the great depth of water, the eagle bearer of the Tenth legion, with a fervent appeal to the gods that what he was about to do might turn out for the good of the regiment, shouted to his comrades to jump overboard unless they wished to see the eagle in the hands of the enemy. "I, at any rate," he exclaimed, "shall not be found wanting in my duty to my country and general." With these words, he flung himself out of the ship, and, eagle in hand, made straight for the enemy. This act roused the legionaries from their stupor, and calling on one another not to permit so ineffaceable a disgrace, as one man they leaped into the sea. The other ships quickly caught the infection, and soon the entire expeditionary force was pressing forward to meet the enemy.

The battle was fiercely contested on either side. The Romans found it impossible either to keep any formation, to secure a firm foothold, or to advance by companies; since every man, no matter from what ship he came, at once formed up round the first standard he encountered, to the no little confusion of all concerned. The enemy, on the other hand, knew every shallow, and watching from the shore, seized every opportunity that offered itself. If single men were noticed leaving a ship, they would dash in with their horses and fiercely attack them while they were still battling with all the difficulties of landing. Isolated groups would be surrounded with larger numbers of their own, while all along its unguarded flank the main body would be swept with a murderous cross fire of iron missiles. Perceiving the success attending these tactics, Caesar ordered the boats belonging to the men-of-war, with the small scout ships attached to the fleet, to be manned with legionaries, and to go to the assistance of any who were observed to be in difficulties. Once firm on dry land, with all ranks pressing on behind, the troops quickly charged and routed the enemy, but could not pursue them far, since the cavalry of the army had failed to keep its course at sea and to make the island. In this single respect Caesar's proverbial good fortune had played him false.

Vanquished in battle, the enemy, as soon as they were sufficiently recovered from their flight, immediately thought of peace; and envoys with promises of hostages and submission to Caesar's orders now appeared. Accompanying them was the Atrebatian king Commius, who, it will be remembered, had been sent into Britain by Caesar to herald his approach. After disembarking, he had, in his role of ambassador, been about to deliver the terms of his message, when he was rudely seized and thrown into prison; and it was only after the decision of the battle that they decided to send him back. In suing for peace, they threw the blame for this outrage upon the ignorance of the populace, and on that ground begged for quarter. In his reply, Caesar justly complained of the inconsistency of first sending across to the Continent uninvited to ask for peace, and then without any provocation making war; but attributing it to want of proper knowledge, promised to overlook it, and then ordered hostages. Some of these they surrendered outright; the rest they declared they must fetch from the more distant regions of the country, but would deliver in a few days. Meanwhile they directed their followers to return to their work upon the land, and their leading chiefs from all parts began waiting on Caesar, anxious to put both themselves and their people at his disposal.

As a result of these measures peace seemed firmly secured, when, on the fourth day after the arrival in Britain,[1] the eighteen transports carrying the cavalry, and already mentioned more than once, put out to sea before a gentle breeze from the upper harbor. On their nearing the coast of Britain and coming into sight of the Roman camp, there suddenly arose so fierce a storm that not one could keep its course; but while some were driven back to their port of sailing, others were blown down channel to the more westerly parts of the island, at imminent risk to their own safety. Here they anchored and endeavored to ride out the gale; but, swept by the big seas, with night fast coming on, they were forced once more to stand out from shore, and to run across for the opposite side.

[1] Either including or excluding the day of arrival.

That night it happened also to be full moon, a day which always brings with it the highest tides on shores washed by the Ocean, though of the fact the Romans were ignorant. Wind and wave were thus united in the work of destruction. The Roman galleys which had acted as escort to the expeditionary force, and which had afterward been beached, were quickly swamped by the rising tide; while at the same time the transports lying off shore at anchor were exposed to the full fury of the hurricane, without any possibility on the part of the troops either of working them into a place of safety or of rendering them any aid. Morning showed a long line of wrecks, and even those which had escaped were totally unfit for navigation, being stripped of hawsers, anchors, and other tackle; and as a consequence (under the circumstances only natural), a profound gloom settled over the entire army. Other visible means of making the return voyage there were none; not a single appliance was available for repairing the shattered ships; and, most disquieting thought of all, nothing had been done toward securing winter supplies on the British side of the Channel, since it was universally agreed that the better course was to winter in Gaul.

The effects of this disaster were presently seen in a marked change of attitude on the part of the natives. Those of their chiefs who had waited on Caesar after the decision of the battle, on suddenly waking to the fact that the Romans were without either cavalry, transports, or provisions, and, to judge by the insignificant size of their camp (all the smaller because the legions had crossed without heavy baggage), that their numbers were in nowise formidable, now jumped to the conclusion, after talking the matter over together, that their best chance lay in once more taking up arms and in starving out the invaders. Could this be systematically done till winter, and the present expedition be either crushed or cooped up within the island, then beyond a doubt no other attempt to land on their shores with a view to conquest would ever be made. Secret pledges were then given and taken, and gradually withdrawing themselves from camp, they covertly began to call off their followers from the land.

These treacherous designs were for the present undetected by Caesar, though recent occurrences all pointed to their likelihood, and the fate of the fleet, along with an ominous suspension in the delivery of hostages, made him suspect the truth. He was accordingly resolved to provide against all possible emergencies. The camp was daily replenished with corn from the surrounding fields, and the repair of his damaged ships was effected by taking the timber and copper of all the worst of the wrecks and using it upon those that were more or less sound, as well as by fetching over from the Continent materials and other accessories for the work. In the task now set them, so great was the ardor displayed by the troops, that, with a total sacrifice of twelve, the other vessels were soon made tolerably seaworthy. It was during these operations that, as usual, one of the two legions, on this occasion the Seventh, was sent out to gather corn. No suspicion of hostile movements had as yet arisen, and the countryside was still peopled by its inhabitants, several of whom still continued even visiting the camp, when suddenly the outposts stationed before the gates reported to Caesar that a cloud of dust, greater than occasion warranted, could be distinctly seen in the direction previously taken by the legion. At once suspecting what had occurred, viz. that some new plot had broken out among the natives, Caesar ordered the battalions forming the pickets to proceed with himself to the point of danger, two others to relieve these, and the rest to arm and follow with all speed. After marching a considerable distance from camp, it became possible to make out that the Romans were being desperately put to it by the enemy, that they were barely holding their own, and that the legion was fighting in a cramped position, exposed on all sides to a torrent of spears. What had happened was that the enemy, on observing that in every district but one the crops had now been reaped, had not unnaturally anticipated the route to be followed by the legion, and had overnight secretly occupied the woods. Waiting then till the men had become scattered, as, with arms laid aside for the sickle, they were busily engaged with their harvest, they had suddenly attacked, and after killing a certain number, had thrown the rest into dire confusion, through partial loss of formation, and had finally surrounded the whole party with their cavalry and chariots.

The chariot fighting of the Britons is of the following description. Beginning with a wild gallop down the whole field of battle, to the accompaniment of dense volleys of missiles, they generally succeed in this part of the action in creating disorder among the opposing ranks simply by the terrifying aspect of the horses and the loud rattle of the wheels; then, after worming themselves between the squadrons of the enemy's cavalry, they leap from their cars and fight on foot. Meanwhile the drivers gradually draw clear of the press, and take up a position a little outside the battle, such as will give a ready line of retreat to their fighting men, should these be overpowered by numbers. As a fighting force, they thus combine in themselves the steadiness of infantry with the mobility of cavalry; and so accomplished do they become by constant practice and maneuvering, that on broken and precipitous ground, even when in full career, they can keep perfect control over their horses, pull them in at a moment's notice or turn their heads, run out along the pole, stand astride the yoke, or regain the car, with a nimbleness and dexterity most astonishing.

Warfare so novel in its methods had sorely tried the discipline of the troops, when Caesar, at a moment than which none could have been more opportune, brought timely relief: the enemy at once began to pause in their attack, and the legionaries to recover confidence. For anything more than this,—for taking the offensive, and fighting a pitched battle,—the Roman commander did not consider the circumstances to be propitious; and so, after maintaining his own position for some time in face of the enemy, he returned with his troops to camp. Meanwhile those of the natives who still remained out upon their lands had taken the opportunity presented by this incident, when everyone's attention was fully engaged on the Roman side, to slip quietly away. There followed a period of incessant rain, and consequently enforced inactivity on either side, during which the Romans kept their camp, and the enemy abstained from attacking it. The latter, however, employed the interval to send round all the country a full description of the weakness of the Roman force, and a spirited call to seize the opportunity now offered, by expelling the Romans from their entrenchments, of amassing loot and of winning for themselves a lasting freedom. As a result of this appeal large forces of foot and horse were quickly raised, who now advanced upon the camp.

Although fully aware that the experience of the past few days would only repeat itself, and that the enemy at the moment of defeat would by the quickness of his heels escape all real punishment, yet, having now been joined by the thirty troopers brought over, as already recorded, on his mission by Commius the Atrebatian, Caesar resolved to accept battle, and marshaled his two legions a little way in front of his own camp. The opening of the action quickly demonstrated the inability of the enemy to stand before a Roman charge, and turning their backs to flee, they were pursued by the Romans as far as their unaided powers of running would take them. Numbers having been killed, and the farms of all the district laid in ashes, the troops returned triumphantly to quarters.

Before the day had closed, envoys appeared from the enemy prepared to discuss terms. In his reply, Caesar doubled the number of hostages previously imposed; and as the equinox was close at hand and he was reluctant in the present untrustworthy condition of his ships to put off the time of sailing to the winter months, he ordered these to be brought over to him in Gaul. Waiting only for a fair wind, he then set sail shortly after midnight, and had the satisfaction of seeing every one of his vessels safely make the opposite coast; the sole exception being two of the transports which, failing to reach the same harbors as the rest, were carried a trifle farther down channel.

The troops from these two, some 300 in all, had effected their landing and were making the best of their way to headquarters, when they were suddenly confronted by a party of hostile Morini. Though left by Caesar, when starting for Britain, in a state of comparative quiet, yet the temptation to plunder now proved too strong for this wild people, and surrounding the little detachment at first with only a moderate force, they ordered it, if it wished to escape destruction, to lay down its arms. At this threat the Romans formed up into a hollow square, prepared to defend themselves, and soon the noise of battle brought together some 6,000 other tribesmen. As soon as the news reached Caesar, he at once dispatched the full strength of his cavalry to their assistance. They meanwhile, with the utmost gallantry, had stood at bay for four long hours, and at the cost to themselves of a few wounded had killed large numbers of the enemy. At last the Roman cavalry appeared in sight, and then the assailants, rapidly throwing away their arms, abandoned themselves to flight, in which a heavy toll was taken by the pursuers. The day following, Caesar sent T. Labienus, his chief of staff, with the two legions lately returned from Britain, with orders to chastise those of the Morini who had been guilty of so flagrant an act of rebellion; and as these no longer had the same retreat open to them as in the previous summer, owing to the dry state of the marshes, almost the entire party fell into his hands. The similar expedition against the Menapii under Q. Titurius and L. Cotta had not been quite so successful; but after devastating the country, destroying the crops, and burning all homesteads, it found that the enemy had hidden themselves in impenetrable forests, and therefore returned to Caesar. The winter camps for the year were then determined on, all of them lying within the Belgic frontiers. As to the hostages ordered from Britain, two tribes alone fulfilled their obligations: the rest ignored the command. Thus ended the year's campaign, on a full account of which being received at Rome through the Governor's dispatches, a public thanksgiving of twenty days was ordered by the Senate.

BOOK V

SECTION I. SECOND EXPEDITION TO BRITAIN

THE CONSULS FOR THE NEW YEAR, L. DOMITIUS AND APPIUS CLAUDIUS, had already taken office when Caesar, following his usual custom, quitted the army's winter camps for his visit to North Italy. Before leaving, he ordered the generals commanding the separate legions to see that as large a fleet of transports as possible was built during the winter, and that the necessary repairs to the old ships were also carried out. The new vessels were to be of a special design, which he now explained. A slight reduction was made from that customary in the Mediterranean in the amount of freeboard allowed: this was done to ensure quickness in loading, as well as for convenience in beaching; experience having proved the seas in the British Channel, owing to the frequent changes of tide, to be smaller than those elsewhere. On the other hand, since it would be necessary to carry very heavy cargoes, including large numbers of horses and mules, a somewhat wider beam was given them than that ordinarily used by the Romans on other seas. With regard to the means of propulsion, all vessels, without exception, were to be equally well fitted for rowing and for sailing, for which conversion their nearness to the waterline gave no little facility. The various stores required for the proper equipment of the fleet were ordered to be brought overland from Spain.

Having finished his judicial duties in Italy, Caesar was called away to his province of Illyricum, where the frontier was reported to be suffering from bands of marauding Pirustae. On his arrival, he called out the local levies, appointing a place for their concentration; upon which the governing authorities of the tribe immediately sent word to disclaim all public responsibility for the raids, and to announce their readiness to make every reparation in their power. These explanations he thought proper to accept, and having ordered hostages to be delivered by a certain day, told them plainly that their failure to comply with these terms would at once bring down upon them a punitive expedition. His orders were scrupulously obeyed and the hostages surrendered by the time prescribed; after which arbitrators were appointed to assess the damages between the two states, and to determine the amount of fine.

This question satisfactorily disposed of, and the assize business of the province finished, Caesar returned to Northern Italy, and from thence rejoined the army in Belgic Gaul. A tour of inspection of the various camps showed that the men had not been idle. In spite of an almost complete dearth of proper appliances for the task, about 600 vessels of the type described, together with twenty-eight ships of war, had been built by all but superhuman effort, and at the time of his arrival were within a few days of being launched. After a warm tribute of praise to the troops for their devotion, and to the officers who had directed the operations, Caesar explained his instructions, and ordered the whole flotilla to assemble at the port called Itius, proved by experience to be the best for the passage to Britain, from which it is distant some twenty-eight miles.[1] For the work of transportation an adequate force was then left behind, and meanwhile, with four legions, in light marching order, and 800 cavalry, he himself proceeded to the country of the Treveri (*Trèves*). For such an expedition the reasons were partly their constant neglect to attend the annual councils of the Gauls, and to recognize his authority, partly the

[1] i.e. English miles.

report lately current that intrigues were proceeding between them and the Germans east of the Rhine.

The cavalry possessed by this people surpasses that of all others in Gaul.[2] To it also they can add a large force of infantry; and, as already explained, they border on the Rhine. At this particular epoch they were torn between two rival factions under two chiefs named Indutiomarus and Cingetorix, each of whom claimed the headship of the tribe. The news of the coming Roman invasion made it necessary for each to adopt a definite attitude. Cingetorix at once came to put himself in Caesar's hands, and after a strong declaration of loyalty on behalf of himself and his immediate followers, and a promise given to adhere faithfully to the side of Rome, proceeded to describe accurately the present political condition of his country.

Indutiomarus, on the other hand, lost no time in preparing for hostilities: horse and foot were rapidly collected, and all under military age were sent away for protection to the great forest of Ardennes, which runs as a huge barrier from the Rhine right across the country of the Treveri to the frontiers of the Remi (*Rheims*). But his followers melted away before his eyes. Several of the chiefs, partly out of regard for Cingetorix, partly through increasing fear at the steady advance of the Romans, now left him and came to make private terms with Caesar, since, as they expressed it, they were not allowed to save their country from disaster. Such widespread disaffection threatened to leave him in unpleasant isolation, and before long Indutiomarus also sent in his submission. His envoys explained that it was only a deep concern for his people's loyalty that had hitherto prevented him quitting the center of affairs in order to pay his respects to Caesar, since he naturally feared that in the absence of all the principal men of the country the commons might be moved to embark on some fatal policy. The result was he now held the country firmly in his grasp, and with Caesar's permission, therefore, he would do himself the honor of visiting the Roman commander in his camp, and would

[2] See II. 24.

there submit both his own and his country's future to the friendly judgment of his superior.

The true meaning of such language was not lost upon Caesar, who thoroughly understood the reason that had caused his change of attitude; but not wishing to spend the summer among the Treveri, when all was ready for his British expedition, he contented himself with ordering Indutiomarus to appear before him and to bring with him 200 hostages. All these, including a son and the whole of his nearer kindred, who were specially named in the terms imposed, were duly delivered, and the chieftain was himself then sympathetically urged to abide loyal to his engagements. At the same time Cingetorix was singled out for special commendation from Caesar, and before a general assembly of the head men of the tribe, the interest of each was warmly enlisted on his behalf. Such a step was no more than the chieftain's due, though doubtless policy also demanded that the position held among his own people by such a wholehearted supporter of Rome should be enhanced to the utmost. But the act was bitterly resented by Indutiomarus, who saw in it a deliberate slight to his own authority; and from having entertained beforehand no very friendly feelings toward Rome, he now became fired with the far more deadly hatred and a longing for revenge.

This settlement effected, Caesar returned with the legions to the Itian port. There he learned that sixty vessels built in the country of the Meldi (*Upper Marne?*) had been driven out of their course by contrary winds, and compelled to put back to their point of sailing, though the rest were all ready to start and fully equipped. There had also arrived a force of 4,000 cavalry, the flower of Gallic knighthood, under chiefs representing every individual tribe, a select number of whom, as being men of undoubted loyalty, Caesar intended to leave behind in the country; the rest he had resolved to take over with him as hostages, and to serve as a precaution against a not unlikely rising in his rear.

Among their number was the Aeduan prince Dumnorix, whom earlier in this narrative we have had occasion to mention. Of all those now present there was not one whom Caesar was more determined to have with him than this firebrand, of whose restless intrigues, boundless ambition, daring spirit, and far-reaching influence over the Gauls he already had had ample proof. Another reason for his detention had lately arisen when, before the Aeduan assembly, he had openly declared that by Caesar's orders he was appointed sole ruler of the country; a statement which the tribal leaders, though they much resented it, dared not question by sending either a dis-avowal or remonstrance to Caesar. That it was uttered, however, Caesar had received private assurances from his friends among the Aedui. Dumnorix now exhausted every form of appeal to be allowed to remain in Gaul. "He was no sailor, and he dreaded the sea; besides, he had religious reasons for not undertaking a voyage at that time." Finding his request inflexibly rejected, and hopeless of carrying his point, he began to intrigue with the Gallic nobles; and taking each of these aside, he urged upon them not to quit the mainland, driving home his appeal by the cunning use of fear. "Did they suppose it was without an object that Gaul was to be bereft, at a stroke, of all its aris-tocratic class? No, it was Caesar's design to get them over to Britain, and once there, to murder them in a way he dared not do while under the eyes of their own countrymen." Then turning to the rest, he pledged all to mutual support, and demanded that all should take an oath that whatever course should commend itself as for the best interests of their country they would in unison carry out. All this was divulged to Caesar by various informants.

Assured of the facts, Caesar resolved that, so far as his own jealous regard for the interest of the Aeduan government was concerned, the ambitious designs of Dumnorix should at all costs be put under restraint; but on its becoming manifest that the arch-plotter was committed to yet wilder and wilder schemes of sedition, it became a matter of importance to see that nothing should seriously threaten either his own or the public safety. Accordingly, as the expedition happened to be delayed about three weeks at Port Itius, owing to the strong northwest wind which in this part of the world is so prevalent at all times of the year, Caesar, while at much pains to hold Dum-norix to his sense of duty, yet took every opportunity to discover the projects passing through his brain. At last the weather mended, and the order was given for both infantry and cavalry to go on board. Under cover of the general preoccupation this occasioned, Dumnorix with his Aeduan horsemen quietly left camp, and, all unknown to Caesar, made off toward home. On the alarm being sounded, Caesar at once countermanded the order to sail, and postponing every other consideration, sent off in pursuit a powerful force of cavalry, strictly enjoined to bring back the fugitive. In the event of his proving refractory and showing fight, his orders to the men were at once to kill him; there being small ground for expecting that one who had so openly flouted him to his face, would in his absence act in a reasonable manner. These surmises turned out only too correct. Summoned to surrender, Dumnorix prepared for resistance and threw himself into an attitude of defense, appealing all the while to his companions not to forget their pledge, and crying out again and again that he was a free man and a citizen of a free country. Acting on their instructions, the horsemen then surrounded and cut him down, whereupon the whole of the Aeduan cavalry returned quietly to Caesar.

This episode concluded, the work of embarkation could once more proceed. Three legions with 2,000 cavalry were left on the Continent under Labienus, whose orders were to keep open the harbors, to maintain supplies for the expeditionary force, to watch events in Gaul, and generally to take such measures of defense on his own responsibility as time and occasion might demand. Then with five legions and a cavalry force equal to that left behind, Caesar himself set sail at sunset, and before a gentle southwest breeze stood out into the Channel. About midnight the wind dropped, and the vessels being unable any longer to keep a course, were carried rather too far down by the tide; so that when day broke, the coast of Britain could be made out on the port bow, steadily receding from them. On the tide turning again, and taking the ships with it, oars were got out and a great effort was made to strike the island at the point which last year's experience had shown to be the best for landing. In this undertaking it is impossible to praise too highly the spirit shown by the troops, who, seated at the oar in their heavy and cumbrous ships of burden, without once taking a spell of rest, succeeded in holding their own for speed with the trained crews of the long-pointed sloops of war. The coast was finally reached by the whole fleet near the hour of noon, no sign of an enemy being anywhere visible, the reason for which was discovered afterward from prisoners. Armed forces, it seemed, had at first assembled in considerable strength to oppose the landing; but the sight of the vast flotilla (which, counting last year's ships, and those added by individuals for private uses, reached a number well over 900, all visible at a single glance), had filled them with dismay, and quitting the shore, they had now secreted themselves in a strong position farther up the country.

As soon as the army was landed, and a site chosen for a camp, Caesar, ascertaining from prisoners the precise whereabouts of the enemy, a little after midnight set out in search of them. Over the naval station he placed a garrison of ten battalions with 300 cavalry, and, in leaving the neighborhood of the sea, felt the less anxiety about his ships, because the anchorage where they were riding was an open and sandy bay. The officer appointed to the maritime station was Q. Atrius. After a night march of some twelve miles, the enemy's forces were discovered; and these, now advancing with cavalry and chariots to the banks of a certain river, endeavored from this point of vantage to bar the passage of the Romans, and to force them to an engagement. Routed by the Roman cavalry, they next fell back to the protection of their woods, among which they had secured a most formidable position, of immense natural and artificial strength, and from all appearances built on some earlier occasion for use in one of their native wars, since every approach to it was strongly guarded by masses of felled trees. From the wood their skirmishers kept up a running fight, with the object of preventing the troops from passing the line of fortifications. Thereupon the Seventh legion, locking their shields above their heads, whereby to take cover, quickly raised a bank against the outside wall of the stockade, and swarming over, carried the place at the sword's point, and at the cost to themselves of a small number of wounded drove the enemy from the woods.

Further pursuit was forbidden by Caesar; the country before him was all unknown, it was late in the day, and he wished to leave sufficient time for the proper entrenchment of a camp.

But on the following morning the pursuit was taken up in earnest, and organizing three flying columns, each composed of infantry and horse, he sent them after the fugitives. The advance had proceeded some distance, and the troops were already in touch with the rearmost bodies of the enemy, when dispatches overtook them from Q. Atrius, bearing news of great gravity. In a terrific storm along the coast on the previous night, nearly the whole of the transports had been torn from their moorings and driven on shore: anchors and hawsers had failed to hold, and crews and captains had found it impossible to cope with the fury of the gale. The result of the vessels being thus violently dashed ashore had been a disaster of the very first magnitude.

Upon this intelligence, Caesar at once ordered the recall of all arms, and bidding the troops remain on their present ground, returned himself to his ships. Personal investigation confirmed in most respects the report of the messengers; some forty vessels were found to have gone to pieces, the rest might conceivably, by an enormous expenditure of labor, be put into repair. To the work of reconstruction each legion now gave up its section of engineers, others being also summoned from the Continent; while written instructions were sent to Labienus to build all the vessels that he could with the legions on his side of the Channel. On considering the naval problem as a whole, Caesar arrived at the conclusion that, in spite of the immense toil involved in such an undertaking, the most satisfactory solution was to haul up every one of the ships on to dry land, and then to incorporate them with the main camp in a single system of defenses. These operations took up about ten days, and during this time not even the night watches brought any cessation of work to the tired troops. At length all the vessels were beached and safely housed within a naval camp of unassailable strength; after which, leaving the same composite force as before in garrison, Caesar again set out to the point from which he had returned. There he found that during his absence the enemy had been largely reinforced from various parts of the island, and that by universal consent they had appointed as their commander in chief, with supreme control of the war, a king named Cassivelaunus, whose territories were separated from the maritime districts of the south by a river called the Tamesis (*Thames*), situated about seventy-five miles from the sea. Between him and his neighbors there had existed in the past a state of perpetual war; but the common menace of Roman invasion had temporarily healed all local feuds, and he was now installed by the British as the acknowledged chief and champion of his country.

And here a word or two on the island of Britain and its people may not be out of place. Its inland parts are inhabited by a race pronounced by their own tradition to be aboriginal; whereas the population of the south along the coast are Belgic immigrants, who at first crossing for the sake of war and plunder, afterward remained to settle and till the soil, and are still known in the large majority of cases by their earlier tribal names. The island is densely populated, and everywhere houses meet the eye, very similar in type to those of Gaul, while flocks and herds abound. The coinage of the country is usually copper, but gold also is current, and bar iron, weighed in definite quantities, is likewise used as a substitute for money. The two principal metals produced in the island are tin in the midlands, and iron along the coast, although of the latter the supply is extremely small: copper, on the other hand, they have to import. Of timber, apart from the fir and beech, the species found are just those of Gaul. Of their animals, they have a conscientious scruple against eating either the hare, domestic fowl, or goose, though all of these are kept for amusement or as pets. The climate is more temperate than that of Gaul, and the frosts not so severe.

The island is triangular in form, and on one of its sides looks out upon Gaul. This side is terminated eastward by the corner of Cantium (*Kent*), the usual place of landing for ships from the Continent, and at the farther end by a point that turns toward the south. The length of this side is about 460 miles. The second or western side leans more toward Spain, and off it is situated the island of Hibernia (*Ireland*), generally supposed to be about half the size of Britain, and separated from it by a sea passage equal to that from Britain to Gaul. Halfway across this channel lies an island called Mona (*Man*), in addition to which, if report speaks true, there are other small islands near the coast, about which certain writers have alleged that for thirty days round the winter solstice there is unbroken night. Though we ourselves inquired carefully into the matter, we could glean no information; and the only evidence we can adduce is that according to the accurate measurements of the water clock the nights there were seen to be shorter than on the Continent.[3] The length of this western side, to borrow again the reckonings of the same authorities, is 640 miles. The third side faces north, and is without any adjacent land: its extreme point may perhaps be said to face toward Germany, and its length is computed at 735 miles. We thus get a grand circumference for the whole island of 1,835 miles.

Of the inhabitants, those of Cantium (*Kent*), an entirely maritime district, are far the most advanced, and the type of civilization here prevalent differs little from that of Gaul. With most of the more inland tribes, the cultivation of com disappears, and a pastoral form of life succeeds, flesh and milk forming the principal diet, and skins of animals the dress. On the other hand, the Britons all agree in dyeing their body with woad, a substance that yields a bluish pigment, and in battle greatly increases the wildness of their look. Their hair is worn extremely long, and with the exception of the head and upper lip the entire body is shaved. In their domestic life they practice a form of community of wives, ten or twelve combining in groups, especially brothers with brothers and fathers with sons. The children born of such wedlock are then reckoned to belong to that member of the partnership who was the first to receive the mother as a bride into the household.

While still on the march, the cavalry with the Roman column was exposed to constant fierce attacks from the horse and chariots of

---

[3] Sc. in summer.

the enemy. Beaten at all points, however, these were at last driven back into the hills and woods with heavy loss, until the Romans, by a too incautious pursuit, suffered some casualties. There followed a lull, during which nothing was seen of the enemy; but on the troops proceeding with careless confidence to the construction of a camp, they suddenly burst out of hiding once more, and charging down upon the outposts stationed before the camp, engaged these in a fierce hand-to-hand encounter. Caesar at once ordered up two battalions to their relief; but though these were the first in their respective legions,[4] happening at the time to be posted but a small distance apart, the unwonted form of attack so completely shook their nerve, that the enemy, with a boldness than which nothing could have been finer, drove right through the center of the mass, and then wheeling round, made good their retreat. Among those who fell that day was Q. Laberius Durus, a young commissioned officer attached to one of the legions. Only with the arrival of further reinforcements was the enemy at last driven from the field.

To those watching the engagement, which took place in full view of everyone, before the gates of the camp, it was sufficiently clear that in fighting of this kind the Roman infantryman, with his heavily weighted armor, was no proper match for so nimble a foe as the British. If they retreated, he could not follow; if they attacked, he dared not break the strict formation of his line. The dangers attending a cavalry combat were no less serious; for more often than not the enemy would purposely yield ground, and having drawn their opponents away to a distance from the legions, would suddenly leap from their chariots and engage their pursuers on foot in what was now a very unequal contest. While such tactics were being adopted by the enemy's mounted force, the peril attending a pursuit was just as formidable as that of a retreat. When it is also remembered that they never fought in close, but always in open order, with considerable distances between the ranks, and had detachments posted in reserve with which by a system of constant reliefs tired men could instantly

---

[4] Probably containing more numerous and more seasoned troops than the rest.

be replaced by others who were fresh, the difficulties of contending
with such a foe will be readily understood.

On the next day the enemy kept the hills, merely showing
themselves in small groups at a long distance from camp, and making demonstrations against the cavalry, though with far less
determination than the day before. But toward noon, on a force
consisting of three legions and all the mounted troops leaving
camp in search of fodder, under the general C. Trebonius, they
suddenly swept down from every side upon the foragers, and even
ventured up to the standards, prepared to cross swords with the
legions. The latter delivered a spirited charge, before which they
broke and fled, hotly pursued by the infantry. After this the cavalry, with the confidence born of the near support of the legions
whom they could see close behind, took up the pursuit. The retreat
was turned into a rout, in which the slaughter was great, and no
opportunity was given to the fugitives either of rallying their shattered ranks, or of stopping to practice their favorite device of
dismounting from their cars. The immediate result of this defeat
was the dispersal homewards of the various local levies that had
flocked to the campaign; nor did the enemy after this ever again
venture to oppose the Romans openly in the field.

Their change of tactics was not unknown to Caesar, who now
continued his advance toward the Thames, with the object of pene-
trating the country of Cassivelaunus at the single point where this
river is just fordable on foot. On reaching it, large bodies of the enemy
were observed in position on the opposite bank, which moreover was
strongly fortified by a bristling array of pointed stakes fringing all the
riverside, and by others of a similar kind let perpendicularly into
the bed of the river and hidden beneath the stream. These facts were
disclosed by prisoners and deserters; and acting on their information,
Caesar ordered the cavalry to lead, and the legions to follow immediately behind. Though up to their necks in water, the troops went
across with irresistible dash and spirit; and the enemy never once
standing to await the combined charge of infantry and horse, quickly
deserted the banks and sought shelter in a general flight.

Finding it useless to meet the Romans in a pitched battle, Cassivelaunus, as already indicated, after dismissing the greater bulk of his
forces, and retaining merely some 4,000 chariot men, determined in
future to confine himself to guerrilla warfare. For this purpose he
would hang tenaciously upon the Roman line of march; and having
previously driven off from the cultivated lands to the surrounding
forest all the cattle and inhabitants of the district through which he
knew the army must pass, he would ensconce himself a little off
the main road in any piece of broken and wooded ground. Then,
as the Roman cavalry spread themselves more freely over the country for purposes of waste and plunder, this silent retreat would
suddenly become alive with swarms of chariots racing down every
path and by-lane, to the infinite peril of the Roman force, who had
frequently to fight when widely scattered. The constant menace of
such attack narrowly restricted the area of cavalry operations, and
the only course left to Caesar was to forbid all distant expeditions
from the column; though, in doing this, he of course reduced the
damage that could be inflicted on the enemy, by means of fire and
pillage, to the measure of the stamina and powers of marching possessed by the heavy infantry of the line.

Meanwhile there came an offer to surrender from the tribe
called the Trinobantes (*Essex*), probably the strongest of all in that
part of the island. A young representative of their nobility, a chief
named Mandubracius, whose father had once held the throne
among his own people, but had met a violent death at the hands of
Cassivelaunus, the son only escaping by taking to flight, had already
joined Caesar in Gaul, and put himself unreservedly under his protection. Their envoys, while pledging the tribe's obedience to any
demands that might be made, begged Caesar to intervene on behalf
of Mandubracius against the violence of Cassivelaunus, and to send
him back to them as their accepted lord and ruler. Caesar replied
by first demanding forty hostages and corn sufficient for his army:
Mandubracius he sent back as desired. These orders they promptly
obeyed, rendering the full tale of hostages, and delivering the corn
in camp.

Their example was quickly followed by others, for on observing that the Trinobantes were adequately protected, and scrupulously guarded against all ill usage by the troops, the Cenimagni, Segontiaci, Ancalites, Bibroci, and Cassi sent in similar offers to surrender. In doing so, they informed Caesar that not far from his present position lay the capital of Cassivelaunus, a natural stronghold of the surrounding forest and swamps, into which large numbers both of cattle and men had already flocked. Though called a "town," it was so only in the British acceptation of the term, by which is meant no more than a central rallying point from hostile incursion, formed of some inaccessible piece of woodland that has been fortified by a high rampart and ditch. To this place, therefore, the march of the legions was now directed. It was found to be a position of extraordinary natural and artificial strength, but nonetheless preparations were at once made for assaulting it at two separate points. The enemy, though they clung to their cover for some little time, did not venture to await the final charge, but broke away by another quarter of the town. Inside large quantities of cattle were found, and in the pursuit that followed many of the islanders were killed and captured.

During these operations inland Cassivelaunus had made a desperate effort to create a diversion in the Roman rear, by means of a rising in Cantium (*Kent*). This district, it will be remembered, lies near the sea, and was at this time ruled by four petty kings, named Cingetorix, Carvilius, Taximagulus, and Segovax. To these, therefore, instructions were now sent from the British headquarters to summon all their forces, and flinging themselves without warning upon the naval station of the Romans, to carry it by assault. The garrison, however, were quite ready for the attack, and as the enemy approached, issued from their lines; and after inflicting on them heavy slaughter and capturing a leader named Lugotorix, a prince of royal blood, effected their retirement without loss to camp. It was now plain to Cassivelaunus that resistance had reached its limit. His last attempt had ended in failure, he had been repeatedly worsted in battle, his lands were all ravaged, and now, to crown all, his chief supporters were beginning to fall off. Having

enlisted, therefore, the friendly offices of the Atrebatian king Commius, he sent his ambassadors to Caesar to treat for peace. To the
Roman commander his surrender was not inopportune. The season was far advanced, and what remained of it could easily be
frittered away without decisive results; while the constant liability
of Gaul to sudden outbreaks had already led to the decision to winter on the Continent. After imposing hostages, therefore, and
fixing the amount of tribute which Britain was to pay annually to
Rome, Caesar closed the negotiations by solemnly warning Cassivelaunus to abstain from all unprovoked attack against either
Mandubracius or the Trinobantes.

On surrender of the hostages, the army retraced its steps to the
sea, there to find the transports all fully repaired. But as soon as these
were launched, it became clear that their number was scarcely adequate to the work of transportation: not only had several foundered
in the gale, but the numbers of the Romans had meanwhile considerably increased through the many prisoners they had taken. Under
the circumstances Caesar determined to take back the army in two
voyages instead of one. And here it may be remarked that on neither
of the two British expeditions, either this year or last, was a single
vessel ever lost out of the entire fleet while carrying troops on
board, though the trips made across channel were so numerous:
whereas, on the other hand, in making the return passage from the
Continent when empty, only a very small number succeeded in
gaining the coast, whether of those which now took over the first
batch of the troops, or sixty others subsequently built under the care
of Labienus, nearly all of which were driven back by stress of weather.
And so, having vainly for several days waited their appearance,
Caesar at last resolved to bow to the inevitable; and rather than risk
being made a prisoner in the island, when the equinox should have
suspended for the winter all further navigation, determined to over-
crowd his remaining boats. Fortunately there followed a season of
exceptionally fine weather; and setting sail soon after 9:00 p.m., by
the first of the dawn he had made the opposite coast, and eventually
brought every one of his troopships safely to land.

As soon as these were safely docked, he called a national council of the Gauls at Samarobriva (*Amiens*), and then proceeded to make his military dispositions for the winter. Owing to the continued drought there had been this year a considerable failure of the harvest throughout Gaul, and he was therefore compelled to depart from his usual custom, and to parcel out the legions over a more extended area. Of these one was sent to the Morini under command of C. Fabius, a general of division; a second accompanied Q. Cicero to the district of the Nervii; a third L. Roscius took to the Esubii; a fourth went with T. Labienus to the Remi (*Rheims*), with orders to winter on the frontiers of the Treveri (*Trèves*); while, lastly, three more were stationed in central Belgium under command respectively of M. Crassus, the Paymaster, and the generals L. Munatius Plancus and C. Trebonius. A single legion, recently raised in Italy north of the Po, together with other details amounting in all to five battalions, was sent to the Eburones, at that time governed by two chiefs named Ambiorix and Catuvolcus, whose territories lay for the most part between the Meuse and the Rhine. This last force was under command of two general officers, Q. Titurius Sabinus and L. Aurunculeius Cotta. Such was the distribution of his army, which in Caesar's judgment best remedied the existing scarcity of corn; a distribution that, apart from L. Roscius's force, which had gone to a part of the country where peace and order had been fully established, placed all the camps roughly upon a circle, whose diameter at any point was well under 100 miles. The Roman commander also determined not to quit Gaul, until he knew that each of these corps had reached its destination, and was securely entrenched behind its fortified lines.

At this point an incident happened necessitating a slight modification of these arrangements. Among the Carnutes (*Orleans*) was a highly aristocratic chief of the name of Tasgetius, a member of what had once been the ruling house. A man of striking courage and of wholehearted devotion to Roman interests, Caesar had found his services throughout these campaigns invaluable, and for reward had restored him to his ancestral throne. In this, the third year of his reign, at the instigation of his numerous enemies who had left the country, a plot was formed against him which ended in his murder. On the crime being reported to Caesar, he at once saw that the fact that many were concerned in it might easily result in the public defection of the tribe; and he accordingly ordered L. Plancus to move rapidly from Belgium with his legion upon the Carnutes, and to pass the winter in their country, and at the same time to seize the persons of those whom he found guilty of the murder, and to send them under escort to himself. While this was being done, dispatches came to hand from each of the commanding officers of the legions, announcing his safe arrival in winter quarters and the fortification of his camp.

Section II. Attack on the Winter Camps

ABOUT A FORTNIGHT AFTER THE TROOPS HAD GONE INTO CANTONMENTS, the first symptoms of revolt were seen in a sudden outbreak among the Eburones, headed by their two chiefs Ambiorix and Catuvolcus. They had journeyed to their southern frontiers with the express object of waiting upon Cotta and Sabinus, and had actually brought the stipulated corn into camp. Then, listening to secret overtures from the embittered Treveran leader, Indutiomarus, they called together their tribesmen, and having surprised and overpowered a Roman fatigue party which was out gathering wood, swept on, a now formidable force, toward the Roman station, to carry it by assault. In this, however, they were foiled. The garrison, rushing to arms, quickly manned the walls, and launching the Spanish horse at one point of the lines, completely routed the cavalry opposed to them, whereupon the enemy, despairing of success, drew off from the encounter. With characteristic change of front, they then called loudly for someone from the Roman side to come out to parley. They had, they said, important proposals to make in the interests of either party, which, they hoped, would do much toward settling the differences between them.

Upon this two persons left the Roman lines, C. Arpineius, a Roman knight and personal friend of Sabinus, and a certain Spaniard named

Q. Junius, whom Caesar had frequently employed as his agent in his past dealings with Ambiorix. In their presence Ambiorix then made the following statement. Beginning with a defense of his own position, he acknowledged the undoubted debt of gratitude which he owed to Caesar for his great services to him in the past, mentioning especially his liberation from the tribute formerly paid to his powerful neighbors the Aduatici, and the restoration of his son and nephew, whom that people had exacted as hostages and afterward kept in imprisonment. In the recent assault on the camp, according to his own account, his share had been forced upon him by his fellow countrymen, directly against his own wishes and better judgment: for, according to the law of their constitution, king and commons formed two equally balanced authorities in the state. What then, he might be asked, had driven his people to take up arms against Rome? It was simply their powerlessness to withstand the great national upheaval that had so suddenly shaken the country. Did the Romans doubt this explanation, let them consider the insignificant position held by his own tribe among Gallic peoples, and they would acquit him of the simplicity of supposing that, single-handed, it was a match for the might and majesty of Rome. The real situation was something very different. The whole of Gaul was united in a single determined purpose; and on that day a simultaneous attack was to be made on every one of Caesar's winter quarters, in order to preclude any possibility of mutual assistance among the legions. In such circumstances it was surely too much to ask from Gauls that they should reject the appeal of brother Gauls, when the object of the movement was well known to be the recovery of their independence? "But," he continued, "the claims of patriotism are now satisfied, and I have next to consider my duty as Caesar's grateful friend. Convey my warning to Titurius— nay, implore him as one who has been my honored guest—to act in this emergency like a wise man in the best interests of himself and his troops. A large body of German mercenaries has crossed the Rhine, and in two days will be here. You Romans have now to decide whether or not you will evacuate your present camp, and, before the surrounding tribes can hear of it, make your way either to Cicero or to

Labienus, one of whom is some fifty miles away, the other a little more. For my part, I promise and solemnly pledge my word of honor to grant you a safe passage through my territories; for in doing so I not only benefit my country, which is thereby relieved of the great burden which your presence in it entails, but also requite the past kindnesses of Caesar to myself."

At the close of this speech he took his departure, and Arpineius and Junius returned to report what they had heard to the commanding officers. They, not unnaturally perhaps, had lost under the suddenness of the emergency something of the power of collected judgment; and though the words were those of an enemy, yet they thought them worthy of consideration, especially as it sounded ridiculous that a tribe so undistinguished and unimportant as the Eburones should dare to provoke an armed conflict with Rome, unless supported from without. Accordingly they brought the matter before a council of war, and there a fierce discussion of views took place. L. Aurunculeius and the vast majority both of commissioned and noncommissioned officers of senior rank held strongly that nothing hasty should be done, and that under no circumstances could it possibly be their duty to evacuate their allotted winter quarters, without express orders from Caesar. They maintained that behind entrenchments such as theirs they could defy even Germans, no matter what their numbers; and in proof of this contention pointed to their gallant repulse of the enemy's first attack, which had involved those who made it in no little loss. They were not at present pressed for stores, and before very long help would doubtless arrive both from Caesar and the camp that lay nearest. Nothing, they argued finally, could be a greater confession of weakness or a more undeniable ground of disgrace, than to allow themselves to be dictated to on questions of vital policy by the unsolicited suggestions of a foe.

In opposition to this, Sabinus loudly protested that it would then be too late to act, when the enemy's forces had swollen by their juncture with the Germans, or when disaster of some kind had overtaken the neighboring camp. It was, he insisted, emphatically a question of making up their minds at once. His own conviction was that Caesar had left Gaul for Italy; for on no other hypothesis than the commander in chief's absence, would either the Carnutes have hatched their plot against Tasgetius, or the Eburones have had the effrontery to march upon a Roman camp. To the taunt that he looked to the enemy for his advisers, he opposed the evidence of facts; and reminded his hearers that the Rhine was after all not so far away, that the Germans had long nursed bitter resentment against the Romans for the death of Ariovistus as well as for subsequent defeats, and that Gaul was at that moment burning to avenge the repeated humiliations she had suffered, humiliations which had brought her into the wide dominions of Rome, and had caused her to lose forever her old proud title to military fame. Finally, he asked if anyone honestly believed that Ambiorix, had the facts not been as he stated, would have acted toward the Romans in so extraordinary a manner. "My own plan," he then concluded, "has the merit of meeting both alternatives. If things are no worse than we hope, then there will be no danger in proceeding to the next legion; if, on the other hand, there is this understanding between Gaul and the German tribes, then our only chance lies in instant action. To the plans of Cotta and others who differ from me, I can see no satisfactory conclusion. If they escape present danger, they leave us the grim prospect of a protracted siege, and in the end starvation." After a fierce discussion on either side, as Cotta and the leading centurions still persisted in their opposition, Sabinus at length took the votes. "Decide it as you will," he remarked; and then raising his voice so as to be audible to a large part of the troops, "You need not imagine that to a soldier like myself death has any special terrors. The men here will understand, and (this to Cotta) in case of disaster will hold you responsible; since but for your perverseness, by the day after tomorrow, they might even now form a junction with the next division, and with it face the common lot of war, instead of being left in this heartless fashion to perish far away from comrades, either by sword or famine."

On the breaking up of the council, both officers were besieged by an eager throng of excited soldiery, earnestly begging them not to imperil the situation by a foolish insistence each on his own opinion. "With agreement and harmony of view, it mattered nothing whether they went or stayed—either course was equally practicable; dissension, on the other hand, must extinguish even the last ray of hope." The dispute dragged on its weary length till midnight, and then Cotta at last yielding the point, Sabinus's view carried the day. The word was passed that at dawn the march would begin. What remained of the night, instead of being wisely spent in sleep, was allowed to be wasted by the troops in anxious deliberation on what portion of his little property each could carry away with him, and what part of the camp furniture he must leave behind. No step, in short, was omitted on that fatal night, by which the further retention of the camp became a positive danger, while at the same time the actual peril of the troops was increased by the weariness induced by a nightlong vigil. With the first streak of day the work of evacuation began. To judge by appearances, it might have been supposed that Ambiorix, on whose advice they were acting, was not the foe, but the staunchest friend of their country: the length of column and the amount of baggage taken were alike tragic in their significance.

Meanwhile the noise and other signs of wakefulness in the Roman lines had apprised the enemy of the decision to march; and in a cunningly concealed spot among the woods some two miles farther on, they formed their ambuscade, and in two divisions waited the arrival of their enemy. The place they had selected was a deep gorge, into which the greater part of the column had no sooner plunged than, suddenly disclosing their presence at either end, one party pressed hard upon the Roman rear, while the other strove to prevent their van from climbing clear at the opposite end. No position could well have been worse in which to fight a battle.

It was then the hour that proclaimed the man. Titurius, like one taken altogether by surprise, could everywhere be seen hurrying wildly up and down, striving to deploy his companies into line; yet acting all the while in a weak and nerveless manner that inevitably betrayed his complete bewilderment,—the sure penalty of those who put off deliberation to the moment of action. Cotta, on the other hand, who had fully expected some such occurrence on the road, and had therefore condemned the idea of evacuation, now became the heart and soul of the defense: his calm and encouraging demeanor and the brilliant example he set in battle alike proclaimed him a born leader of men and a gallant soldier. Owing to the unwieldy length of the column, it soon became evident that no real control could be exercised over the progress of the action, or the needful measures taken in the various quarters of the field by the officers in charge; and the order was therefore passed along to cut off the wagons and to form all ranks into a hollow square. For such an order at such a time there is perhaps much to be said: in this particular instance it had disastrous consequences. Rightly or wrongly regarding it as an open confession of impotence and despair, the legionaries at once began losing heart, and the enemy to attack with redoubled energy; while another inevitable consequence was a general breaking of the ranks, in a wild scramble to recover what each man most valued among the baggage. On all sides the air was rent with shouts and cries of disappointment.

On the other hand, the self-control exhibited by the Gauls was astonishing. Acting on their leaders' instructions, not a man among them left his place in the line; but concentrating every effort upon victory, they rested content with the knowledge that the plunder was as good as theirs, and that everything abandoned by the Romans must inevitably revert to them. In courage and in reckless determination to fight they were also worthy foemen.[1] Their opponents, meanwhile, deserted though they were by Fortune and by one of their own generals, were fighting as men fight who know they have themselves alone to look to, and at every charge delivered by a battalion the pathway back to the square was marked by rows of the enemy's dead. Such punishment caused Ambiorix to order his followers to avoid close fighting, and raking the Romans at longer range with volleys of spears, at once to retreat whenever the latter left their lines for a charge. The reason for this, as he

---

[1] I conjecture *animo* for MSS. *numero*.

explained to them, was that their own light armor and soundness of wind and limb rendered them practically invulnerable, and as their antagonists fell back to the standards, they could once more follow them up.

These directions they obeyed to the letter, and whenever after this any battalion sallied out from the square to come to grips with the enemy, they would scatter before it like chaff before a blast of wind. Every such attempt also necessarily exposed the unshielded side of the battalion, a disadvantage of which the enemy were not slow to avail themselves, and to enfilade it with a withering fire of spears; and when again it retreated to its old position in the line, it was to find itself hemmed in, not only on its front by those who had a moment ago scattered before it, but also by converging masses on either flank. Supposing, on the other hand, they decided to stand their ground and to remain on the defensive, then the brave man was every whit as defenseless as the coward; and in their close and serried order it was difficult to parry the spears of so dense a multitude. Tormented by these and countless other troubles, with many of their number already sorely wounded, the little Roman band, in spite of all, still made good its defense; and though the fight had raged from early dawn to one o'clock of a winter's afternoon, yet through all those hours not one act was committed on their side of which any of them had cause to feel ashamed. At this point there occurred three disasters which in the event proved irreparable. In the first place T. Balventius, a noncommissioned officer who the year before had led the senior company of his legion, and whose personal courage was not more conspicuous than his commanding influence over his comrades, was rendered *hors de combat* by a javelin that transfixed both his thighs. Then Q. Lucanius, another sergeant of the same company, in attempting to go to the rescue of his son, who had become surrounded, was killed while fighting most gallantly; and lastly, the general, L. Cotta, was struck full in the face by a sling, as with words of cheery confidence he moved in and out among the battalions, an example and an inspiration to all.

These threefold losses so deeply affected the spirits of Sabinus, now left in sole command, that recognizing Ambiorix in the background rallying his men to the attack, he sent out under a flag of truce his interpreter, Cn. Pompeius, with a formal appeal for quarter both for himself and his troops. Thus accosted, the Gaul replied that while he had no objection to discussing terms with the Roman general, the ultimate fate of the Roman rank and file must rest with his people; who, however, he hoped would not prove unmerciful. As to Sabinus himself, he had nothing to fear, and for his safety he pledged his word of honor. Titurius then consulted with his wounded colleague, and suggested that, with his approval, both should leave the battle and repair in company to the presence of Ambiorix for the purpose of a conference: there, as he hoped, terms favorable alike to themselves and the troops might be arranged. To this Cotta simply replied (and nothing would turn him from his purpose) that to an enemy with arms in his hands he would never consent to go.

Sabinus therefore collected what officers were immediately near him, and together with the senior centurions, ordered them to follow him. As they approached Ambiorix, a peremptory order greeted the party to throw down their arms. This order Sabinus obeyed, and directed his companions to do the same. The discussion of terms then proceeded, and in the meanwhile, as the wily chief purposely spun out his presentation of the case, the Roman general was stealthily surrounded and cut down from behind. Then with a shout of triumph at their bloody deed, they raised the hideous war cry of their nation, and flinging themselves upon the Romans, carried confusion and dismay into the ranks. Here it was that L. Cotta fell, still wielding a sword, and here the great majority of the troops met their end. The rest fought their way back to the deserted camp; conspicuous among them being the eagle bearer of the legion, L. Petrosidius, who, finding himself surrounded by a dense swarm of foes, first flung the colors over the rampart, and then, fighting with calm heroism, turned to meet death outside the fortress. Within the lines, the little band of survivors just managed to keep off their assailants till nightfall: then, under cover of darkness, as all hope of saving themselves was now gone, each man died by his own hand. A few stragglers finally made their way from the battle through the pathless tracks of the forests, till, reaching the camp of Labienus, they informed that commander of all that had occurred.

Determined now to fly at higher game, and flushed with his first success, Ambiorix straightway started with his horsemen for the neighboring kingdom of the Aduatuci, riding night and day across the country, and instructing his infantry to follow immediately behind. The story he had to tell served to rouse that people to rebellion, and by the next day he had reached the Nervii. Calling on these to seize the opportunity now offered them of shaking off forever the yoke of bondage, and of wreaking on the hated Romans vengeance for all that they had suffered, he pointed out that already two of the enemy's most distinguished generals had been slain, and a large part of their army annihilated; and that to make a sudden descent upon the legion in winter quarters with Cicero, and to crush it at a blow, was a task well within their powers, in which they might rely on his hearty cooperation. Needless to add that in the Nervii also he found ready listeners.

Instructions were accordingly posted at once to the Ceutrones, Grudii, Levaci, Pleumoxii, and Geidumni—all of them tribes acknowledging Nervian sway—to raise the largest contingents each could furnish; and then before any word of Titurius's death could reach the ears of Cicero, they suddenly made their appearance before his camp. Here too a similar though unavoidable fate overtook a small party of legionaries, who having gone at the time to the forest in order to cut firewood and timber for the stockade, were now snapped up by the swift descent of the enemy's horse. Fresh from this first taste of blood, the three confederate tribes, Eburones, Nervii, and Aduatuci, forming with all their subject and client states a most formidable array, then opened their attack upon the legion. The Romans flew to arms and quickly lined the walls; but the enemy, who looked throughout for the success of their movement to a few lightning-like strokes, and felt that victory here would render them invincible hereafter, pressed home the attack with such impetuous fury that the strain of this first day proved well-nigh unendurable.

Dispatches were at once sent off by Cicero to Caesar; but though large bribes were offered to any successful carrier, the roads were all found to be so completely in the hands of the enemy that every messenger was stopped. The night was spent in strengthening the defenses; and from the stocks of timber fortunately accumulated in camp for engineering purposes, the troops, by almost superhuman efforts, actually succeeded in raising no less than 120 towers along the rampart, while at the same time all defects discoverable in the earthworks were carefully made good. Morning showed the enemy strongly reinforced; the attack on the camp was again renewed, and a bold attempt was now made to fill the ditch. The garrison met their assailants by the methods of the day before, and this struggle was repeated with little variation day after day, for several days in succession. Through all this period the night work imposed upon the troops was incessant, and neither sick nor wounded could get an hour of sleep. The preparations against the morning's attack had to be finished before dawn, and the night was occupied in manufacturing piles of sharpened stakes to serve as artillery bolts, and large quantities of heavy siege javelins; in fitting the towers with floors, and protecting them by breastworks and parapets formed from hurdles of wattle, firmly plaited on. Though in an extremely indifferent state of health at the time, Cicero yet set a splendid example to his men, refusing even at night to allow himself any rest; and ultimately he had to be forcibly restrained by their earnest remonstrances from overtaxing his strength.

The Nervian leaders now tried the effect of artifice, and those of their number whose personal intimacy with Cicero justified them in approaching him by word of mouth, expressed their wish to negotiate. Leave being granted them, they repeated in so many words the story that Ambiorix had already played off upon Titurius, viz. that the present armed rising extended throughout Gaul, that the Germans had passed the Rhine, that Caesar and all the other winter camps were at that moment under investment. To this tissue of lies they appended the one fact of Sabinus's death; and in proof of this statement proudly displayed Ambiorix to their foes. Then expatiating on the folly of relying on those whose own position was by this time all but desperate, they impressed upon the Roman officer that both toward Cicero and the Romans generally their feelings were perfectly friendly except on the single question of the winter camps, and these they did not desire to see made a permanent institution. "As far as we are concerned, therefore," they concluded, "you may safely evacuate your present quarters, and without fear of molestation proceed to any part of the country that you like." To these proposals Cicero's sole rejoinder was that Rome was not accustomed to accept conditions from an armed foe. If, however, they chose to disband their armed forces, he promised his hearty cooperation in addressing an appeal to Caesar, and assured them that, as far as his opinion went, they would find that Caesar, with his well-known sense of justice, would reject no reasonable demands.

The result of this disappointment was that the Nervii proceeded to carry out a regular circumvallation of the Roman camp, erecting for the purpose a continuous earthwork nine feet high, lined by a ditch fifteen feet wide. The military skill required for so considerable a work had been gathered by their increasing familiarity with Roman methods throughout the previous years, as well as from the instruction of certain prisoners originally captured from the Roman army, and still secretly detained in their midst. Of iron implements, however, necessary for the task, they were quite destitute, and they could now be seen cutting out the sods with their swords and carrying away the loads of earth in their hands and military cloaks. Their action afforded an excellent indication of their numbers; as in a space of less than three hours they had constructed walls of circumvallation three miles in circumference, which they afterward followed up by building on succeeding days movable towers proportioned to the height of the Roman ramparts, powerful hooks for disintegrating the stockade, and battery sheds under which to advance—all of them devices learned from the prisoners alluded to above.

The seventh day of the siege was ushered in by a violent hurricane; and the enemy, seizing the occasion, opened fire upon the long lines of soldiers' huts, which after the usual Gallic fashion had been roofed with thatch, with white-hot balls of molded clay, discharged from slings, and with hand grenades that were formed by highly heated spears. The huts quickly caught alight, and, fanned by the strong wind, the fire soon spread its way throughout the camp. With screams of exultation at the success of their plot, and feeling now sure of victory, the Gauls next pushed up their towers and battering sheds, and fixing ladders, began to scale the ramparts. But the Roman infantry, steady and cool as if on parade, though scorched by the flames which everywhere roared behind them, while on their front the spears flew in clouds, and knowing all the while that the regimental baggage and all their own belongings were fast being consumed, stood grimly to their task; not a man among them left his post, scarcely a man so much as turned his head; but in all alike the hour served only to call forth the deepest springs of resolution and the loftiest embodiment of courage. Though to the garrison the most critical of all the siege, yet to the enemy this day proved unexpectedly disastrous, and on no other was their list of killed and wounded quite so heavy. This was owing to the tremendous crush immediately below the ramparts, where those in front found it impossible to escape for the pressure from behind. It happened that at one point during the fight, one of the movable siege towers had so far advanced as actually to touch the fortifications; and as at the time there was a lull in the fierceness of the fire, the centurions commanding the third cohort, which was here posted, drew back from their place in the line, and calling off their men, beckoned and shouted to the enemy to step across if they dared. Nobody was found bold enough to accept this challenge, and the Romans opening a murderous crossfire of stones upon their assailants, drove them from their position, and then set fire to the tower.

Among the noncommissioned officers of this legion were two men named T. Pullo and L. Vorenus. More gallant soldiers it would be difficult to find; and in the case of either a distinguished career was about to be crowned by promotion to the first battalion of the regiment. Between the two there had throughout been a constant and bitter rivalry on the question of precedence, and year after year a fierce competition had taken place for priority of rank. When the fight round the trenches had reached its height, one of these two men, viz. Pullo, gave the following challenge to his rival. "Come, Vorenus, it's all or nothing. If you've got your eye on that captaincy, let's put it to the test. Today shall settle all differences between us." So saying, he calmly strode outside the earthworks, and selecting the point where the enemy's ranks were thickest, dashed forward straight upon it. Vorenus was not the man to hang back after such a challenge, and dreading the public opinion of his regiment, was soon hard upon the other. Nicely calculating his distance, Pullo delivered his javelin with full force at the enemy, and striking one who was dashing out to meet him ahead of the others, brought him to the ground. Stunned by the blow, the wounded man was covered by his comrades' shields, who with one accord then turned their spears upon their bold assailant, cutting off his retreat. Pullo next had his own shield rent by a spear, and the spearhead most unluckily sticking fast in his belt, shifted his scabbard and sorely interfered with him as he strove to draw the blade; thus giving the enemy time to close in upon him while still struggling with his difficulties. At this critical moment his old antagonist, running up to his relief, drew off upon himself the attention of the enemy, who were firmly convinced that Pullo had been killed on the spot by the spear. Making brilliant play with his sword, Vorenus in a fierce hand-to-hand encounter had already cut down one of his numerous opponents, and was steadily driving the others before him, when, in his eagerness to press home the attack, his foot caught in a sudden depression of the ground and he came heavily down. He was quickly surrounded by the enemy, but in his turn was rescued from his perilous position by Pullo; and the two men, after accounting for numbers of the enemy, and covering themselves with glory, fell back unscathed to the fortifications of the camp, fighting side by side. Thus, in endeavoring to terminate their dispute upon the field of battle, each of the two rivals, by successive turns of Fortune's wheel, was made the means of helping and rescuing the other; and the question, which of the two was the better man, had perforce to remain unsettled.

Every day now increased the strain and suffering of the siege. The gravest cause for anxiety was the rapidly lengthening list of wounded, which threw the burden of defense upon a constantly diminishing section of the garrison; and though with the rise of the danger messengers with dispatches were sent off with greater and greater frequency to Caesar, many of these were caught outright, and in full view of the Roman camp were tortured to death. At last a more successful means was found. Within the fortress was a certain distinguished Nervian named Vertico, who having deserted to Cicero at the earliest stage of the siege, had since proved to that commander his undoubted trustworthiness. This man, by a lavish promise of reward and the hope of emancipation, induced one of his slaves to carry a letter through to Caesar. Tied up inside a spear, it was conveyed without the lines, and the bearer, passing unsuspected as a Gaul among Gauls, safely conveyed it to its destination. In this manner Caesar learned for the first time the critical condition of Cicero and his legion.

The message reached him within an hour of sunset. A mounted courier was at once dispatched to his paymaster Crassus, whose camp lay among the Bellovaci (*Beauvais*), twenty-five miles from headquarters, ordering the legion there to march at midnight and to join him with all speed. Crassus left upon the word. A similar summons was sent off to the general C. Fabius, directing him to move with his legion down to the country of the Atrebates (*Arras*), through which the relief expedition was bound to pass. Lastly, a written communication was addressed to Labienus, commanding that officer to proceed with the legion under him to the frontiers of the Nervii, if on a general review of the situation he deemed it practicable. His remaining divisions, as lying a little too far distant, he decided not to wait for. Cavalry to the number of about 400 sabres were drafted in from the nearest camps.

About half-past nine the following morning Caesar's advanced scouts reported Crassus to be in sight, and before the close of that day he had marched twenty miles. Crassus he left at Samarobriva (*Amiens*). In that town were the bulk of the army's baggage, the hostages of the various Gallic tribes, important state papers, and immense stocks of grain accumulated for winter consumption by the troops: a garrison was therefore absolutely necessary, and for this duty Crassus, with the legion under him, was best detailed. Proceeding on his march he was joined by Fabius and his legion, with no great amount of delay. Labienus's position was more difficult. He had recently learned of the fate of Sabinus and his battalions; the Treveri were swarming in his neighborhood; and to leave his present quarters under circumstances which so strongly savored of flight might well render him powerless to ward off the attack of an enemy known to be flushed with victory. In his written reply to Caesar, therefore, he explained to his commander how serious must be any immediate movement of his troops; and after giving a full account of the late disaster among the Eburones, finished by stating that the entire forces of the Treveri, horse and foot, had encamped on a site only three miles distant from himself.

Although this decision ended his hopes of three legions, leaving him with only two, Caesar yet approved of his subordinate's action, and now had to trust to speed, and speed alone, for saving the situation. Rapid marching brought him to the frontiers of the Nervii, where prisoners informed him of the true position of affairs outside the camp of Cicero, and of the deadly nature of his peril. In order to open communications with the beleaguered garrison, he prevailed on one of the native horse, by the offer of a handsome reward, to go with a letter to Cicero; and in order to guard against the revelation of military secrets to the enemy in the unfortunate event of capture, the letter was written in Greek characters, and its bearer instructed, should he fail to get close up, to tie it to the leather handstrap of a javelin and to throw it in this manner over the trenches. It contained the simple statement that Caesar had started with the legions, and might be expected to arrive shortly; and ended with an earnest appeal to his lieutenant to show himself the true soldier that hitherto he had always been. Fearful of the risk he ran, the Gaul threw the javelin as

directed; but by an unlucky chance it impinged itself on one of the
wooden turrets of the camp, and in this position was for two days left
unnoticed. On the third it was seen by one of the legionaries, taken
down, and carried to Cicero. Having carefully perused its contents,
the Roman commandant publicly read it out to the assembled troops,
and his words sent all ranks beside themselves with joy. A little later,
and the sight of distant smoke, rising in vengeance over the burning
country, told that the legions were indeed upon their way.

Informed by their scouts of the new condition of affairs, the Gauls
at once raised the siege of Cicero, and in full strength hastened to
fling themselves upon Caesar. Their numbers may have been anything short of 60,000 fighting men. Following on their withdrawal,
Cicero again applied to the Nervian chief Vertico, who has already
once been mentioned in a similar connection, for the loan of a Gallic
slave as letter carrier to Caesar. The need of care and circumspection
upon the road was duly impressed upon the man; and the letter
informed the commander in chief that the enemy had dispersed
from before the camp, and that the full strength of their host was
now doubling back upon himself. This letter was delivered in Caesar's camp about midnight, and its contents were at once laid before
his assembled officers, who were then warned to hold themselves in
readiness for the coming fight. With the first streak of dawn on the
following day camp was struck, and after a march of three or four
miles, the enemy's masses were observed crowning the farther slopes
of a valley intersected at its bottom by a stream. Against a position so
formidable, it would have been highly dangerous with so puny a
force to engage in action: and, the knowledge that Cicero was now
relieved justifying to some extent an abatement of speed, Caesar
decided to form an encampment, and was soon firmly entrenched
on the most convenient site discoverable. The new camp, which had
only to accommodate something under 7,000 men, without heavy
baggage, would under no circumstances have been of imposing size;
but with the object of bringing it into supreme contempt in the
mind of the foe, Caesar directed the roadways across it to be so
contracted as to reduce to the utmost the total dimensions of the

ground. Meanwhile his scouts were searching the country in all directions to find the most suitable route across the valley.

Apart from a few petty cavalry skirmishes for the possession of water, the day passed without event, each side having its own reasons for remaining on the defensive. The Gauls were still expecting reinforcements, and pending their arrival preferred to make no movement; while with Caesar two considerations at present counseled inactivity. His main hope was that the enemy, through his feigning fear, might be inveigled across to his own side of the valley, where he might fight on favorable terms, resting on his fortifications: failing that, he would at least gain time for a careful study of the roads, and so be enabled to make the passage of the river and valley with less danger than it now involved. In this expectation he was not disappointed. At dawn on the next day the enemy's horsemen passed the stream, and advancing toward his position, were soon engaged with the Roman mounted troops. These had orders to retire before the threatened attack, and to fall back upon camp; at the same time the legionaries were instructed to raise the height of the rampart all the way round, to block up all gates, and in the execution of these orders to throw over their movements an appearance of such excessive haste as would raise a presumption of abject fear.

These numerous decoys succeeded in their object, and transferring their forces to the farther side, the Gauls now formed for battle on ground well below the level of their opponents. On perceiving, however, that even upon these terms the Romans, instead of fighting, only evacuated their ramparts, they advanced within still closer range, and on all four sides began contemptuously tossing their spears over into camp. Their heralds were thereupon ordered to go the round of the Roman lines, and publicly to announce that any Roman or Gaul who chose to come over to their side before nine o'clock that morning might freely do so; after that hour the invitation would be withdrawn. So truculent did their bearing grow, that, thinking it impracticable to rush the gates (which though they appeared from outside to be stoutly blocked, were in reality only piled up with a single layer of turves), some began actually to wrench away the materials forming the rampart, while others started to fill the ditch. Then at last, Caesar gave the word. Issuing from all four gates, the legionaries, with the cavalry following hot in pursuit, quickly routed their assailants; and meeting with not even a semblance of a stand, inflicted heavy slaughter, finishing by stripping all the dead of their arms.

Where swamps and forests so abounded, and where, from the nature of the case, no additional punishment could be inflicted, further pursuit must necessarily have been hazardous: the recall was therefore sounded, and on the same day the relief expedition, without having lost a single man, marched into Cicero's camp. As he passed the siege towers, the covered ways for the sappers, the imposing lines of fortification erected by the enemy, Caesar's admiration was unbounded; and when the warworn regiment was at length paraded for inspection, and less than ten percent of its effective strength was found to remain unwounded, no more eloquent testimony could have been forthcoming, alike of the appalling danger and of the heroic courage that had marked the siege. In recognition of his great services, Cicero and the legion were then publicly thanked by the commander in chief; after which a few words were addressed personally to each of those centurions and officers whose gallant behavior had been specially singled out by their general. The news of the disaster to Sabinus and Cotta was now confirmed by prisoners, and it became necessary to apprise the troops. Before the assembled forces, therefore, Caesar on the next day gave a full account of what had occurred; and while sympathizing with the men in the great blow that had fallen on the army, gave every reason for a confident outlook on the future. The disaster, he pointed out, had been due solely to the ill judgment and recklessness of the officer in charge, and, regarded as a check to Roman arms, had, through the auspicious overruling of Providence and their own valor, already been fully retrieved. In the light of subsequent success, therefore, they might view with calmness the errors of the past; and the thought of the short-lived triumph of their foe should sensibly relieve their natural feeling of regret.

Meanwhile across the intervening country of the Remi (*Rheims*) the news of Caesar's victory was speeding on its way to Labienus. Very nearly sixty miles separated his position from that of Cicero, which, it will be noticed, Caesar only reached after one o'clock in the afternoon; yet so marvelous was the rate of traveling, that before midnight the shouts announcing the intelligence and the congratulations of the Remi upon the event, could be heard outside the gates. Though a general assault on the Roman lines had been planned by Indutiomarus to take place on the morrow, yet the night saw him in full retreat, and subsequently the whole Treveran muster melted away to their homes. The pressure of immediate danger being thus removed, Caesar had leisure to remodel his dispositions for the winter. Fabius he sent back with his single legion to his old quarters among the Morini; the other three he concentrated in three separate camps in the immediate neighborhood of Samarobriva (*Amiens*), his own headquarters; while, owing to the serious nature of the outbreaks that had just occurred in Gaul, he determined to remain with his army throughout the winter. The need for his continued presence was indeed paramount. The loss to Roman prestige inflicted by the massacre of Sabinus and his force was already found to be far-reaching in its effects. State after state, as the story reached its ears, leaped instantly to thoughts of war; everywhere across the country secret agents were moving from tribe to tribe, actively discussing future plans, and eagerly seeking a convenient center from which to raise the standard of revolt: night revealed the Gauls met in solemn conclave at lonely districts of the countryside. For Caesar the winter was, with rare exceptions, a period of unrelieved anxiety, during which reports of Gallic plots and Gallic risings became of almost daily experience. Among these was the intelligence forwarded by L. Roscius, commanding the Third legion, that large bands of what are known as the Armorican tribes had lately gathered for an assault upon his camp, but that when no more than eight miles distant, the news of Caesar's victorious march had caused such a sudden dispersal of their forces, that they seemed like a defeated army flying from the field of battle.

In spite of all, however, Caesar succeeded by a wise and judicious choice of methods in preserving at least an outward semblance of loyalty over a large proportion of the country. Summoning to headquarters the prominent members of each tribe, he either, according to the circumstances, administered a severe fright by telling them plainly that their plans were all well known to himself, or, addressing them in friendly words, urged them to persevere in the course of duty. Not the least flagrant case was that of the Senones (*Sens*), quite one of the most powerful tribes, whose influence over the Gallic world is second to none. Their present ruler was a prince named Cavarinus, a nominee of Caesar's and a member of their ancient royal house, whose brother, Moritasgus, had been on the throne at the time of Caesar's advent into Gaul. A public attempt to assassinate him only miscarried through his discovery of the plot; and on his taking to flight, he was pursued to the frontiers by his intended murderers, who then formally pronounced his banishment from both kingdom and home: and though they had the grace to send explanations of their conduct to Caesar, yet an order from him to assemble at his camp the whole of their tribal council was contumaciously ignored. The same tendency to defy authority was visible elsewhere. With the sole exception of the Aedui and Remi, both of which states were the constant recipients of distinguished marks of favor at Caesar's hands—the one because of their ancient and unbroken loyalty to Rome, the other for their more recent services in the Gallic wars— there was hardly a tribe this winter throughout the length and breadth of the wide territories of Gaul that did not fall under deserved suspicion; so strongly, it appeared, was the native mind impressed by the fact that someone had at last been found bold enough to take up arms, and so strikingly had it altered the attitude of all. That such should have been the case was perhaps not wonderful. Many courses doubtless cooperated to produce the change; but not the least potent was the deep-seated sense of indignation that a race, whose warrior spirit was ranked first among all the nations of the world, should have so far belied its previous history as to sink without a struggle beneath the conquering arm of Rome.

Meanwhile the disbanded Treveri under their leader Indutioma-rus had not been idle, and had allowed no part of that winter to go by without making every effort to stir up the Germans beyond the Rhine. In addition to the ordinary money bribe, the tribes were further incited by deliberate misrepresentations of the strength of the Roman forces. A large proportion of these was said to be already annihilated, leaving only an insignificant fraction still to be accounted for. These arguments, however, proved signally unavailing: not a state could be induced to cross the Rhine, and the invariable answer to all appeals was that two attempts had already been made, one in the campaign under Ariovistus, the other at the migration of the Tencteri, and that they were not at present disposed to risk a third. Undeterred by this rebuff, Indutiomarus continued his preparations as before: armed bands were busily raised and drilled, horses bought from neighboring states, and to attract the outlaws and desperadoes from all the remotest corners of Gaul, the most alluring terms were held out. By such methods he rapidly made himself the cynosure of all eyes in the Gallic world of his day, and envoys bent on obtaining his friendship and assistance, either in a public or a private capacity, flocked from all quarters to his court.

His projects indeed seemed to be now in a fair way toward consummation. He himself was evidently regarded as a leader; a firm basis of disaffection had, thanks to a common participation in past guilt, been laid in Central Gaul among the Senones (*Sens*) and the Carnutes (*Orleans*): in Belgium the Nervii and Aduatici were preparing to make war on Rome; and clearly he had only to show himself outside his frontiers for volunteers to crowd to his standard. Under such favorable circumstances he determined to take a step which, to all intents and purposes, is the Gallic equivalent of a formal declaration of war, and to summon what is known as an "Armed Council." At every such council the adult males of a population are bound by a universal obligation to appear with weapons in their hands; and so strictly is this duty enforced, that the last comer invariably pays the penalty with his life, and is executed with every refinement of cruelty before the eyes of the assembled host. At this council the first business of Indutiomarus was to attack the Romans through their protégé, Cingetorix, his own son-in-law and head of the rival political faction, who, it will be remembered, had openly espoused the cause of Caesar, with whom he had since remained. He was now condemned as the avowed enemy of his country, and his property declared confiscated to the state. That done, he formally announced to the assembly the invitations received from the Senones, Carnutes, and other states of Central Gaul; proclaimed his intention to proceed thither through the territories of the Remi, plundering these as he went, and lastly, as a preliminary step to these measures, his resolve to carry by storm the neighboring camp of Labienus. The proceedings closed with a careful enunciation of his orders.

To Labienus the prospect of attack was in no sense disconcerting. Safely entrenched behind a position, which both in natural and artificial strength was practically impregnable, he had no fears either for his own or his legion's safety: his sole anxiety was lest he should lose some chance of dealing a really decisive blow at his enemy. Apprised, therefore, of the speech just delivered at the tribal gathering by Indutiomarus, which Cingetorix and his friends duly reported, he at once sent off agents to the surrounding tribes, summoning them to supply him with drafts of cavalry, to assemble all together upon a fixed day. Meanwhile cavalry demonstrations on the part of the enemy became almost of daily occurrence, and spreading his forces immediately below the Roman camp, Indutiomarus would now make a nice observation of the strength of the position, now would endeavor to get a word with the garrison, now once again would try to overawe them by imposing appearances, on most of which occasions his horsemen would ride up and deliberately shoot their spears into the lines. In answer to this challenge Labienus resolutely kept his troops behind their earthworks, and by every device in his power fostered the belief in his own timidity.

The contemptuous bearing of the enemy in approaching the camp became day by day more marked, until upon one particular night the cavalry reinforcements sent for by the Roman commander from the various Gallic states were quietly admitted within the lines: after which so strict was the watch kept upon all ranks, that by no sort of contrivance could intimation or report of their arrival be conveyed outside to the Treveri. On the morrow Indutio-marus again paid his customary visit, and spending the larger part of the day in the neighborhood of the camp, his horsemen amused themselves by throwing spears over the rampart and by challenging the Romans in the foulest language to come out and fight. No answer being vouchsafed on the part of the garrison, the enemy toward the close of the afternoon rode leisurely back, observing no sort of formation, but broken up into groups. Then from two sepa-rate gates Labienus suddenly launched the whole of his brigade. Accurately foreseeing the panic and wild confusion that this would cause among the enemy, and determined if possible to prevent their ringleader from escaping in the general melee, he had given strict orders to all his men to make Indutiomarus the one object of their attack, and that no one was to strike a single other blow until he had seen the Gallic leader dead before him: at the same time liberal rewards were offered to the party who killed him, and several infan-try battalions were pushed up to support the cavalry. It was a case of Fortune smiling approval on human prescience: for the rebel chief, singled out in this manner for universal pursuit, was caught in the very act of fording a river, cut down, and his head brought back to camp. Returning from the pursuit, the victorious troopers gave chase to various other parties of fugitives, several of whom they suc-ceeded in accounting for. The sudden downfall of their leader at once reacted on the other centers of rebellion; and the bands of Ner-vii and Eburones who had lately taken the field against the Romans now melted rapidly away, leaving Caesar to enjoy a period of com-parative tranquility throughout Gaul.

BOOK VI

SECTION I. PUNITIVE EXPEDITIONS
IN THE NORTHEAST

THE SITUATION, HOWEVER, PRESENTED STILL MANY DISQUIETING FEATURES, and indications of a yet wider movement of revolt were not wanting. With the object, therefore, of strengthening the military forces at his disposal, Caesar commissioned three officers, M. Silanus, C. Antistius Reginus, and T. Sextius, to raise further levies in the Italian portion of his government; and also made a special request to the proconsul, Cn. Pompeius (who for reasons of state still remained after his year of office in the neighborhood of the capital, with full civil and military authority) that he would order those recruits in North Italy who had been recently sworn for service under himself when consul, immediately to join the colors and to proceed as reinforcements to the army of Gaul.[1] In acting thus he had an eye also to the importance of impressing for the future upon the Gallic imagination a vivid idea of the inexhaustible resources of Italy, and of showing that the wastage suffered in war she could not only rapidly make good, but could even, if called upon, replace her first by still larger military establishments.

---

[1] In 55 Pompeius as consul had been empowered by the Senate to raise troops in North Italy, though this was part of Caesar's government. These men, amounting to a legion, and now lent to Caesar, were afterward, on the pretext of a Parthian invasion, demanded back on the eve of the civil war (50).

On public and on personal grounds alike Pompeius acceded to this request; and being well served by his officers in their conduct of the levy, Caesar had, before the close of winter, three new legions all fully organized and conducted to their destination. Thus, by exactly doubling the number of battalions that had perished with Sabinus, he gave convincing proof, both by the extent and rapid concentration of the new forces, how immense was the strength that underlay the discipline and the wealth of Rome.

To return to the narrative. On the death of Indutiomarus, the circumstances of which have already been related, the headship of the tribe was transferred by the Treveri to the kinsmen of the fallen chief. These, steadily persisting in his old policy of intrigue among the Germans of the Eastern Rhineland, found that their appeal, though supported by copious promises of pay, was but coldly received by all the nearer tribesmen, and had therefore to turn to those at a greater distance. A certain number of these were at length discovered ready to make the attempt, and the compact having been sealed by an interchange of oaths between the contracting parties, and hostages given as present security for future pay, last, but not least, Ambiorix was admitted as a partner to their joint schemes by a formal treaty of alliance. To Caesar, as the reports came to hand of these successive movements of revolt, it was plain that on all sides the clouds of war were fast gathering. The Nervii, Aduatici, and Menapii, with the whole of the German region lying westward of the Rhine, had already taken the field; the Senones (*Sens*) still ignored his express summons to appear, and with the Carnutes (*Orleans*) and other neighboring states, were busily concerting measures intended to defy him; the Treveri (*Trèves*) were sending embassy after embassy into Germany to gain adherents to their cause. The times thus calling for exceptional activity, he resolved to forestall to some extent the date he had usually observed for the reopening of hostilities.

Winter was not yet passed, therefore, when orders for concentration were quietly issued to the four legions lying nearest to headquarters, and a sudden dash was made into the Nervian district. Prevented from either massing for defense or from scattering for refuge, the tribe was obliged to look helplessly on while the Romans overran the country, seizing large numbers of men and cattle, which the soldiers were permitted to retain as their lawful prize. Surrender soon became imperative, and hostages for future good behavior were then reluctantly handed over. At the close of this short but very successful expedition the troops once more returned to winter quarters. According to precedent, the general assembly of Gaul was due to take place with the opening of spring, and to the summons of the Roman governor all gave ready obedience, except the representatives of the Senones, Carnutes, and Treveri. Rightly interpreting this as an open defiance of authority and a virtual declaration of war, in face of which all other business of the council must stand over, Caesar at once transferred the place of meeting to Lutetia (*Paris*), the capital city of the Parisii, not far from the frontiers of one of the three recalcitrant tribes. The Parisii indeed not only marched with the Senones, but within the last generation had entered into political union with them; though in the recent decision taken by their rulers the Parisii were believed to have had no share. A formal declaration to this effect having first been publicly made by the Roman governor from his presidential seat at the adjourned congress, on the same day the legions were put into motion for the country of the Senones, to which a series of forced marches quickly brought them.

Their approach becoming known, the ringleader of the anti-Roman movement, a chieftain of the name of Acco, at once gave orders for the population to abandon the open country and to fall back on their fortified towns; but before this measure could be adequately carried out, they were surprised in their attempt by the news that the Romans were already in their midst. Compelled to relinquish their contemplated plan of defense, they presently sent delegates to the Roman camp, with instructions to throw themselves absolutely on the mercy of Caesar. In this appeal they were supported by the Aedui, for many years their acknowledged suzerains, whose intervention gave Caesar an opportunity for which at the moment he was peculiarly grateful. With an important war immediately before him, he had no wish to spend the summer months in a

troublesome investigation of political charges; and it was with much
satisfaction, therefore, that he accepted their explanations and con-
doned their misconduct, after first stipulating for one hundred
hostages, for whose custody the Aedui were made responsible. Without further advance on the part of the army, another deputation,
sent with a similar object and also accompanied by hostages, arrived
from the other refractory tribe, the Carnutes. These, as being politically dependent on the Remi, had secured for themselves the
powerful intercession of that people, and gained by means of it
the same terms as the others. A requisition for cavalry laid on the
component tribes then brought the assembly to a close.

The restoration of order in this part of Gaul had now set free
the unimpeded activities of Caesar for the war with Ambiorix and the
Treveri. First of all, however, the late fugitive chieftain, Cavarinus,
was bidden to accompany the Senonian contingent of horse; for otherwise, either from the man's own natural rage at the authors of his
overthrow, or from the bitterness that his restoration had since
aroused against him, a grave risk would have been run of a renewed
outbreak. This difficulty overcome, it was now possible to formulate
a plan of action against the Eburonian rebel. That he would not venture to oppose the Romans in the field might safely be taken for
granted: what other designs he might contemplate had therefore to
be the more thoroughly scrutinized and anticipated. Lying on his
northern frontiers were a people, the Menapii, whose endless alter-
nation of forest and fen afforded so strong a natural protection, that
it had emboldened them, even after other tribes had all sent in their
representatives, still to withhold their submission to Caesar. Between
them and Ambiorix there were known to exist ties of most friendly
intercourse; while with the Germans beyond the Rhine the Treveri
had been the intermediaries, as was clearly revealed by the information to hand, in bringing about a close understanding between that
people and the Eburonian monarch. Prudence therefore suggested
that before striking at the rebel chief in person, his two principal
sources of probable support should first be detached; since it went
without saying that the escape of the insurgent chief in his despair to

the trackless wilds of the Menapii was a contingency as much to be avoided as was his juncture with the German tribes lying east of the Rhine. The plan of operations being thus decided on, the whole of the army's baggage was first sent away under two legions to Labienus, who was still among the Treveri; after which the remaining five, now unencumbered by heavy transport, marched northwards for the district of the Menapii under the personal leadership of Caesar. No open resistance was attempted by the tribe, but relying on the natural fastnesses of their country, they at once fled to their woods and marshes, taking with them into hiding all livestock and other valuables.

Three columns under separate commands were now organized by Caesar, the other generals being C. Fabius and his Quaestor, M. Crassus; and rapidly constructing bridges, the three forces advanced into the heart of the Menapian country, burning and plundering as they went. Large captures both in men and cattle were quickly made, and finding themselves helpless before such tactics, the tribesmen petitioned for peace. In taking hostages from them, the Roman commander made it quite plain that they would be considered to have put themselves in the position of enemies, should they harbor anywhere within their territories either Ambiorix or his emissaries. This settlement effected, a force of cavalry was left under the Atrebatian chief, Commius, with which to keep order in the country, and the Roman forces then proceeded southward to deal with the Treveri.

That people had themselves taken the initiative in renewing hostilities. Having raised strong bodies both of horse and foot, they had, concurrently with the operations just related, marched forth to attack the single legion under Labienus, which throughout the winter had been quartered in their country. Arrived within two days' march of their destination, they had heard of the junction of the legions sent by Caesar, and upon this information had decided to camp on a site fifteen miles removed from the Roman position, in order to await their German auxiliaries. These tactics Labienus resolved, if possible, to frustrate by so working on the impulsive nature of his opponents as to force them to a general engagement. Leaving five battalions to guard his stores and baggage, he set out with the remaining twenty-five and a strong force of cavalry toward the enemy's position, and having arrived within something approaching a mile sat down behind entrenchments. The two hostile camps confronted one another across a stream, the steep banks of which made its passage so hazardous, that the Roman general had neither the intention of crossing it himself nor any expectation that his enemy would do so. With every successive day bringing nearer the expected arrival of the foreign auxiliaries, he then openly announced before his assembled council that in view of the reiterated reports as to the German approach, he had decided not to incur the grave risk of endangering both his own stores and those of the whole Roman army, and that, therefore, early on the following morning he would strike camp. This declaration was at once conveyed outside to the enemy, as indeed was only to be expected: among so large a number of Gallic horse, ties of blood were sure to lead some to espouse their nation's cause. During the night a meeting of his principal officers was summoned by Labienus to receive their final instructions for the execution of his plan; and in order to perfect the simulation of panic within the Roman lines, the order was given to increase the noise and clamor on moving camp above that usually associated with Roman methods. The departure of the troops was by this ruse made to resemble nothing so much as that of an army in rout, a circumstance that, thanks to the short distance separating the camps, had before daybreak been also fully reported to the enemy by their scouts.

The sight of their expected prey thus slipping from their grasp effectually dispelled all previous hesitation on the part of the Gauls. It was now admitted on all sides that to wait longer for the promised German support when the Romans were already stricken with panic, was but a needless waste of time; and that to shrink, with their large numbers, from attacking so insignificant a force, which was in the act of running away, besides being greatly hampered in its movements, was intolerable to their self-respect. Hardly, therefore, had the tail of the column drawn clear of the trenches, than they began to move across the stream, only too eager to give battle even

158 ► CAESAR'S GALLIC WAR

on ground that was sorely to their disadvantage. Their action had been fully anticipated by Labienus, and still masking the true purpose of his retreat, in his anxiety to inveigle the entire body over to his side of the valley, he still kept steadily on, without any sign of hostile movement visible in the ranks. When all were at length across, the word was passed for the transport to draw clear on the front, and to take up its position on a neighboring height; after which, the general, turning to his troops, gave them the chance which they had so long and so eagerly expected. "They now saw their foes trapped and caught upon ground where they must struggle for a foothold: let the men only show the same devotion under his leadership as had so often carried them to victory under their commander in chief, in whose presence and before whose eyes they must now imagine themselves to be acting." At the word of command the Roman column made a turn which brought it facing the enemy, and then deployed in line: a few squadrons of horse were told off to guard the baggage, the rest were massed on either wing. A wild cheer ran through the ranks of the legionaries, as with eager haste they launched their heavy javelins, and then prepared to charge. For such a charge at such a time the enemy were but little prepared: the sight of the supposed fugitives suddenly wheeling and bearing down upon them in serried order of battle had filled them with dismay, and at the first shock they broke and fled, seeking the shelter of the nearest woods. The cavalry then took up the pursuit, and a few days later, having lost heavily in killed and prisoners, the whole tribe surrendered at discretion. The German auxiliaries who were on their way, on hearing that the Treveri had been routed in battle, at once turned homewards; and in company with them there also went those relatives of Indutiomarus, who, as the real authors of the rebellion, now thought it prudent to quit the country. In succession to them, the headship and rule of the tribe was conferred upon Cingetorix, of whose unswerving loyalty to the Roman cause throughout these troubles evidence has already been adduced.

In the meantime, Caesar with the main army had, after his expedition against the Menapii, joined his subordinate in the south.

There he decided that for two important reasons a second crossing of the Rhine had become a military necessity. In the first place, the tribes needed to be chastised for their recent support of the Treveran rebellion; in the second, he had to secure himself against the possible escape of Ambiorix in this quarter. The decision once taken, no time was lost in bridging the river, a little above the site of his first passage; and as past experience had now made the design familiar, and all hands displayed the utmost willingness, a few days sufficed for the completion of the work. A strong guard was left on the Gallic side both to hold the bridge and to overawe any attempted rising by the Treveri in the rear; after which the rest of the forces, both mounted and foot, crossed the stream. Among the first to greet the appearance of the Romans on the farther shore was a deputation from the Ubii, a tribe which had previously given in its surrender and delivered hostages. They now came forward to disclaim responsibility for the dispatch of auxiliary bands to the Treveri, and to declare that in no sense had they violated their plighted word. In the indiscriminate hatred by the Romans of every one called a German, they feared that they, though innocent, might be confounded with the guilty, and they therefore begged the governor for a merciful consideration of their case. Finally, they professed their readiness to increase, if so desired, the number of their hostages already in Roman hands. Careful investigation by Caesar proved that the real responsibility for supplying auxiliaries lay with the Suebi; and, satisfied with the explanations offered by the Ubii, he proceeded to collect information as to the roads and principal lines of advance leading to the country of that people.

Within a few days it was reported to him by the Ubii that a general concentration of the Suebic military forces was in progress, and that all their subject tribes had received strict injunctions to dispatch to the seat of war fixed contingents of horse and foot. Upon this information, the Roman commander completed his arrangements for supplies, and then carefully selected a site for a camp. At the same time the Ubian authorities were enjoined to clear their country of livestock, and to convey behind the walls of their towns everything

of any value to an enemy; it being common experience that in warfare with primitive tribes the strain imposed by the want of customary
food will often bring on an engagement even where conditions are
most adverse. The importance of keeping constant watch by means
of spies upon the Suebic territories was duly emphasized, and any
movement there in progress was at once to be reported to the Roman
general. These instructions the friendly Germans loyally observed,
and at the close of a few days they returned with the following report.
The Suebi, after waiting for more accurate information as to the
Roman advance, had, with all their forces, both national and allied,
retired to what was well-nigh the farthest boundary of their kingdom, an immense forest tract known as the Bacenis; which, running
far up into their country, like a solid wall, interposed by nature
between them and their chief rivals, the Cherusci, effectually prevented both from raiding and from preying upon one another. Upon
the fringe of this great barrier they had decided to await the oncom-
ing of the Romans.

SECTION II. ETHNOGRAPHY OF GAUL AND GERMANY

AT THIS POINT OF OUR NARRATIVE IT WILL NOT PERHAPS BE THOUGHT inopportune if we pause to consider in some detail the national life of Gaul and Germany, and to show the more important aspects in which the two races differ from each other. To begin with the Gauls. The most remarkable feature about their political organization is the existence everywhere of two great antagonistic parties. Not merely do these parties divide each independent tribe, but the cleavage extends to every territorial division and subdivision, and may almost be said to permeate every individual household. In all cases the party leaders are appointed from those who are recognized by their constituents as the most prominent of their members, and to their judgment and decision every question of fact or policy is of necessity referred. In such a system would seem to lie the true explanation of a time-honored custom throughout Gaul, which ensures for every poorer member of the community protection against more powerful neighbors; since every party leader is quick to resent and revenge any wrong or oppression that may be perpetrated on his clients, and indeed only holds his position of authority among them on condition of fulfilling this primary obligation. These characteristics of the internal state of each tribe obtain also in the country taken as a whole, and the same spirit of political partisanship splits it into two permanently hostile camps.

The respective heads of these two factions were, at the time of Caesar's arrival in the country, the Aedui and the Sequani. The former held an assured position of power by virtue alike of ancient prerogative and by their formidable list of subject communities; so that the Sequani, too weak to maintain the contest single-handed with the forces at their disposal, turned in the hour of their extremity to foreign alliance. At ruinous cost to themselves, both present and prospective, they induced Ariovistus and his Germans to cross the Rhine to their assistance; after which a succession of victories in the field, which swept away the whole of the Aeduan nobility, gave them such a predominating position over their rivals, that these for the time were virtually extinguished. Not only were considerable numbers of their supporters compelled to transfer their allegiance to the victorious party, and they themselves to give their chieftains' sons as hostages, but in their crippled state they had to swear to abstain in future from all unfriendly acts against the Sequani, to allow a strip of border territory to be forcibly occupied by their conquerors, and to see these firmly installed as the paramount power in Gaul. It was at this dark hour of his country's fortunes that Divitiacus undertook his mission to Rome in order to appeal to the Senate; but his effort was unavailing, and his return left matters where they were. The arrival of Caesar, however, caused a complete revolution in the conditions governing the contest. The Aeduan hostages were now given back to them, their ancient supporters renewed their former ties, and through the powerful influence exerted by Caesar, fresh states were induced to join the alliance (observing as they did that the members of the Aeduan confederacy enjoyed fairer terms and a juster rule than those elsewhere); while in every direction and by every means their authority and prestige was fostered and extended, until slowly but surely the premiership of the league passed from the hands of the Sequani. Their successors in the leadership were the Remi; and under this state, when once it was realized that Caesar's support was still bestowed as generously as before, many of those whose ancient feuds with the Aedui made a combination with that people intolerable, enrolled themselves as vassals to the Remi. Their new overlords, scrupulously upholding their rights as subjects, soon succeeded in building up for themselves an assured position of political power, that was as novel as it had been sudden in its growth. Thus at the period we have now reached, while the first place in public estimation belonged, without question, to the Aedui, the second was no less definitely conceded to the Remi.

That part of the Gallic population that is of any practical account may everywhere be divided into two heads: the position of the commons, who might form a third estate, may for our purposes be disregarded, since it is virtually that of slaves, powerless of themselves to initiate any political action, and wholly unrepresented in the councils of the nation. The majority, indeed, are so crushed down by debt and excessive taxation, or so much the victims of aggression by the rich, that they are glad to enter into voluntary servitude under some one or other of the great nobles, who then exercises over them all the rights of a master over slaves. The other two classes are those of the Druids and the Knights. Of the first the special province is religion in all its aspects. Every sacrifice, whether public or private, is conducted under their auspices, every manifestation of divine agency is brought to them for interpretation: they are the eagerly sought instructors of vast numbers of the nation's youth, and to the reverence accorded them there is hardly a limit. A dispute can scarcely arise, either between individuals or states, which is not referred to them for judgment. The graver criminal charges, such as murder, no less than such civil cases as those of inheritance or boundary disputes, are laid before the same tribunal; they it is who determine rewards and punishments, and to their decision should either party, whether a people or an individual, refuse obedience, it is excommunicated from all the religious life of the community. Than this dread penalty none is known among them more severe. Those on whom such sentence has been passed are regarded by their fellows as men polluted and accursed: their society is universally shunned; none will visit them, no one will speak to them, for to do either is to risk the fall of some dire calamity; the courts of law are closed to them, and from the public services they are rigorously excluded. At the head of all stands a single chief, the Archdruid, invested with supreme powers. Upon his death the succession either passes to the next in eminence, or, where there are several candidates of equal merit, the election is determined by vote of the Druids, and even occasionally by force of arms. Every year at a fixed date there is held a general assembly of the order at a sacred spot among the Carnutes, popularly believed to be the center of Gaul; and to this grand assize all make their way who have outstanding quarrels, to abide by the decisions there given. The Druidical cult is generally supposed to have originated in Britain, and from thence to have been transplanted to Gaul; and today those who desire to learn the more esoteric side of the doctrine cross to that island in order to complete their studies.

As a class the Druids take no active part in war, and pay none of the ordinary taxes for that purpose: not only from direct military service but from other state burdens also they are uniformly exempt. Through the attractions held out by such a career no less than from private choice, large numbers join the ranks of the priesthood, and are sent by their parents and relatives to undergo the necessary training. In their schools they are said to learn by heart an extraordinary number of lines, and in consequence sometimes to remain under instruction for as many as twenty years. Although for most other purposes, in both their public and private accounts, they have adopted the Greek alphabet, yet they still retain a superstitious objection to committing the secrets of their doctrine to writing. In acting so they would seem to be guided by two main considerations. The first is their natural repugnance to the unrestricted publication of their tenets; the second is a fear lest their pupils, by too close a reliance on the written text, should relax the cultivation of their memory; experience generally showing that the constant presence of a manuscript serves only to weaken the natural powers of application and retention possessed by the mind. With regard to their actual course of studies, the main object of all education is, in their opinion, to imbue their scholars with a firm belief in the indestructibility of the human soul, which, according to their belief, merely passes at death from one tenement to another; for by such a doctrine alone, they say, which robs death of all its terrors, can the highest form of human courage be developed. Subsidiary to the teaching of this main principle, they hold various lectures and discussions on astronomy, on the extent and geographical distribution of the globe, on the different branches of natural philosophy, and on the many problems connected with religion.

The second great division is that of the Knights. These form the warrior class, and live exclusively by the sword: war makes their opportunity; and as, previous to Caesar's arrival, wars of provocation or retaliation were the normal state of things, they were in those days constantly engaged. Their order of precedence depends exclusively upon the number of followers and retainers they can lead into the field, and that in its turn depends upon the eminence of each either in descent or in worldly circumstances. Rank or title of any other kind is not recognized among them.

In the formal observances of religion, the Gauls are as a nation almost excessively devout. This instinct leads them on such occasions as grievous bodily illness, impending battle, or similar dangers, to offer or to vow a human sacrifice in place of animal victims, the Druids being called in to officiate at the rites. Of this practice the underlying belief is that only by the substitution of one human life for another can the inexorable demands of heaven be satisfied; a principle that obtains in much of their public ceremonial also. Others keep by them a grotesque and gigantic image of some favorite god, into whose huge limbs of wickerwork those destined for sacrifice are packed alive; fire is then placed beneath the pile, and the souls of the victims pass away amid a torrent of roaring flames. Though ready enough to admit that the gods are better pleased when such punishment is inflicted on those convicted of theft or brigandage or other similar crime, yet, on the failure of this particular source of supply, they do not hesitate to seek the instruments of atonement even from the innocent.

Of all the gods, the one whose worship is most in vogue is Mercury. Everywhere the most conspicuous by the number of his images, he is commonly regarded as the revealer of all useful sciences, as the trusty guide to wayfarers and travelers, and as the all-important partner in trade and commerce. Next to him come Apollo, Jupiter, and Minerva, and about them their ideas correspond fairly closely with those current among the rest of mankind; viz. that Apollo expels diseases, that Minerva teaches the principles of domestic arts and crafts, that Jupiter wields the scepter over heavenly beings, that Mars holds in his hand the arbitrament of war. To the last-named god, on the eye of a big battle, they not infrequently devote the spoils of the campaign, and then whatever of the captured livestock remains on the termination of the war is publicly slaughtered in his honor, while all other kinds of booty are collected and heaped together in a single place. Of such dedicated piles of loot standing in sacred enclosures it is possible to see examples among many of the tribes; and rare are the cases where contempt for sacrilege has led either to the concealment at home of a piece of plunder, or to the theft of what has once been offered. For such an offence the punishment is the most terrible that torture can inflict.

Their supernatural descent from Father Dis[1] is the unanimous tradition of all Gauls, based, as they declare, on the teaching of the Druids. One curious result of this is that intervals of time are reckoned, not in days, but in nights; and similarly birthdays or the first day of any new month or year are observed in such a fashion as to make the preceding night always part of the festal day. Among other social customs, perhaps the most noticeable is their seclusion of children. Boys are never allowed to go and meet their sires, and for a boy of tender years to be seen in public by the side of his father before he is capable of bearing arms is regarded as a great disgrace.

What money a husband receives in dowry from a wife is always doubled by an equal portion taken from his own estate, strict valuation being made on either side. Of this combined sum a common account is kept, and all profits from it set aside; whichever partner then outlives the other takes both shares, together with the interest accumulated during their married life. Over their wives, no less than

---

[1] God of the dark underworld.

over their children, husbands exercise the power of life and death;
and whenever any member of their more distinguished families dies,
if there be reason to suspect foul play, at the meeting of the male
relatives which then takes place the wife is rigorously examined
according to the process usually adopted with slaves, and if proved
guilty, is put to death by burning and other refinements of cruelty.
The obsequies of the Gauls are, in proportion to their standard of living, both costly and magnificent, and at them all objects believed to
have been dear to the heart of the departed, including even animals,
are flung upon the pyre: indeed, only a little while before the present
account was written, at every properly conducted funeral slaves and
retainers known to have been loved by the dead man were commonly burned with their master.

Those of the tribes whose government passes for something
more enlightened have a special enactment that any rumor or
report on matter of vital interest, which may have been picked up
across the frontier, shall be instantly carried to the authorities, and
not divulged in other quarters; so frequently has it been found the
case that this people of strong passions and weak judgment can be
swept away by unreasoning panic, driven into the perpetration of
crime, and hurried into a fatal course of public conduct, solely by
their acceptance of some lying tale. When such information reaches
them, the magistrates decide what they will guard as state secrets,
and what they may with advantage issue to the public; and outside
the council chamber, it has to be remembered, no discussion of
political questions is permitted.

Turning now to the Germans, we find among them a form of
national life in sharp contrast to the one just described. Of anything
like a religious caste, such as we see in the Druids, there is a complete
absence, and a corresponding indifference to the multiplication of
sacrifices. The only deities they recognize are those visible powers
of nature whose kindly influence upon human labor is clearly
manifest; viz. the Sun, Moon, and God of Fire; of the existence of
any others they seem to be aware not even by hearsay. To them the
business of life is summed up in hunting and the art of war, and their

training in feats of hardship and endurance begins with earliest childhood. The postponement in a boy of the age of puberty is always a coveted distinction, and is believed to be a sign either of unusual height or of immense bodily strength. Sexual intercourse below the age of twenty is considered a disgrace to manhood; though, on the other hand, they are singularly free from all false modesty on this subject, and not only bathe together in their rivers, but even wear nothing more upon their bodies than a thin covering of deer or other skin, which necessarily leaves the greater portion bare.

The cultivation of the soil, in the strict meaning of the term, is little practiced by them, and their diet consists for the main part of milk, cheese, and flesh. Neither the exclusive enjoyment nor the private ownership of land is permitted; but instead an annual distribution of it is made by the government officials and local chiefs, who determine both the extent and situation of the portion of land to be allotted to each class and family-association living together: every one of these groups being required to remove elsewhere a year afterward. Of this practice the explanations given are various. It is said sometimes to owe its origin to a fear lest the charms of a fixed tenure should beget in the people a preference for the peaceful life of the farm over the more violent pleasures of war; to the covetousness inseparable from private ownership, which tempts the strong to oust the weaker from their holdings; to the desire of discouraging any elaborate form of building for protection against the natural vicissitudes of heat and cold; to the dread of arousing the latent love of money—that pernicious root of all discord and class hatred; or finally, to the conviction that their system alone reconciles the lower orders to their lot, when every man sees his own share of the national riches equal to that of the very highest in the land.

Among the tribes there is no more coveted distinction than to live in the center of a vast wilderness, that has been carved out with their own swords along each and all of their frontiers. In their minds the true test of national greatness is the power of compelling all neighbors to retire before their face, and to keep at a respectful distance from their settlements; such devastation, moreover, acts as a form of security, since undoubtedly it relieves them from the constant fear of raids. Upon the outbreak of war, whether offensive or defensive, the conduct of hostilities is entrusted to a board of magistrates, specially elected, and wielding capital jurisdiction; in peace the place of a central government is taken by the local chiefs, who dispense justice and regulate disputes each in his own division or subdivision of the country. Open brigandage, provided its victims be not fellow tribesmen, carries with it no disgrace; rather is it held up to admiration as a natural outlet for the activities of youth, and a useful remedy against sloth. Whenever, therefore, any chief announces before the tribal council that he is ready to lead an expedition, and calls for volunteers to follow him, those who approve of both the man and his measure leap to their feet with offers of assistance, winning much popularity by their action: should any of these then fail to make good their promise, they will be branded as renegades and traitors, and confidence in their sincerity will be forever afterward shaken. Their observance of the ties of hospitality is invariably most strict, and any foreign visitor, no matter what the object of his journey, may always rely on their loyally protecting him against abuse, as though his person were inviolable, and as long as he chooses to stay, the houses of all and the tables of all are freely at his disposal.

There was a time when the German race was distinctly inferior in martial qualities to the Gauls, and when the latter, habitually the aggressors, on account of their dense population and deficiency of land at home, sent offshoots of their own to the other side of the Rhine. It was in this way that some of the richest land in all Germany, lying round the great Hercynian forest (or, to give it the name by which it is known to Eratosthenes and other Greeks, the "Orcynian"), passed into the hands of the Tectosagan Volcae; and even today, thanks mainly to the double reputation they enjoy for fair dealing and hard hitting, that tribe is still maintaining itself in its adopted home, though sunk to the level of the surrounding population, and reproducing the well-known features of German poverty, destitution, and general discomfort, with the same rough style of living and of dress. The Gauls, on the other hand, have steadily progressed, and owing to the nearness of the Roman provinces and their introduction to articles of seaborne commerce, the national wealth has tended constantly to increase, and the standard of comfort constantly to rise. Thus the growing sense of their own inferiority arising from repeated overthrows in the field has resulted today even in their own admission that in warlike qualities they are no longer a match for their German foes.

This Hercynian forest, to which reference has been made, has a width, north and south, equal to a nine days' march for an ordinarily fast traveler; than this no more accurate computation can be given, and in it the length of a day's journey is left purely conjectural. From west to east it starts from the latitude of the Helvetii, Nemetes, and Raurici, and follows the line of the Danube as far as the frontiers of the Daci and Anartes. There it turns northwards and leaves the neighborhood of the river, skirting in the course of its immense length a large number of different tribes, until it finally loses itself at some remote point never yet penetrated, even after sixty days' journey, by any German of these parts, with whom, therefore, its eastern limit remains still shrouded in mystery. The forest itself is well known to exhibit a fauna in many respects peculiar; and therefore to set down the most typical and interesting examples may not be thought altogether inappropriate.

The first species is that of an ox shaped like a deer.[2] From the center of the forehead, between the ears, springs a single horn, higher and straighter than those of the deer in our country, and at its summit widely palmated and branched. The females closely resemble the males, and both are to the same extent antlered.

Another is that called the Elk. In outward form and in the particoloration of its skin, this has much in common with the Italian wild goat, though in build it is slightly heavier. Its horns are mutilated and its legs marked by an absence of any natural protuberance or joint; it never lies down to rest, and if accidentally cast, is powerless to recover its position or to raise itself from the ground. Its lairs are the trunks of

---

[2] Generally identified with the Reindeer.

trees, leaning against which, with its body slightly out of the perpendicular, it will go off to sleep. On discovering from their tracks any
of these animals' favorite haunts, the huntsmen either undermine all
the trees of the immediate neighborhood, or else cut them through
just far enough to leave them apparently still firmly standing. The
elks then return and lean against these as usual, and their weight
proving too much for the weakened trunks, they and their supports
come crashing to the ground.

The third species is that called the Urus (*aurochs*), in size a little
below the elephant, in appearance, color, and shape resembling a
bull. Their strength and speed are equally remarkable, and if once
discovered, neither beast nor man is safe from their attack. The trap-
ping in pits and the killing of these fierce animals forms a favorite
pastime with the natives, who find in it not only an admirable training school for the nation's youth, but also a highly popular form of
sport; and those who succeed in killing the largest number are, upon
the public exhibition of the horns as proof, acclaimed the heroes
of the hour. Unfortunately the species is quite useless for domestica-
tion, and all attempts to tame them, even when they have been taken
quite young, have hitherto proved unsuccessful. Their horns differ
both in size, shape, and general appearance from those of the Italian
domestic cattle; they are always in great demand, and, decorated
with a silver band at the mouth, are used as drinking cups at all their
more imposing banquets.

Section III. The Hunting of Ambiorix

THE INFORMATION BROUGHT IN BY THE UBIAN SCOUTING PARTIES THAT THE Suebi had all withdrawn to their forests determined Caesar to stay his advance: in the heart of Germany, where, as already noted, there exists a natural repugnance to tillage, little corn was likely to be found, and he had no wish to endanger his supplies. At the same time it was expedient not to relieve the natives altogether of apprehension as to his return, as well as to check the flow of auxiliaries to the western bank. As soon, therefore, as the army had recrossed the river, the order was given to cut away the farther end of the bridge, where it touched the Ubian shore, to a distance of 200 feet; after which at the extreme point of the part left standing a wooden artillery tower was erected of four stories high: twelve battalions were stationed at the bridge head in a strongly fortified redoubt, and the whole place with its garrison put under command of a young officer, C. Volcatius Tullus. These precautions taken, it became possible to proceed with the campaign against Ambiorix, especially as the corn was now beginning to ripen. In the immediate neighborhood there lay the great forest of the Ardennes, stretching from the Rhine and the Treveri (*Trèves*) across to the country of the Nervii, and thus covering a distance of some 500 miles.[1] In the hope of gaining whatever advantage

---

[1] Possibly a textual error, though it seems as old as Strabo.

swift action and lucky circumstance might combine to offer, Caesar sent forward through this forest the full strength of his cavalry, under its commander, L. Minucius Basilus; strict injunctions being given to forbid all fires whenever they camped, for fear of betraying their approach to any distant watcher, along with an assurance that he himself with the main army would follow closely behind.

These orders Basilus faithfully carried out. Marching very rapidly, before any had time to realize the fact of his presence, he made a large number of prisoners out on the open lands; and then, acting on the information these supplied, quickened his course in the direction in which Ambiorix, the rebel chief, with a few horsemen, was said to be in hiding. In war, however, even more than in other things, there is always the uncertain element of Fortune to be reckoned with. By an astonishing stroke of good luck, the Roman officer rode straight upon the Eburonian leader while the latter was lulled in a false sense of security, and before any word or rumor had had time to reach the party, his men were actually upon them. By a piece of misfortune no less inexplicable, the insurgent chief, after all the military equipment which he had by him had been seized by the troops and his horses and carriages secured, managed just to elude his impending fate. His escape was due to the fact that the house in which he lay was (according to the favorite Gallic custom of seeking the neighborhood of woods and streams as a protection against heat) surrounded by dense forest, and in the narrow clearing round about it his friends and adherents were able for a few seconds to hold off the attack of the cavalry; in that brief interval one of his followers lifted him into a saddle, and the woods then hid his retreating form. Thus, whether one considers the circumstances that brought about his peril or those that rescued him from it, the disposing hand of Fortune is equally apparent.

The reasons which determined Ambiorix not to concentrate the forces under him are veiled in some obscurity. It may have been due to settled policy, under conviction that any general engagement was to be avoided; or he may have concluded that his opportunity for so doing was already gone, and his freedom of action destroyed by the rapid advance of the Roman horse, which, as he was well aware, was the certain forerunner of the Roman army. Be that as it may, his next movement was to send a proclamation broadcast throughout the country, ordering a *sauve qui peut*. His people at once scattered in all directions. Some sought the deep shelter of the Ardennes, some hid themselves in the lonely wastes of the marshland, others nearer the great Ocean crossed to the low-lying flats scoured out by the natural action of the tides, numbers fled the country altogether, and among races in every respect strangers to their own[2] begged the protection of their lives and property. The ruler of the other half of their kingdom, a prince called Catuvolcus, who had allowed himself to become entangled in the treacherous designs of Ambiorix, proved unequal to the severe strain now imposed by the double fatigue of war and flight; he was already far advanced in years, and after solemnly cursing his colleague with every imprecation that language could command for the ruinous folly into which he had been dragged, took poison of yew (a plant very common in both Gaul and Germany), and so ended his life.

At this point there waited on Caesar a deputation from the two tribes of the Segni and Condrusi, who, situated between the Eburones and the Treveri, are by virtue of their extraction generally reckoned as German. The object of their mission was to deprecate any hostile treatment by the Romans and to combat the mistaken notion that a single policy ruled all the Germans west of the Rhine; the truth being that in their case they had never contemplated the taking up of arms, or dispatched any auxiliaries to the help of Ambiorix. After carefully sifting the evidence of prisoners on the point, Caesar demanded that any Eburonian fugitives who had harbored in their country should be brought into camp, but, provided that was done, assured them that their lands would not be devastated. The Roman military forces were then formed into three divisions, the baggage of the entire army being sent away to a fortress called Aduatica. This place, situated somewhere about the center of the

[2] The Eburones were German (II. iv).

Eburonian country, had the previous winter been the headquarters of Titurius and Aurunculeius, and apart from other advantages had the additional recommendation that, its old fortifications being still intact, its occupation would considerably lighten the labors of the troops. To hold this depot one of the three legions lately raised in Italy, the Fourteenth, was left behind, and strengthened by a detachment of 200 cavalry was, along with the camp itself, put under the command of Q. Tullius Cicero.

Of the separate divisions thus formed, the first, consisting of three legions under Labienus, was sent to scour all that part of the Eburonian country that borders on the Menapii, another also of three legions under C. Trebonius took the district extending to the Aduatuci, having orders to pillage and burn; while the last under Caesar himself, again of three legions, was intended to penetrate to the river Scheldt, a tributary of the Meuse, and to the outer fringe of the Ardennes, where rumor had it that Ambiorix with a few horsemen had betaken himself. Upon marching, Caesar gave a distinct understanding to his subordinate that the seventh day would see his return; that being the day on which, as he knew, fresh supplies would be due to the legion garrisoning the fort. Labienus and Trebonius were similarly urged, should circumstances render it possible, to return with their columns by that date, in order that the three commanders might again confer together, and concert such fresh measures between them as a study of the enemy's methods might show to be desirable.

As already indicated, the enemy were without a single organized band in the field, without one fortified post or town that was prepared to defend itself by force of arms; it was a war against a whole population scattered to the four winds. Wherever a hidden gorge, a wooded clump, or a treacherous marsh held out hopes either of concealment or defense, there they lay ensconced; and such places being the common knowledge of the countryside, the situation was one demanding the closest care; not indeed for the general safety of the army (for nothing that a demoralized and disorganized rabble could effect could seriously endanger that), but for guarding the lives of individual soldiers, a matter, however, in which, as will be seen, the safety of the army was to a large extent bound up. For it would constantly happen that the desire of loot drew men away to an unwise distance from the ranks, while the tangle of the forest, with its elusive or hidden paths, made it impossible to advance in anything like close order. If the work was to be done thoroughly, and the treacherous race to be extirpated once and for all, then the number of parties working the woods must be increased, and the line dangerously extended: if, on the other hand, as all Roman military method and practice demanded, the advance was to be made by order of companies, then any difficult ground became in itself a sufficient protection to the natives, isolated groups of whom were always ready to dart out from ambush, and fall upon the stragglers. Under conditions so harassing, all that watchful foresight could suggest was carefully carried out; and though the troops were burning for revenge, it was thought wiser to forgo some portion of the punishment intended for the enemy than to inflict it at the cost of valuable lives. Accordingly, messengers were dispatched to all the surrounding tribes, with a general invitation from Caesar to flock to the plunder of the Eburones, and to the certain prospect of loot. This device would at all events substitute Gauls for Roman legionaries in the risky work among the woods, and at the same time, by covering the country with dense hordes of men, would make doubly sure that the treacherous tribe should pay for its abominable crime by the utter extirpation of its name and race. From all parts of the country a large force was rapidly assembled.

While these operations were in active progress from one end of the district to another, the seventh day, previously fixed by Caesar for his return to the legion guarding his base, drew steadily near. And now occurred a remarkable illustration of the extraordinary power wielded by Fortune in the game of war, and of the incalculable nature of her surprises. The enemy, as has been made abundantly clear, were broken and crushed beyond hope of recovery, and throughout the whole field of operations there was not a single armed band on foot sufficient to raise even a qualm of apprehension. Suddenly to

the ever-ready ears of the Germans across the Rhine came the startling report that the Eburonians were being plundered, and that
anyone who liked might come and share the booty. Instantly 2,000
horsemen were ready to march from the Sugambri, a tribe that lies
nearest the Rhine, and that has already come before us as having
harbored the Tencteri and Usipetes when these were chased out of
Gaul. Crossing the river by means of boats and rafts, 30 miles below
the bridge and garrison established by Caesar, they quickly reached the
frontiers of the Eburones, where they picked up numerous small
bodies of fugitives, and (what is always dearest of all to the native
mind) large quantities of cattle. From that point the lust of spoil
drew them still farther on; and, bred up as such men are from their
cradles to war and rapine, they made small difficulty of either forest
or morass. Questioning their prisoners as to the whereabouts of
Caesar, they learned that the Roman commander in chief was far
away to the south, and that the Roman forces had all left the neighborhood. Then one of the prisoners made them a happy suggestion,
and asked why they remained contented with such meager and beg-
garly loot when wealth, beyond the dreams of avarice, might easily
be theirs. Aduatica was within a three hours' ride, Aduatica, where
lay the accumulated treasures of the whole Roman army. So weak,
moreover, was the garrison, that they could scarcely man the walls,
and so frightened that not a man dared show his face outside the
lines. At a prospect so dazzling, the Germans hastily hid out of sight
such booty as they had already seized, and taking as their guide the
same man who had tendered the information, set off eagerly in
the direction of the fort.

There for six long days Cicero had scrupulously observed the
parting injunctions of Caesar, and strictly confining his men to
camp, had allowed not even a sutler to pass the lines. On the seventh,
doubts began to trouble him as to the ability of his commander in
chief to keep his pledge with regard to the number of days. Rumor
said he was far away, and no word of his return had as yet reached
camp. The men were beginning to chafe under the long spell of
enforced inactivity, and openly to declare that, if all leave was to be

indefinitely stopped, the state of things was that of a regular siege. And indeed, with nine legions of Roman infantry in the field, supported by an overwhelming force of cavalry, and all operating against a broken and all but annihilated foe, the risk of any disaster occurring within a three miles' radius of camp appeared to the Roman commandant a negligible one. Leave was accordingly granted to five of the ten battalions to proceed to the nearest wheat fields, separated from camp by nothing more than a single hill, in order to get provisions. Originally left behind in the fort there had been also a large number of sick belonging to the other legions; and a section of these, amounting in all to some 300 men, grown convalescent during the past few days, went out also with the colors. Lastly, a crowd of followers and their mules, room for which had been found within the camp, obtained the desired permission to accompany the force.

It was precisely at this conjuncture of events that the German horsemen appeared upon the scene. Maintaining the same furious rate that had marked all their ride, they at once prepared, without slackening rein, to rush the defenses of the camp hard by the postern gate. The view on this side was obstructed by a belt of trees, which so effectually screened the enemy's approach that, when at last they were distinguished, the petty traders whose tents were pitched only just outside the line of ramparts had not even time to run for shelter inside the fort. The surprise and overwhelming nature of the attack caused general bewilderment, and only with great difficulty did the battalion on picket duty outside the gate hold off the opening rush. The enemy quickly spread themselves round the remaining faces of the camp, eagerly scanning all approaches; but though the holding of the gates strained all the powers of the defenders, in other quarters the elaborate fortification of a naturally strong position proved sufficient protection in itself. Within the area of the camp meanwhile the wildest disorder reigned. Men were rushing madly about, eagerly asking one another the meaning of the uproar: no one seemed to know the whereabouts of the attack, nobody could say where his own presence was required. Now it was confidently affirmed that the camp was already captured, now someone would passionately declare that the whole Roman army had perished with its commander, and that this was but the advance guard of the triumphant foe, who had ridden on from their victory. The great majority became victims of superstitious terrors, conjured up by the associations of the place, and with fevered imagination saw impending on themselves the same fate that in this fort had overtaken Cotta and Sabinus. Where panic was so unreasoning and so general, the confident belief of the Germans, with which their prisoner had instilled them, that no guard was kept within the Roman lines, was naturally confirmed; and calling on one another not to throw away so admirable a chance, they redoubled their efforts to force an entrance.

Among the sick left behind in the fort had been P. Sextius Baculus, a centurion who during his service with Caesar had held the command of the senior company in his regiment, and of whose conduct in earlier battles of these campaigns mention has already been made. This man at the time of the attack had been without food for five days, but believing that all was now over both with himself and all others in the fort, he sallied forth from his tent without his weapons, and there saw the enemy all but through the defenses, and the position as desperate as it was possible to be. Seizing arms from some bystanders, he boldly planted himself in the gateway of the camp, and was followed in so doing by the centurions of the battalion on picket duty at the time; and together these brave men for a few moments held their assailants at bay. Desperately wounded, Baculus then fainted, and with difficulty was rescued through being dragged out of the *mêlée*. But the short respite so gallantly gained had been long enough to steady the remaining troops, who at all events now dared to take their places on the wall and to offer some semblance of defense.

Meanwhile the foraging party had just completed its labors, when the roar of battle coming from the direction of the camp fell upon its ears; and the cavalry racing forward to observe the cause took in at a glance the full gravity of the position. Here was no shelter of fortified entrenchments with which to cover a frightened soldiery: lately raw recruits, and wholly unaccustomed to act for themselves, the men turned with mute appeal to their commanding officer and centurions, anxiously waiting for the word of command to issue from their lips. The sudden nature of the emergency had unstrung the stoutest heart. On their side the Germans, seeing the gleam of Roman standards showing in the distance, at once broke off the assault, convinced at first that the legions of whose departure their prisoner had spoken had unexpectedly returned. A few moments' observation, however, quickly undeceived them, and revealed the true proportions of their new foe, whereupon with feelings of profound contempt they charged down from every quarter.

The sutlers with the force immediately bolted to the nearest hill, and when quickly driven out of that, hurled themselves in wild confusion upon the troops, who were now drawn up around the standards, thereby changing their existing state of nervousness into one of downright terror. On the course to take the officers were not at all agreed. Some thought that with the camp so near they should form a wedge and cleave their way through the ring of hostile horsemen, arguing that even if a section got cut off, the main body could yet be saved; some, on the other hand, wished to take up a position on the hill range, and there meet their fate together. To this view the strongest opposition came from the small group of veterans who, it will be remembered, had accompanied the force. Calling on one another to make a supreme effort, and headed by C. Trebonius, a Roman knight who was acting as commanding officer of the contingent, they boldly cut their way through the heart of the enemy, and safely reached camp to a man. Close in their rear, with the impetus of the same rush, the sutlers and cavalry, thanks to the intrepid conduct of these veterans, were carried into safety. In painful contrast to this boldness was the vacillating conduct of the division on the hill. Even now their soldierly instincts had not returned to them, and lacking the resolution either to adhere to their first resolve of clinging to the higher ground, or to follow the example of swift and courageous action which they had seen so splendidly vindicated in the case of others, they attempted to carry out a regular retreat to camp, and in so doing fell upon difficult ground. Their centurions behaved in a manner worthy of all admiration. The senior compa-nies in this legion had in many cases been given to men specially promoted for valor from the lower commands in others, and the brilliant reputation they had already gained they were now deter-mined not to lose. Fighting till they dropped, they succeeded in temporarily relieving the pressure of the attack, and by their noble self-sacrifice enabled a portion of their men, to their own utter sur-prise, to regain the shelter of camp: the rest were cut off and perished amid the throng of natives.

Seeing that the garrison had by this time manned the walls, the German raiders quickly abandoned whatever hopes they might have entertained of storming a Roman camp, and after recovering their spoil from the woods in which it had been hid, started off for the Rhine toward home. Though, however, they were gone, the panic inside the Roman lines continued unabated, so that when toward the close of the same day the Roman cavalry, under C. Volusenus, rode into camp, having been dispatched in advance by special orders, that officer found it impossible to establish a belief that Caesar, with the main army safe and well, was himself close at hand. So complete a mastery had fear gained over their minds, that like men distraught they would have it that the Roman forces had been utterly annihi-lated, the cavalry alone escaping in the rout, and insisted that, had the army still been in existence, the Germans would never have dared to assault the camp. Only the timely arrival of Caesar put an end to this state of panic.

Familiar as he was with the surprises of war, Caesar's single adverse criticism, on his return, fell upon the decision which had allowed the battalions to leave their appointed post inside the fort, at a time when every circumstance demanded that no opening should be left for running even the shadow of a risk. The most prominent agent throughout the whole incident appeared to him to have been For-tune. She it was who had contrived the startling appearance of the Germans before the camp, and her they had to thank for so strangely turning them back just at the moment when rampart and gates seemed to be in their hands. But of all the various aspects of the case none was certainly more remarkable than that the Germans, who had crossed the river for the express purpose of plundering the possessions of Ambiorix, should by their sudden deflection toward the Roman camp really play so completely into his hands.

Once more the systematic harrying of the enemy recommenced, and numbers of volunteers having flocked in from the neighboring states, these were now dispatched to every corner of the kingdom. Villages and farms wherever seen were ruthlessly burned, and everywhere long trains of plunder filled the land; and though the standing crops were mostly consumed by the army of men and animals now engaged upon the work, wherever this was not the case the late season of the year and the heavy autumn rains had already beaten them to the ground. Even, therefore, should a certain number succeed in evading the bands now operating against them, it was practically certain that, with the withdrawal of the army, any survivors must perish from the total destitution that would ensue. Many were the occasions on which the efforts of the crowds of horsemen quartering the country seemed about to be crowned with success. Prisoners would declare that only a moment ago they had seen Ambiorix fleeing for his life, and straining their eyes to the horizon would insist that even yet he was not clearly out of sight. Then officers and men would be fired with fresh zeal at the prospect of overtaking the rebel chief, and buoyed up at the thought of earning the lasting gratitude of Caesar, would undergo such endless fatigue as apparently to triumph over even the limits imposed by nature. But the fulfillment of their desires, so ardently pursued, ever receded before their grasp; and again and again the hunted king would from some secret nook in a forest glen watch his enemies go by, until under the friendly covering of night he could steal away to another part of his wide dominions, never accompanied by more than three or four horsemen, to whom alone he dared entrust his life.

The devastation of the country having by these methods been completed, the army, weakened by the loss of two battalions, returned to Durocortorum, the capital of the Remi (*Rheims*). To this place the general assembly of the Gauls was summoned, and at it

Caesar prepared to hold a judicial inquiry into the recent insubordination among the Senones and Carnutes. Upon Acco, the ringleader of the movement, the heavier sentence of the law was passed, and the penalty inflicted that usage has made habitual; while of his accomplices many fled the country from fear of judicial proceedings, and were then formally condemned to outlawry. After this the legions were free to go into winter quarters. Two were posted at the frontier station of the Treveri, two among the Lingones (*Langres*), and the remaining six at Agedincum, the capital of the Senones (*Sens*). Arrangements for their supplies having been satisfactorily settled, Caesar, in accordance with his annual custom, then left Gaul for Italy, to resume his civil duties in the courts.

BOOK VII

SECTION I. THE RISING OF VERCINGETORIX

THE CALM THAT NOW LAY OVER GAUL HAD ENABLED CAESAR TO FULFILL HIS original plan of visiting Northern Italy, and superintending in that part of his government the civil administration of the courts. There he heard of the murder of Clodius (Jan. 20), and acting upon the consequent resolution of the Senate which called on all the adult population of Italy to take the oath of military service, he proceeded to order a levy throughout the province. These unusual movements were of course at once reported to the Gauls beyond the Alps, and their true significance being purposely exaggerated and perverted by interested mischief-makers, Caesar was represented as forcibly detained in Italy owing to the disturbances at Rome, and as unable to rejoin his army through fear of an armed outbreak. So good an opportunity was eagerly embraced by those who had long resented the yoke of foreign rule, and fresh thoughts of war, on a bolder and grander scale, now began to stir their minds. Secret councils were convened in remote districts of the forestlands, at which the national leaders, taking the death of Acco for their text, cunningly incited others to rebellion by the insinuation that his fate might very probably be theirs, and by generally lamenting the woes of their unhappy country. The great point was to discover some tribe to lead the way, and, induced by the sure prospect of generous reward from its fellows, though at the imminent risk of its own existence, to work out the common salvation of Gaul. The importance of severing Caesar from his army before their secret negotiations got abroad was fully recognized; but this feat was declared easy of accomplishment because, just as in the absence of their commander in chief, the legions would not think of stirring from their cantonments, so neither could he without an escort make his way to them. And come what might it was universally agreed that to fall fighting on the field of battle was infinitely better than to endure the loss of their ancient military renown, and of their sacred heritage of freedom as a people.

As a result of these discussions the Carnutes stepped forth with the bold announcement that they were prepared to risk everything for the welfare of their country, and to take upon themselves the responsibility of beginning hostilities. It seemed inadvisable, however, at the present juncture to interchange hostages, as such a step might well lead to disclosure; they therefore requested all present solemnly to bind themselves by the most sacred rite known to their people, viz. the interlocking of their military ensigns, and to swear that, when once they had set their hand as leaders to the task of national redemption, other tribes should not leave them in the lurch. Loud was the applause at this patriotic conduct of the Carnutes; and every member present having given the required oath, a date was fixed for carrying out their schemes, and the council then dispersed to their respective homes.

As dawn broke upon the fateful day, the Carnutan authorities gave the signal, and under the leadership of two desperadoes named Cotuatus and Conconnetodumnus, an armed mob burst upon the town of Cenabum (*Orleans*), where they first massacred the Roman mercantile residents, and then proceeded to distribute their property. Among the victims was a Roman knight of distinguished family, C. Fufius Cita, who at the time was holding a commission from Caesar in the commissariat department of the army. The story of this deed of blood was quickly carried into every corner of Celtic Gaul. In these regions the report of any event of uncommon interest or distinction is usually conveyed by being shouted across the countryside, each man in turn catching it up and passing it on to the next. Thus on the present occasion an incident which happened at Cenabum at sunrise was made known before the close of the first watch of the night by this method to the Arverni (*Auvergne*), over a distance of a hundred and fifty miles.[1]

Among the Arverni it took instant hold on one of the most prominent of their younger chiefs, a man named Vercingetorix. This man's father, a certain Celtillus, had once been the titular head of all Gaul, and because he aspired to monarchical power, had been put to death by his own people. The son now summoned his personal retainers round him, who were easily caught by his own infectious zeal, and as his designs became more widely known the whole tribe flew to arms. On the other hand, he encountered stout opposition from most of the ruling chiefs, headed by his own uncle Gobannitio; and as these all strongly disapproved of his policy at such a time, he soon found himself expelled from the capital, Gergovia. In no wise daunted by this rebuff, he next proceeded to rouse the countryside, and to enlist to his standard every needy adventurer that offered himself: with this band to support him, he then paid various visits to such of his fellow countrymen as he hoped to secure for allies, pleading with them to take up arms for their country's cause; until, having accumulated quite a formidable force, he returned to oust from their position those political opponents by whom he had himself been rudely dismissed. Proclaimed king by his followers, he next dispatched agents to all four quarters of the Gallic world, begging the various states to stand loyally to their pledge; and soon the Senones (*Sens*), Parish (*Paris*), Pictones (*Poitou*), Cadurci (*Cahors* on the *Lot*), Turoni (*Tours*), Aulerci (*Perche-Maine*), Lemovices (*Limoges*), Andi (*Anjou*), and all the maritime tribes of the northwest had announced their adhesion to his cause. Having been by universal consent appointed commander in chief, he proceeded in virtue of his new powers to exact hostages from all the tribes above, to apportion military contributions for each member of the confederacy, and to fix the quantity of arms that each tribe was to

[1] i.e. in 14 hours.

manufacture at home, together with their date of delivery. Especially did he take measures to raise a really powerful cavalry. Tireless and unsparing of himself, he demanded from others a discipline almost savage in its rigor; and insubordination was stilled at the thought of the punishment awaiting it. All the more serious offences were visited with death by fire and other racking tortures; in the case of minor delinquencies, the culprit first had his ears cropped, or one of his eyes put out, and was then sent back to show himself to his friends, as a lasting warning through the severity of his punishment to all other would-be evildoers.

In spite of, or maybe because of this sternness, an army was rapidly collected; whereupon half of his forces he dispatched under a certain Cadurcan named Lucterius, a bold and resolute leader, to the country of the Ruteni (*Rodez*) in the south, while with the remainder he himself advanced northward against the Bituriges (*Bourges*). That people at once sent a message to their political suzerains, the Aedui, requesting their assistance in the task of repelling the enemy. The Aedui, upon the advice of those Roman officers who had been left by Caesar in charge of the army, replied to their appeal by sending off to their relief a mixed body of horse and foot. On reaching the river Liger (*Loire*), which forms the boundary between the Aeduan and Biturigan territories, this force halted for several days, being afraid to cross. Returning home, the men then reported to the officers that they had discovered a treacherous plot on the part of the Bituriges, who meant first to inveigle them across the river, and then to crush them between the two converging armies of themselves and the Arverni. Whether the alleged cause was the true one, or whether their action was prompted by disloyalty, in the absence of clear proof one way or the other, need not be here decided. Their retirement was at once followed by the secession of the Bituriges to the Arvernian cause.

These movements reached the ears of Caesar while he was still in Italy; and coming at a moment when, thanks to the vigorous measures adopted by Cn. Pompeius, affairs at the capital had been reduced to something approaching order, they made it possible for him to recross the Alps into the further Province. Arrived there, he was at once confronted by the exceedingly difficult problem of how best to reach his army. To summon the legions southward into the Province would be to send them into action upon the road in his own absence; to make a dash northward in order to join them was to entrust his person to the safe conduct of still nominally friendly tribes, and this at so critical a juncture would scarcely be advisable.

Meanwhile, however, circumstances had combined to solve the problem for him. The Cadurcan leader Lucterius had so far succeeded in his mission to the Ruteni as to win over that tribe to the national cause, passing thence to the Nitiobriges and Gabali,[2] from each of whom he exacted hostages; and now, after strengthening himself by several fresh contingents, he was ready to descend upon the Roman Province with the object of striking at the town of Narbo (*Narbonne*). The news of this movement determined Caesar to relegate all other issues to secondary consideration, and to proceed at once to the threatened town. There he soon put fresh heart into the waverers, and then proceeded to erect a chain of forts along those sections of the Ruteni that lie on the Roman side of the frontier, the Arecomican Volcae, the district of Tolosa (*Toulouse*) and the environs of Narbo, all of which lay directly in the enemy's line of attack. At the same time a portion of the Provincial levies, as well as the new drafts lately come from Italy, were ordered to concentrate upon the Helvii, who are situated on the southeastern flank of the Arverni (*Auvergne*).

These measures sufficiently checked the further advance of Lucterius, who, finding the ring of fortified posts too strong to pierce, presently beat a retreat, thus leaving Caesar free to go on to the Helvii. On the Cevennes, the mountain range that blocks the Helvii from the Arverni, midwinter had spread a pall of deep snow over the face of all the country, that sorely hindered progress: but, working with tireless energy at the task of clearing the drifts, that were often six feet high, the troops gradually laid bare the roads, and soon the army was upon the frontiers of Auvergne.

[2] Between the Dordogne, Garonne, and the Cevennes.

Its inhabitants were overwhelmed by the extraordinary suddenness of the attack. The Cevennes had always been regarded as an
impregnable barrier of defense, and never within the memory of
man had the passes been open at this season even to a single wayfarer.
Pressing his advantage, Caesar ordered his cavalry to scour the country to the utmost limits of their powers, and to overawe the enemy
wherever found. The report that the Romans had taken the field was
quickly communicated to Vercingetorix, and, as a first consequence,
he was quickly surrounded by a crowd of terror-stricken Arverni,
begging him to go to the rescue of their property before it was looted
by the enemy, and reminding him that to him had been entrusted
the sole conduct of the war. To these arguments he yielded a grudg-
ing recognition, and breaking up his camp among the Bituriges,
began to move southward toward the Arvernian district.

Meanwhile Caesar, who had expected some such result in regard
to Vercingetorix, after remaining two days in the neighborhood,
gave out that the need of obtaining fresh drafts of infantry and cavalry now summoned him away, and then quietly took his departure
from camp. The command of the forces was left with one of the
younger generals, D. Brutus, who had orders to continue the sweeping movements of the cavalry about the country during the
commander in chief's absence, which would not, as he hoped, be
extended beyond three days. These dispositions effected, without any
suspicion even by his own attendants of the object of their journey,
he traveled through with all haste to Vienna (*Vienne*), where, picking
up a division of cavalry which had been sent on thither some days in
advance, and was therefore now rested, and barely drawing rein
either by day or night, he raced across the country of the Aedui
toward the Lingones (*Langres*), where were two legions in winter
quarters. In this way he trusted to his speed to frustrate any designs
upon his own person that the Aeduan authorities might likewise be
harboring. Arrived at his destination, he at once sent word to the
remaining legions, and before any inkling of his presence in these
quarters had reached the Arverni, the concentration of the Roman
army was complete. At this unexpected news Vercingetorix once

more fell back upon the Bituriges, from whence he moved to attack
the town of Gorgobina, at this time inhabited by that section of the
Boii which after the Helvetian war had been settled there by Caesar in
political dependence upon the Aedui.[3]

The enemy's new movement raised a serious difficulty for Caesar
as to what course he should pursue. To keep the legions together for
the rest of the winter while a city belonging to Aeduan subjects was
openly carried by assault, was to confess before the Gallic world that
the Romans were unable to defend their friends, and to risk, therefore, the universal defection of Gaul: on the other hand, to move
from winter quarters earlier than usual, with transport a matter of
much trouble, would probably lead to a breakdown in his supplies.
Yet it seemed preferable to endure any degree of hardship than, by a
tame acquiescence in such a humiliating ignominy, to alienate the
sympathies of every Roman supporter: and therefore, after urging
on the Aedui the importance of maintaining a regular succession of
convoys, he sent word to the Boii that he himself was marching to
their relief, bidding them at the same time stand firmly to their allegiance and present a bold front to the enemy. Then leaving two
legions at Agedincum (*Sens*) along with the stores and baggage of the
whole army, with the remaining forces he set out for the Boii.

The second day's march brought him to a town of the Bituriges
named Vellaunodunum,[4] and in order to leave no enemy in his rear
who might afterward threaten his communications, he prepared for
its assault, and in two days had completed the necessary lines. On the
third the enemy opening negotiations, they were allowed to surrender on condition they gave up all arms, brought out all draft animals,
and handed over hostages to the number of six hundred. The carrying out of these terms was entrusted to C. Trebonius, a staff officer,
and the army with the commander in chief then resumed its forward movement. Its next objective was Cenabum (*Orleans*), the capital
of the Carnutes, for whose defense that tribe was only now preparing

[3] I. 28.
[4] Possibly Montargis or Beaune.

to introduce a garrison; since they had expected the siege of Vellaunodunum, of which they had just heard, to be an affair of some time.
Two days' march brought the legions before the town; but, it being
too late to deliver the assault that night, it was decided to defer it till
the morning, and meanwhile the army camped outside the walls.
The necessary preparations for attack having been carefully completed by the troops, as there was reason to fear that the enemy
might, under cover of darkness, attempt to escape by the bridge
connecting Cenabum with the farther bank of the Liger (*Loire*), two
legions were ordered to remain under arms throughout the night.
This expectation was abundantly realized, and shortly before midnight the inhabitants quietly began the evacuation of the town by
crossing the stream; but the movement being reported by his scouts
to Caesar, the two legions, who by his orders were ready for any
emergency, were at once directed to fire the gates and to enter the
town. The victory was all but complete: along the bridge and narrow
roads debouching upon it the crush had been so dense, that very few
indeed of the enemy's masses had succeeded in making their escape.
The town was first plundered and then burned; and the troops having
been rewarded with the spoil, the army now crossed the Liger and
found itself in the country of the Bituriges.

The news of its approach caused a modification of plans on the
part of Vercingetorix, and breaking off the siege then occupying him,
he boldly advanced to throw down the gage of battle to Caesar himself. The latter meanwhile had interrupted his advance in order to
attack the Biturigan town of Noviodunum,[5] lying upon his line of
march. A desire to negotiate had already been expressed by the garrison, and Caesar, anxious to complete his work with the same
expedition which had hitherto proved so effective, had, in answer to
their appeal for pardon and preservation, at once commanded the
delivery of arms, animals, and hostages. Some of these had already
been surrendered, and centurions with a file of soldiers had even
entered the town for the purpose of completing the arrangements

[5] Between Orleans and Bourges, but of uncertain identification.

and of collecting the arms and animals, when suddenly on the horizon the cavalry corps preceding the army of Vercingetorix was seen to be approaching. No sooner was the discovery made by the townspeople, than realizing that possible help was at hand, they raised a loud shout of defiance, and rushing to arms, shut all the gates and surged forward to man the walls. The centurions in the town, observing from the signals passing between the Gauls that some untoward circumstance had arisen, at once drew their swords, and having secured possession of the gates, ultimately withdrew every one of their men without loss.

Upon Caesar's orders the cavalry advanced from camp and at once engaged the enemy; but finding that they were being worsted he called up as reinforcements a body of some four hundred German troopers, which throughout these campaigns had been a permanent feature of his army. Before their charge the enemy broke and fled, and with heavy loss fell back upon their main column. Their overthrow revived to the full the alarms of the townsfolk, and, having arrested the suspected leaders in the recent renewal of resistance, they sent these out to Caesar under escort and again tendered their submission. This affair satisfactorily disposed of, the advance was continued toward Avaricum (*Bourges*), and as this town is the largest and strongest of all those belonging to the Bituriges, and forms the center of an exceedingly rich and fertile district, there was good ground for believing that its recovery by the Romans would be followed by the surrender of the entire Biturigan people.

So far the war, from the point of view of Vercingetorix, had been one long series of disasters; and when to the fall of Vellaunodunum were added those of Cenabum and Noviodunum, it was time in his opinion to summon his principal supporters and to discuss with them the military situation. The campaign, he now announced, must in future be conducted on very different lines from those hitherto adopted. The supreme object of the Gauls should be to deprive the Romans of fodder and provisions; and owing to their superior cavalry, as well as to the time of year, neither of these tasks should present much difficulty. It was, he truly observed, impossible to cut fodder, and the Romans, to get it at all, must scatter over the country and pillage the private stores; and one by one their separate parties could then be snapped up daily by the watchful Gallic troopers. Bluntly declaring that it was no time to cling to the sweets of private property, he insisted that all villages and farms lying off the high road, within the radius of the Roman foragers, must be ruthlessly burned. They themselves, he argued, would always have enough, as they could freely draw upon the resources of the country forming the area of operations; whereas the Romans must either abandon their task altogether through paucity of provisions, or else spread themselves to a dangerous distance from their base: in which case, as he shrewdly remarked, it was immaterial whether they killed their enemies in the field, or stripped them of those accessories without which war becomes an impossibility. One last sacrifice he also demanded of them. Such towns as were not impregnable either from natural strength or from added fortifications, must be destroyed by fire; otherwise they were leaving convenient shelters for those among themselves who shirked the burden of military service, and a tempting prize to the Romans for the acquisition of stores or loot. Those to whom such a counsel might appear hard or unnatural should consider how infinitely harder it would be to see their wives and children carried into slavery, while they themselves were butchered by the sword. And this fate, were they beaten in this struggle, would inevitably overtake them.

His proposal met with unanimous approval, and on a single day upward of twenty cities of the Bituriges were committed to the flames. A similar step was taken by other tribes, and all round the horizon the flare of the great fires could now be seen. Such a sacrifice, though it cut them to the quick to make it, was yet relieved to some extent by this consideration, that looking upon victory as now assured, they felt confident that a short interval would give them back all that they were at present losing. The fate of Avaricum (*Bourges*) then came up for decision; and before a full assembly of the allies the question of its destruction or retention was warmly debated. Going upon their knees before all their compatriots, the Bituriges passionately pleaded the cause of this queen of Gallic cities—their pride alike and their protection—and begged they might not be forced with their own hands to apply the torch for its destruction. It was, they maintained, easily defensible; and secure amid its maze of river and marsh, and approached if at all at but one point of extreme narrowness, it might safely bid defiance to all attack. Their request was granted; and though Vercingetorix at first stoutly opposed the concession, yet afterward, before the earnest appeal of the Bituriges and the strong sympathy excited by their case, he signified his assent. A trustworthy garrison was then selected for its future defense.

Meanwhile the Gallic commander by shorter stages continued following in the rear of Caesar until, arrived within some sixteen miles of Avaricum, he chose a site strongly fortified by forest and swamp, and there made his camp. Organizing a regular service of secret messengers, he kept himself informed of all that passed within the town, sending back his own instructions to the garrison. All movements of Roman troops in search of fodder or provisions were carefully watched; and if at any time these got drawn too far from their base or became scattered, as was necessarily often the case, they were certain to be attacked. The annoyance thus caused was very considerable, and though various ruses were tried, such as changing the hour and road taken by the foragers, they were mostly unavailing.

Caesar meanwhile had commenced the siege. Fixing his camp at that corner of the town where, as already described, an assault alone is possible through the break in the line of river and marsh, he proceeded to construct a siege embankment, and under cover of mantlets to erect two wooden artillery towers. Circumvallation, which under other circumstances would have been preferable, was in this instance precluded from the peculiar nature of the ground. On the extremely important question of supplies, though frequent appeals were made to the Boii and the Aedui, they effected little. The last-named tribe was but lukewarm in its support, and their help was therefore insignificant: the other, being a small and weakly community, possessed but slender stocks of grain, and so quickly ran to the end of its resources. When to Aeduan indifference and

Boian indigence there is added a third great obstacle in the destruction by fire of all surrounding homesteads, it will readily be seen that the Roman army was reduced to the direst straits for food: indeed, for several days the men never tasted bread, and had to stay the pangs of hunger solely by meat obtained from the herds that were driven in from distant villages. Yet through all this period no word was uttered unworthy of the great traditions of the Roman people, or of their glorious record in the past. Indeed, when the question was put by Caesar in turn to each of the legions, as he went the round of the works and promised to break off the siege if the strain imposed upon the men proved too severe, the unanimous answer was that to do so would be an insult, no less humiliating than undeserved, both to them and their many years of faithful service under himself, and that to break off a task when once begun, such as this siege of Avaricum, was a disgrace they had done nothing to incur. Nay, sooner than fail in the sacred duty owed to the departed spirits of those Romans who had been foully massacred at Cenabum (*Orleans*), they would gladly endure whatever suffering might be necessary. Similar sentiments were expressed by the men to their officers and centurions, with a request that these would convey their wishes to Caesar.

The twin towers of the Romans had all but reached the wall, when through some prisoners the discovery was made that Vercingetorix, having exhausted his present supply of fodder, had moved his camp nearer to Avaricum, and with his cavalry and the light-armed skirmishers who usually fought on foot between the squadrons, had gone off to arrange an ambuscade at a spot where he had reason to believe the Roman foragers were to come next day. Acting on this intelligence, Caesar, about midnight, noiselessly left camp, and early the next morning reached the main position of the enemy. His approach, however, had been promptly reported by their scouts, and after hiding their wagons and heavy baggage in the denser parts of the bush, they were now all drawn up in battle array on a piece of ground that was both raised and open. On hearing this, Caesar ordered his men to pile their knapsacks and to prepare for action.

The hill on which the Gauls were posted, while rising gently from its base, was virtually surrounded by a belt of marsh, which, though not more than fifty feet across, was yet dangerous and treacherous under foot. All connecting bridges had been broken down by the enemy; and with full confidence in their position and ranged in order of tribes, they now quietly awaited the attack, jealously guarding every ford and causeway that led across the swamp, and ready at a moment's notice, should the Romans attempt to rush the intervening space, to fall upon them from their place of vantage as they floundered in the mud. To a spectator, watching merely the narrow interval that separated the two forces, it doubtless would have seemed that the Gauls were asking only a fair field and no favor in order to engage their adversaries; and it was not until he noticed the tremendous inequality of conditions, that he would realize how hollow was their pretense of valor and how empty was their boast. But the sight of their foe thus openly flaunting them to their face at so ridiculous an interval, roused the legionaries to fury, and a clamorous demand was made to have the signal for action. Caesar found it necessary to explain how heavy must be the price of victory, and how terribly long the death roll of brave men; and though, as he told them, he rejoiced to see the spirit of devotion animating them toward himself, and leading them to dare anything for his honor, he yet felt that to sacrifice their lives to his own ambition would justly convict him of most heartless selfishness. Having thus consoled them for their disappointment, on the same day he led his troops back to camp, where the task of completing the various requisites for an assault was once more resumed.

But the incident was not allowed to pass unchallenged so far as Vercingetorix was concerned, and on his return to headquarters he was formally arraigned for treason. The substance of the charge was that he had moved his camp within striking distance of the Romans; that he had gone off with the whole of the Gaulish cavalry; that he had left his large forces wholly destitute of a commander; and above all that, under such favorable circumstances for the enemy, his departure had been promptly followed by the appearance of the Romans on the scene. These facts, it was argued, could not all of them be the result of chance or altogether innocent of design, but plainly indicated that he preferred to accept the kingdom of Gaul as a fief from Caesar, rather than as a gift bestowed by his own people. To such allegations his answer was as follows. Their change of camp had been necessitated by their shortness of fodder, and was indeed openly supported by themselves; while the fact that it brought them nearer to the Romans was, in view of the natural strength of their new position, quite apart from fortifications, immaterial: and as to the cavalry, their services could hardly have been required on the swampy ground, while on the other hand they had proved most valuable on the particular work to which he had transferred them. His neglect to appoint a deputy commander on leaving camp had been intentional; for, knowing their natural repugnance to strenuous toil and their impatience to have done with it, he had been afraid that any subordinate might be driven by their impulsiveness to offer battle. The sudden appearance of the Romans had at least had some good results: it had enabled themselves, as it were from a bird's-eye point of view, to discern the weak numbers of their opponents, and also to show their supreme contempt for men who lacked the spirit to enter on a stand-up fight, but who, like curs, returned to the protection of a fortified camp. Whether, therefore, their arrival had been due to chance or to the invitation of some renegade, the allies might at least be grateful for the good it had effected—to Fortune in the one case, to the particular informer in the other. Again, their taunt about accepting sovereign power from Caesar as the price of treachery he repudiated with all his might; for with victory already well in sight—victory not only for himself, but for every one of his compatriots—it would necessarily follow of itself: and he even offered to resign, if they had any suspicion that the title with which they honored him was more than a fair equivalent for the advantages they themselves derived. Then turning on his accusers, "To understand," said he, "that my words are those of an honest man, I will ask you to hear the evidence of Roman soldiers."

With this he led forward a batch of slaves, captured a few days previously on a foraging expedition, and since tortured by starvation and imprisonment. These, having been carefully drilled beforehand in the story they were to tell their questioners, declared that they were Roman legionaries who had stolen from camp, in the fond hope of finding a little corn or cattle about the country, as they could no longer endure their present hunger and distress. The same awful destitution was being suffered by the entire Roman army, reducing it to such a state of emaciation that the men could no longer perform the manual work demanded by the siege; and if no progress were made with the investment, the Roman commander had decided after three more days to withdraw altogether from the place. "Such," concluded Vercingetorix, "are the services of a man whom you now accuse of treachery. Without shedding a single drop of your blood, by my own exertions, as at last you see, I have brought the vaunted army of Rome to the actual brink of starvation, and have also, by my foresight, ensured that, when it turns and runs for its life, it shall not find a single district in all Gaul able to give it succor."

From all sides of the vast assembly loud applause was heard, accompanied by the clash of arms, the invariable method of the Gauls for signifying their approval of a speaker. Vercingetorix was declared to be a heaven-born general, whose loyalty it was treason to doubt and whose strategy it was impossible to improve. A picked force of 10,000 men, drawn from all the confederates alike, was straightway ordered for Avaricum. The salvation of their common country, it was felt, should not be allowed to depend solely upon the Bituriges; and, as was plainly evident, the retention of their capital by that people was the true key to their ultimate victory over Rome.

Meanwhile the siege steadily advanced, the Roman soldiers displaying a heroism that was only equaled by the inventive genius of the Gauls. A more versatile race, in fact, nowhere exists, and in adopting and reproducing all the best methods of other nations they stand unrivaled. The powerful hooks used by the Romans for loosening the wall would be turned aside by means of nooses made fast to windlasses with which to draw them in; the great siege mound was frequently undermined, with all the precision and skill that familiarity with all branches of mining had given them, owing to the large

iron workings in their country; while the whole periphery of wall
had been crowned with a line of storied towers, wrapped round with
skins. Nor did they fail to make constant sallies, by day no less than
by night, during which they would scatter fire upon the logs that
helped to form the embankment, or furiously attack the troops
while busy upon the works. Again, they would cleverly frustrate the
object of the two great movable towers, whose purpose it was to
command the town, by carefully noting the distance these rose with
the daily rise of the mound, and then raising their own to an equal
height, by taking a line through the tall uprights that formed their
framework. Finally, they would endeavor to block the open ends of
the Roman galleries protecting the sappers, and so prevent their
reaching the wall, by driving in timbers sharpened and fire-hardened
at the point, or by pouring down burning pitch and placing in position massive boulders of stone.

The walls of a Gallic town, it should be noted, are invariably
formed as follows. A line of heavy balks at regular intervals of two
feet is first let perpendicularly into the ground and braced together
on the inner side. These are then dressed from behind with a solid
backing of earth, the intervening spaces being crammed with wide-
faced stones. As soon as the first row is firmly fixed and welded
together, a second is superimposed upon it, preserving throughout
the same intervals, but so arranged that its timbers are not continuous with those below, but by means of the exact uniformity of the
spacing are cleverly made to fit into the corresponding stonework
beneath. The rest of the building then follows the same pattern, until
the whole has attained to the height of an ordinary city wall. Such a
type of construction, besides being in no sense unpleasing to the eye,
owing to the variation produced by the alternate courses of wood
and stone, so accurately divided by rectilinear lines, possesses also
very great advantages in the facilities it offers for the defense of towns.
The stonework is of course proof against fire, while the timber
courses, being clamped together on the inner side by single beams,
often forty feet in length, bid easy defiance to the ram, since it is
impossible either to break them up or to wrench them out.

Though checked at every point by the endless devices of the Gauls, and hampered throughout the operations by both rain and cold, yet the indomitable efforts of the troops at last overcame every obstacle, and at the end of five-and-twenty days they had succeeded in raising a mound 330 feet in width and 80 in height.[6] This had nearly reached the wall, when one night, as Caesar as usual was sharing the watch with the men upon the works, urging them to waste no single moment from the task before them, suddenly a little before midnight smoke was seen rising from the embankment, showing that the garrison had fired it from a mine. At the same time a mighty cheer ran from one end of the enemy's wall to the other, and from two of the gates, one on either side of the Roman towers, a sallying party poured forth. To support this attack, others of their number from their post upon the wall began to throw lighted torches and dried timber upon the mound, and to pour on pitch and any other inflammable material. In the first shock of surprise it was difficult to decide where to combat the evil, or what point stood in most pressing need of aid. Fortunately, it was Caesar's practice always to keep two legions on duty at night before the camp, strong drafts from which were constantly on guard in turn upon the works; and owing to this precaution, the attacking parties were quickly met, while with another division of the troops the towers were rapidly hauled out of danger, and the burning pile sundered in twain. At the same time a hurried movement of all arms took place from camp, to assist in extinguishing the flames.

Then for some hours the tide of battle raged on every side, till night had been succeeded by morning. The enemy's, hopes of victory rose with every passing minute, reaching to certainty as they saw that on the Roman towers the breastworks had been burned off by the fire, leaving it difficult for the troops, owing to the exposure, to go to their assistance. Constant relays of fresh men pressed eagerly forward to relieve those who had become exhausted, and the hour of Gallic freedom seemed at last about to strike, when an incident occurred

---

[6] So the MSS. The height given is that at Marseilles. Cf. *Civil War*, II. 1.

under our own observation, which, as being well worthy of record just as it was witnessed by us, we cannot allow to pass unnoticed. Standing before the town gate was a Gaul, throwing on to the fire, in a line with one of the towers, lumps of grease and pitch that were passed out to him by hand. A bolt from one of the mounted pieces of artillery struck him on his right, or unguarded side, and he fell dead. Across his prostrate body one of those nearest at once stepped forward to continue the same duty, until he too by the same method was hit by the artilleryman, and dropped lifeless to the ground. His place was taken by a third, and his by a fourth; nor was it till the fire had been extinguished along the mound, and the enemy had been driven back at every point, and all fighting was over, that the Gallic sharpshooters allowed this particular post to go unoccupied.

The Gauls had now exhausted every expedient; and as each had uniformly failed, on the next day, by the advice and command of Vercingetorix, they resolved to evacuate the town. This step they hoped to accomplish with little loss to themselves, provided they made the attempt at dead of night; for not only was Vercingetorix's camp at no great distance from the city, but the marshes which covered all the intervening space would necessarily impede any pursuit on the side of the Romans. Darkness having fallen, all was in busy preparation for the task, when suddenly the streets were filled with wives and mothers pouring from their homes, who, throwing themselves with tears before their husbands, begged and implored them by every term of endearment not to betray them and their children, their common offspring, to the tender mercies of the foe, simply because age or natural weakness in their case made flight impossible. Then, seeing that nothing would turn them from their purpose, all pity as usual being quenched where danger is supreme, they rent the air with piercing cries intended to inform the Romans of what was going forward; on which the garrison, fearful of discovery and of finding the roads already in possession of the Roman cavalry, abandoned their design.

On the morrow Caesar moved up one of his two towers, and the various works, on the construction of which the troops had been

long engaged, were now placed in position. A fierce storm had ushered in the day, and through the driving rain it was possible to
observe that the guard upon the enemy's wall was being a little less
carefully maintained. Thinking, therefore, that the wildness of the
elements might be well made to further his purpose, Caesar ordered
the troops to present a listless appearance on the works, while at the
same time he issued his real instructions. The legions were brought
down from camp accoutered for action, and having been carefully
screened from observation behind the rows of mantlets, were then
addressed by their commander. Pointing out that at last they had the
chance of reaping the fruit of their long and painful labors by a glorious victory, he promised a handsome reward to those who should be
the first upon the ramparts, and then gave the signal. From one end
of the Roman lines to the other, the legionaries swept across the
intervening space, and in a few brief seconds were upon the wall.

Overwhelmed by the unexpectedness of the assault, and driven
from both battlements and towers, the enemy fell back upon the
market square and the more open spaces of the town; where, forming
in squares, they prepared to meet attack from whatever quarter it
might come, by a swift movement into line. Seeing, however, that no
attempt was made to come down to engage them on level ground,
but that the storming party was rapidly spreading round the whole
circumference of wall, they became seized with panic lest all exit
should be stopped, and flinging away their arms, rushed in wild disorder for the farthest corner of the town. Here part fell an easy prey to
the troops awaiting them at the gates, as they crushed one another
in the narrow entrance, while any who had succeeded in making their
escape from the town were cut to pieces by the cavalry. No one
thought of plunder; but maddened, by the recollection of the massacre at Cenabum (*Orleans*), as well as by the hardship and privations of
the siege, the troops were altogether without mercy. Old and infirm,
women and children, were indiscriminately butchered. When all was
over, it was found that out of a total fighting population of 40,000
men, scarcely 800 had succeeded in making their way to Vercingetorix, these being the few who on the first cry of alarm had made a wild

dash for freedom. The arrival of these fugitives in his camp was thought by Vercingetorix likely to lead to a riot, through the sympathy excited by their pitiable plight. He had therefore taken the precaution to post along the roads, some distance in advance, prominent friends of his own from among the various allies; and these late in the night quietly received them as they came in from their flight, and having sorted them into tribes, took each back to the particular quarter of the camp which had been originally allotted to it.

The next day he called a meeting of his officers, and in a sympathetic but stirring speech protested against all thoughts of gloom or despondency on account of their late reverse. The success of the Romans, he argued, so far from marking them as the better men in a stand-up fight, was attributable solely to their knowledge of siege warfare, a branch of military science that was unfamiliar to themselves. But apart altogether from the mistake of expecting every operation in war to turn out well, he himself, as he reminded his audience, and as they themselves could testify, had never favored the retention of Avaricum; and their present disaster must therefore be set down to the faulty judgment of the Bituriges, and to the too easy acquiescence of the rest. That disaster, however, he assured them, he would quickly retrieve by successes still more striking; for he was already negotiating for the adherence of those who were yet outside the national movement, and endeavoring to effect the unification of Gaul—and Gaul united might face a world in arms. This great object, he continued, was now all but accomplished; and meanwhile, he considered it not too much to demand of their patriotism that they should henceforth make it a practice properly to entrench their camps, so as at least to prevent the repetition of such sudden attacks from the Romans.

The speech on the whole was well received, and the Gauls, who were especially struck by the fact that, in spite of such crushing disaster, their leader had not lost hope, or deemed it advisable to go into hiding in order to avoid publicity, only praised his judgment and foresight the more warmly, as they reflected that he had originally favored the destruction, and subsequently the abandonment of

Avaricum. The curious result thus followed that, whereas other generals are invariably discredited by failure, he on the other hand found his reputation positively enhanced as the result of a military reverse. The hopes of his followers likewise rose, as a consequence of the emphatic statement of their leader, that the other tribes might still be brought in; and for the first time in history there now was seen the sight of Gauls regularly throwing up entrenchments wherever they camped; and so cowed and crestfallen had this constitutionally idle people now become, that every kind of irksome command was willingly submitted to without complaint.

Nor can it be said that Vercingetorix fell short of his spoken word in his efforts to win over the rest of Gaul, and bribes and promises were freely used as baits. Appropriate agents were chosen to do the work; such men as either by the possession of a glib tongue, or through some existing tie of friendship with those they visited, were likely to make efficient pleaders. The fugitives from Avaricum were thoughtfully provided with new arms and uniforms, while to recruit his sorely depleted ranks, fresh requisitions for troops were laid upon each of the confederate tribes, number and date of delivery being in all cases accurately determined. Lastly, orders were now issued that every available archer in the country (archery being at that time much affected throughout Gaul) should be impressed for service and dispatched to the seat of war. By these and other similar methods the losses experienced at Avaricum were quickly made good, and meanwhile, from an unexpected quarter, further assistance had arrived. Teutomatus, son of Ollovico, king of the Nitiobriges, in spite of the fact that his father had been honored by the Roman Senate with the coveted title of "Friend," took this opportunity to declare his adhesion to the nationalist movement; and bringing with him a powerful force of his own cavalry, with mercenaries hired out of Aquitania, marched northwards to join the insurrectionary army.

Section II. The Siege of Gergovia

Meanwhile Caesar was still at Avaricum (*Bourges*). Ample supplies of all kinds had been found in the town, and a stay of several days in the place afforded his troops, after their arduous labors and prolonged shortness of rations, a much needed rest. With winter fast drawing to its close, and the youthful season of the year once more beginning to invite military operations, he had already determined to take the field against the enemy, in the hope of either drawing him from his woods and marshes, or of pressing him by siege. Suddenly from the Aedui there arrived a deputation of leading chiefs, begging for his assistance in what they described as a political crisis of the utmost gravity. And, indeed, the situation, as represented by themselves, was one of profound danger. Their ancient practice, extending now over a number of years, had been, as it seemed, to elect a single magistrate with an annual tenure of something like regal power: but at the present moment there actually existed two heads of the government, each claiming to be legally appointed. One of these, a chief named Convictolitavis, was a man in the prime of life, deservedly holding a very high position; the other, by name Cotus, belonged to one of their very oldest houses, and through his powerful family connections exercised a very wide influence, a brother called Valetiacus having held the same office the year before. As a result of the *impasse*, the whole country was up in arms, not only the governing council, but every prominent individual of the tribe being ranged with his followers into one of two hostile camps. A prolongation of the dispute must end in a fratricidal struggle between the two parties, and so desperate was the situation that, as the envoys declared, nothing but the resourcefulness and authority of Caesar could now save it.

Only too well aware from bitter experience of the evils commonly engendered by civil warfare, Caesar was determined, if possible, to save so important a people as the Aedui, so closely associated with the arms of Rome, so sedulously upheld and protected on all occasions by himself, from drifting into all the horrors of an armed strife: and though much disappointed at having to suspend military operations and his plans against the enemy, yet sooner than throw the weaker party in this dispute into the arms of Vercingetorix, he was ready to sacrifice all other considerations to this end. But as by the law of the Aeduan constitution no magistrate is allowed during his term of office to set foot outside the frontiers, he resolved, in order to show his scrupulous regard for their rights and customs, to pay a personal visit to their country, and at Decetia (*Decize* on the *Loire*), a town near the border, summoned the whole of their council, together with the two principals to the quarrel, to meet him in a conference. To that city accordingly repaired practically the entire community, and he was then made acquainted with the facts of the case. The appointment of Cotus, it seemed, had been of a highly questionable character. The meeting summoned to elect him had been both clandestine and packed; its time and place had been irregular; the returning officer had been his own brother; and the election was further invalidated by the breach of the rule which forbade two members of the same family, within the lifetime of both, not merely to hold the same magistracy, but even to sit in the council of the chiefs. Under these circumstances Caesar compelled him to resign his office, and at the same time confirmed the appointment of Convictolitavis, whose election had, according to precedent, where no magistrates are available, been conducted under the presidency of the priests.

His decision put an end to the dispute, and further to heal the local dissensions, he begged them all to sink their private differences under the supreme object of furthering the conduct of the war, reminding them that on the final subjugation of Gaul they might expect their well-deserved reward. Before leaving, he ordered them to send him with all dispatch the whole of the mounted troops then in the country, and a picked force of 10,000 infantry to be used along the lines of communication. Returning then to the prosecution of the campaign, he decided to make a twofold division of his forces. Four legions were sent northwards under Labienus to operate against the Senones (*Sens*) and Parish (*Paris*); while with the remaining six he himself moved southward against the Arverni (*Auvergne*), and with the object of attacking their capital Gergovia[1] marched up the right bank of the river Elaver (*Allier*). Of the cavalry, part accompanied Labienus, part he retained with his own force. Vercingetorix's answer to these movements was immediately to break down all bridges leading across the river, and then to begin a corresponding ascent on the opposite or western bank.

The two hostile armies were thus advancing on parallel courses, separated merely by the river; consequently not only did each often look on the camp of the other, but they even faced one another across the stream, along the whole of whose banks scouts were now picketed, so as to prevent the Romans anywhere from building a bridge and thereby passing to the farther side. To Caesar the prospect thus presented was one of no little anxiety, because, the Elaver (*Allier*) not being as a rule fordable till autumn, he seemed threatened with detention on the eastern bank for the greater part of the summer. To extricate himself from this difficulty, he chose for one of his camps a certain wooded district in a right line with one of the bridges broken down by Vercingetorix; and on the following day, keeping back two of his six legions, sent on the remainder with all the baggage in the usual formation, but with certain of their battalions so cunningly extended that they would pass muster as containing the original number. This force was bidden to push on that day to the utmost; after which, about the hour when, as he calculated, it ought to be

[1] Ch. 4.

reaching camp, he proceeded to restore the ruined bridge on its old piles, the lower ends of which were still standing. The work was rapidly carried through, and the two legions being by its means conveyed across, and a strong position chosen for a new camp, the other regiments were then recalled. The success of this ruse made Vercingetorix anxious lest he should be brought to battle against his wishes, and quickening his rate of marching, he now hurried on in advance toward his capital.

Caesar, on the other hand, allowed five more marches in which to reach Gergovia. His arrival was followed on the same day by a cavalry skirmish outside the town, during which a careful reconnaissance was made of the place; but finding it to consist of a precipitous hill, virtually inaccessible on all sides, he at once abandoned all hopes of proceeding by direct assault, and before attempting a blockade, decided thoroughly to safeguard his supplies. Vercingetorix meanwhile had pitched his camp not far from the line of the city; and bristling all round him, in tribe after tribe, on every height that guarded the approach, and filling up every avenue visible from the plain below, the allied contingents could be seen posted at slight intervals and presenting an appearance threatening in the extreme. At his tent at sunrise every morning there was held, in obedience to his orders, a joint meeting of all the local leaders, who formed an advisory staff to the commander in chief, and here any important information would be communicated and fresh instructions issued: and seldom did a day elapse without his testing the courage and endurance of his followers, by sending the cavalry into action, interspersed as they always were with bodies of light-armed bowmen. Facing the town, and springing immediately from the base of the central rock, stood an isolated hill,[2] strongly fortified and sharply scarped on every side, the possession of which by Caesar's investing forces bade fair to deprive the enemy of a large part of their water supply, and their free access to fodder. Though garrisoned, it was not held by any force that could be called overwhelming. Leaving camp

[2] La Roche Blanche, on the south side.

therefore in the dead of night, before any succor could arrive from the town close by, Caesar succeeded in driving out the garrison and securing the position; which, after placing it in the permanent occupation of two legions, he linked up with the main encampment by two ditches, each twelve feet wide, so perfectly defended from sudden incursions of the enemy, that even single soldiers could pass along in safety.

Meanwhile, during these operations at Gergovia, serious trouble had again arisen with the Aedui. The disturbing element this time was the political leader Convictolitavis, who, as will be remembered, had but just recently been awarded the chief magistracy by Caesar. Tempted by the bribes of the Arverni, he had been heard to use treasonable language with certain firebrands among the nobility, notably with a certain Litaviccus and his brothers, young men belonging to one of the principal Aeduan families. Prefacing his remarks by dividing with them the money received, he urged them to remember the grandeur of their birthright, which was that of a free and sovereign people. "At this moment," he continued, "there stands between Gaul and certain victory the single obstacle of the Aedui, for it is our example that holds all others to their loyalty. Remove this obstacle, and the Romans will be left without a footing anywhere throughout the country." Then touching on his personal relations with Caesar, he admitted some degree of obligation, but even if this amounted to more than the recognition of his own incontestable rights, it was not in any case, he asserted, to be weighed against the higher claims of patriotism. For what reason was there in the nature of things, that the Aedui should be expected to go for a settlement of their constitutional difficulties to Caesar, rather than that the Romans should come to them? Before this inflammatory speech from their chief magistrate, commended all the more by its accompanying bribe, the young men, who in reality required no prompting from outside, easily succumbed; but as the conspirators had some qualms about their people's readiness to rush into an unprovoked war, some method had to be found for the execution of the plot. The plan finally agreed upon was that Litaviccus should be placed in command of the 10,000

men under orders to proceed to the seat of war, and be made responsible for their safe conduct to Caesar; his brothers meanwhile
preceding him, so as to be there on his arrival. Other measures inci-
dental to the undertaking were at the same time carefully determined.

At the head, therefore, of this Aeduan army Litaviccus had arrived
within some thirty miles of Gergovia, when suddenly calling the
troops together, he asked them, with tears rolling down his face,
whether they realized to what fate they were proceeding. Every one
of their knights and nobles, he declared, then serving with the
Romans had been foully massacred, while their two distinguished
leaders, Eporedorix and Viridomarus, had been accused of high
treason and put to death without a trial. Explaining that grief for
the murder of brothers and kinsmen prevented his telling them the
story in person, he then referred his hearers to those whom he
described as eyewitnesses that had escaped from the very midst of the
carnage. Thereupon certain carefully prepared agents were led forward, and recounting to the assembly the gruesome details of the
picture merely outlined by Litaviccus, told how the Aeduan cavalry
had been done to death on the charge of intriguing with the Arverni,
and how they themselves had only escaped from the scene of slaughter by sheltering behind the crowd of soldiers. A storm of indignation
greeted these words, and a fierce demand was raised that Litaviccus
should at once take measures to secure their safety. "Measures," cried
he, "what need for them, when our plain duty is to hasten forward to
Gergovia, and to throw the weight of all our swords on the side of
the Arverni! Can anyone doubt that the Romans, having stained
themselves by the perpetrations of this hideous crime, are now burning to complete their work of villainy by adding us to the number of
their victims? Indeed, if we have a spark of manhood in us, we shall,
even here and now, avenge the death of our martyred countrymen,
and once for all make an end of these butchers." With these words,
he pointed to a group of Romans who happened to be traveling
under the trusted escort of his party, and who were now seized and
put to death by the most fiendish cruelty, at the same time that large
quantities of stores and provisions under their charge were looted by

GERGOVIA

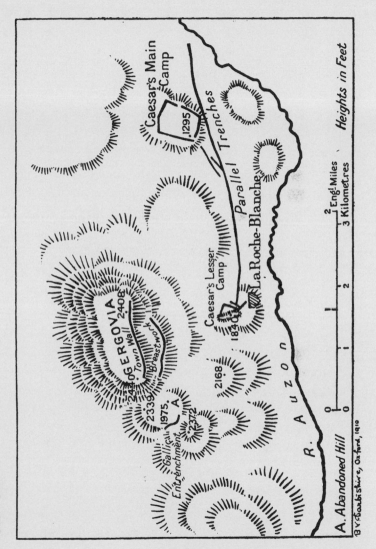

Caesar's Main Camp

.1295

Parallel Trenches

La Roche-Blanche

Caesar's Lesser Camp

1840

GERGOVIA 2408
Town Wall
Breastwork
2339 2410
Galli 1975
Entrenchment
A 2372

2168

A. Abandoned Hill

R. Auzon

0   1   2 Engl. Miles
0   1   2   3 Kilometres

Heights in Feet

B.V.Darbishire, Oxford, 1910

his men. After this, emissaries were dispatched broadcast through the Aeduan land, rousing the people to horror by the same lying tale of their slaughtered knights and chiefs, and urging them to adopt the same methods for the satisfaction of their wrongs.

The two Aeduan leaders referred to above, viz. Eporedorix and Viridomarus, had recently been called out for service by a special summons from Caesar, and had joined the Roman headquarters with the body of native cavalry. Of the two, Eporedorix was a young man of highly distinguished family and of immense influence in his own land. Viridomarus, on the other hand, his equal in years and authority, differed widely as to origin. Originally brought under Caesar's notice by Divitiacus, he had since been raised by him from a position of comparative obscurity to one of highest eminence. Constant political rivals, they had naturally taken different sides in the recent dispute about the magistracy, and had thrown all the weight of their support, the one on the side of Convictolitavis, the other on that of Cotus. When, therefore, the plot of Litaviccus reached his ears, though it was about midnight, Eporedorix at once reported the matter to Caesar, and implored him not to allow the unscrupulous agitation of irresponsible hotheads to sever the friendship between his country and Rome. That result, he went on to declare, must inevitably come about, if once the juncture of so many thousands of his countrymen with the enemy became an accomplished fact; for in that case, not only would the probable fate of these men be a strong inducement with their relatives to cast in their lot with them, but by the government also it could not be disregarded.

The news aroused in Caesar feelings of anxiety that bordered on dismay; for from first to last he had purposely treated the Aedui with special consideration. Without a moment's hesitation as to his course, he gave the word for four legions to hold themselves in readiness, and for the cavalry to prepare for a forced march; and since, at such a time, when everything depended on speed, it was impossible to wait till the dimensions of the camp had been reduced, he had no alternative but to leave the entire position to the defense of two legions, under command of his general, C. Fabius, and himself then started on his march. A vigorous search was made for the brothers of Litaviccus, but they were found just a short time before to have deserted to the enemy. The troops rose to the greatness of the occasion; and to his urgent appeal that at such a crisis they would make light of the fatigue of the march, they replied with so good a will, that after covering a distance of five-and-twenty miles, they were rewarded by the sight of the Aeduan column advancing into view. Thereupon the Roman cavalry was sent forward to harass and retard their progress, with strict orders, however, that on no account were any of the Gauls to be killed. At the same time Eporedorix and Viridomarus, the two supposed victims of the ghastly story, were ordered to display themselves among the troopers and to call aloud on their followers by name. Their recognition revealed to the Aedui the full extent to which they had been duped by Litaviccus, and throwing up their hands in token of surrender, they at once began to drop their weapons and to cry for quarter. In the interval Litaviccus, surrounded by his personal retainers, whom custom compels never to desert their lords however desperate be their plight, got clean away and fled into Gergovia.

The first act of Caesar was to send word to the Aeduan government that, though by all the laws of war their contingent had forfeited their lives, yet by an act of clemency he had allowed them to live. He then gave his men three hours' rest during the night, and having struck camp commenced the return march to Gergovia. Halfway on the road he was met by mounted couriers from Fabius, informing him that during his absence the garrison had passed through a period of much peril. The enemy, it seemed, had taken the opportunity to assail the Roman position in great force, and the defenders, under stress of meeting a constant succession of fresh men along a front whose extended length demanded their continual presence on the ramparts, had become much exhausted. Numbers had been wounded by the showers of arrows and other missiles launched by the assailants—though here, indeed, the Roman artillery had done excellent service in keeping down the fire; and when the messengers left, Fabius was engaged in blocking up all gates of the camp save two, in raising breastworks, and in generally strengthening himself for a repetition of the affair next day. The news acted like magic upon the wearied troops, and before sunrise Caesar was back in camp.

In the midst of these events outside Gergovia, the Aedui had eagerly embraced the earlier reports sent off by Litaviccus, and had left themselves little opportunity for a careful investigation of the facts. Among men whose habitual motives were greed or hatred, or (what is the most characteristic of such races) mere blind impulse, an unfounded rumor easily passed for truth; and Roman residents now began to have their property plundered, their lives sacrificed, or their persons hurried into slavery. Convictolitavis himself added fuel to the fire; and by goading on the populace to fresh outbreaks of violence, hoped to appall them so much by the thought of what had passed, that shame alone would prevent them from returning to their duty. Typical of their madness was the case of M. Aristius, which occurred at Cabillonum (*Chalons-sur-Saône*). This officer was on his way to rejoin his regiment; and having been escorted out of the town under a solemn pledge of safety, accompanied by the Roman mercantile residents of the place who were compelled to go with him, he and his little party were suddenly attacked upon the road. Though losing all their baggage, they nevertheless made a stout resistance, and after enduring a day and night's uninterrupted siege, in which both sides lost heavily, they obliged their assailants to call up larger reinforcements.

In the meanwhile news arrived that all their troops were safely in Roman hands; whereupon, hastily betaking themselves to Aristius, they earnestly disclaimed all public responsibility for what had happened, and, instituting inquiries into the various acts of plunder, confiscated the property of Litaviccus and his brothers, and dispatched commissioners to Caesar to establish their own innocence. In all this their chief concern was the recovery of their armed contingent: their true sentiments were something very different from those expressed. The recent outbreak had involved large numbers in its guilt; and conscious that their hands were deeply stained with crime, but that their pockets had been considerably enriched by the spoil of their victims, these men, when punishment stared them in the face, at once fell back on the desperate expedient of then and there preparing for war, and of fomenting disaffection among other tribes. Though all these facts were perfectly well known to him, Caesar yet received the deputation with all possible courtesy; and assuring them that he was not likely to confuse the impulsive acts of a heedless mob with the deliberate policy of its rulers, promised that nothing should ever prejudice the high regard he entertained for the Aeduan race. That the insurrectionary movement was bound to spread there could, however, be little or no doubt; and if he were not to be caught in the center of a ring of hostile tribes, some scheme for extricating himself from Gergovia, and for reuniting his scattered army, must at once be found. At the same time he had to ensure that a movement, which was necessitated solely by fear of disaffection, should not be mistaken by the enemy for a tacit admission of defeat.

These reflections were suddenly interrupted by an event which seemed to offer some prospect of a military success. Going one day to the lesser camp in order to inspect the works, the Roman commander observed that a certain hill in the occupation of the enemy, hitherto almost hidden beneath the masses of men that crowded it, was now all but empty. Struck by the occurrence, he turned for an explanation to the deserters, who in large numbers daily made their way into his lines. Their answers agreed with one another in all particulars. Describing the summit of the plateau upon which Gergovia stands, they explained, what indeed had been already discovered by the scouts, that though tolerably uniform throughout, it yet narrowed down and became extremely wooded at the point connecting it with the farther quarter of the town. This weak corner, they affirmed, was the cause of no little anxiety to the garrison; for having already seen one hill pass into the hands of the Romans, they were convinced, should they lose another, that the siege would be turned into a blockade, and that all means of obtaining fodder would be gone, through the virtual closing of every outlet. To strengthen the defenses at this narrow neck, all hands had been summoned away by Vercingetorix.

Upon this information Caesar resolved to act. Shortly after midnight several squadrons of horse were dispatched in the direction of the point indicated, with orders to range freely about the country as though bent on a foray. At dawn multitudes of baggage animals and mules were led out from camp, and the muleteers were commanded, after stripping the animals of their trappings, to don helmets, and counterfeiting the manner of regular cavalry, thus to make the circuit of the hills. To complete the illusion, a few genuine troopers were added to the force, so as to give it greater mobility, and all ranks were then bidden to work round by a wide detour to the south, toward the same point as those sent overnight. Since Gergovia commanded an excellent view of the Roman camp, nothing of all this escaped the notice of those in the town, though at the great distance it was impossible to make out clearly the nature of the movements. Next to be dispatched was a regiment of infantry, which, after following for a little the same line along the hills, was then halted on the lower ground and carefully concealed among the woods. This did but increase the suspicion of the Gauls, who now detached the whole of their available forces to the work of fortification. At last, when the enemy's camps appeared plainly denuded of men, Caesar proceeded to develop his real plan. With their military decorations all carefully screened, and regimental colors kept well out of sight, the main body of Roman infantry was stealthily transferred in small driblets, as being still under the eyes of the town, from their principal base to the lesser of the two camps. That done, the scheme of operations was carefully explained to the generals who were to command the several corps; and these were exhorted especially to keep their men well in hand, and to check any tendency to extend the advance, either through the excitement of battle or the hope of plunder. Reminding them that they were about to be placed at a grave disadvantage in position, always a serious consideration in war, he showed how only rapid action could overcome this inferiority, and insisted that their present business was not to fight a battle but to effect a surprise. His instructions issued, he made the signal to the troops, and simultaneously by another route toward the right the Aeduan auxiliaries were sent up the hill.

The distance between the town wall and the point where the ascent from the plain began was, if one took a beeline, and no fold occurred to break the ground, little more than 2,000 yards; any deviation from this, made to ease the stiffness of the climb, proportionately increased its length. About halfway up, the Gauls had built a breastwork of massive stones, six feet high, with which to break the force of any attack, and, according to the natural inclinations of the ground, had extended it from right to left, along the entire mountain slope; everything below this had been left unoccupied, while the space above was crowded with camps reaching right up to the city walls. Mounting the hill upon the word of command, the troops quickly gained this outwork, and rapidly passing it, were soon masters of three out of these camps. As some indication of their amazing quickness of action, we may mention what occurred in the camp of the Nitiobriges. There king Teutomatus was surprised in his tent while taking his siesta, and had barely time to escape from the hands of his pursuers, who were now busily hunting for loot, with his horse wounded and his shirt torn from his back.

Having secured his main object, Caesar ordered the recall, and at once halted the Tenth legion, in whose company he had been when addressing the troops; the others unfortunately did not hear the bugle, owing to a considerable dip in the ground, though, in obedience to his original orders, their officers were now doing all they could to restrain their men. But the near prospect of victory and the actual flight of the enemy had too greatly excited them; and infatuated by their unbroken successes in the past, they now believed themselves to be invincible, and pressing hard upon the pursuit, never paused till they found themselves approaching the gates and walls of the town. Their arrival here was greeted by a universal snout of alarm, and so terrifying was the wild disorder that soon prevailed, that that portion of the garrison which was a little farther off, thinking that the enemy had already forced the gates, fled precipitately from the town. With similar panic their women began stripping off their raiment and jewelry, and tossing them down from the wall; and leaning over with bared breast and outstretched arms, implored they might be spared a repetition of Avaricum (*Bourges*), where the Roman soldiers in their fury had spared neither sex nor age. Many even began to lower themselves down to the ground, helped by those above, and to deliver themselves as prisoners to the Romans. Typical of the reckless courage now animating the troops was the action of L. Fabius, one of the centurions belonging to the Eighth legion. Several had heard him declare on that day that he meant to profit by the lesson of Avaricum, and that if it came to rewards and honors, he would take good care that nobody reached the top of the wall before himself. With the assistance of three of his own company, whom he secured for the purpose, he now hoisted himself to the summit, and then turning round drew up each of the others to a place at his side.

Meanwhile the true position of affairs had been reported to the enemy's main body, which, it will be remembered, had been withdrawn to the western end of the town to strengthen the defenses. Apprised at first by the noise of distant shouting, when message after message followed in quick succession that the Romans were inside the works, they had flung their cavalry to the front, and then like a surging tide came racing back to the point of danger. Forming beneath the wall as fast as each reached the scene of action, they quickly swelled the numbers of the defense, which had soon grown to a formidable army. Thereupon the women, who till now had not ceased to make signals of entreaty to the Romans, seeing the change wrought in the position of affairs, called on their natural protectors to defend them, and in true Gallic fashion displayed their wildly disheveled hair, and held up their children to their fathers' eyes. Alike in numbers and position, the Romans were soon placed at a sore disadvantage; exhausted by their running and wearied by the protraction of the fight, they found it difficult to cope with a fresh and vigorous body of men, such as that now opposed to them.

Observing the unequal conditions of the combat, and the alarming extent to which the enemy was being reinforced, Caesar dispatched an order to T. Sextius, the officer left over the lesser of the two camps, to move with some of his battalions, and to take post at the foot of the hill upon the enemy's right. So placed, he was to hamper the Gauls' freedom of action, should they attempt to pursue in the event of the legionaries being driven down the slopes. At the same time he himself advanced with the Tenth legion a little beyond his previous halting ground, and from this new position watched anxiously the fortunes of the fight.

In the midst of a fierce hand-to-hand encounter, in which to the enemy's reliance on superiority of numbers and position the Roman legionary had nothing to oppose but his own unflinching courage, suddenly on the unguarded flank of the latter appeared the body of Aeduan infantry, which, with the object of weakening the defense, had by Caesar's orders ascended the hill more toward the right. The sudden emergence of this unknown force, armed in all respects precisely like the Gauls, created no small panic among the troops; and though their right shoulders were seen to be bare—the symbol adopted for friendly tribes—yet this in itself was believed to be a ruse, purposely invented to deceive. About the same time L. Fabius, the centurion who had scaled the battlements, was, together with his companions, surrounded and cut down, and their bodies flung over the wall. A second centurion from the same legion, M. Petronius, at the head of a storming party of his own men, had been for some time vainly trying to hew his way through one of the town gates, but was now overborne by numbers. Desperately wounded, he dismissed all hope of saving himself, and turning to his followers, begged they would seize their opportunity while still they had it. "'Tis impossible," he exclaimed in soldierly language, "that all of us should survive this day; and as it was my ambition that brought you into this mess, I at least will get you out." So saying, he hurled himself upon the thickest of the enemy, and having killed two with his own hand, succeeded in clearing for a little a space outside the gateway. Every effort was made by the others to support him, but again he insisted on their departure, and declaring that his strength was now all but spent, and that he was bleeding to death, bade them, while they had the time, to regain their regiment. A few moments later he fell, still proudly fighting, and his gallant death proved the salvation of the rest.

Sorely beset at every point, with no fewer than forty-six centurions slain, the Romans were at length driven in confusion down the heights. On their rear the triumphant foe pressed with haughty insolence; and but for the timely assistance of the Tenth, which had taken post on favorable ground for this purpose, worse disaster must have followed. In this task it was admirably seconded by the battalions of T. Sextius, which having by now moved out from camp, had established themselves somewhat higher up. No sooner, however, did the battered legions feel their feet on the plain below, than at once reforming, with face presented to the foe, they stood firmly to their ground. But Vercingetorix was already satisfied, and having followed his enemy to the foot of the descent, he regained his stronghold on the hills. The day's fighting had thinned the ranks of the Roman army by close on 700 men.

On the morrow the troops were assembled, and Caesar delivered himself of some criticism on their conduct. Their rashness and impetuosity had, he said, cost them dear. In presuming to judge for themselves how far the advance was to be continued, and what movements it might be made to embrace, they had unwarrantably exceeded their duty; and in refusing to halt at the signal of recall, and in getting beyond their officers' control, they had been yet even more to blame. Impressing upon them afresh how serious are the consequences of a disadvantage in position, he reminded them of his own experience at Avaricum (*Bourges*). There the enemy had been surprised without either general or cavalry; and yet rather than inflict upon his men even a minimum of loss, in fighting their way over treacherous ground, he had deliberately sacrificed a victory which was as good as gained. Much, therefore, he continued, as he admired the intrepidity of troops whom fortified, entrenchments, beetling rock, and frowning wall had alike failed to stop, he had no less a detestation for that spirit of overweening self-confidence which imagined that it knew better than the commander in chief where success might be safely pushed, and where operations ought properly to cease. Never should it be forgotten that strict obedience and a power of self-control were not less binding on a soldier than steadfast courage and a daring spirit.

Having administered this rebuke, and closed his speech by some strong encouragement to the troops, he proceeded to give effect to his words. It was important to check at the outset any tendency toward demoralization caused by recent events, and to see that a result which was due entirely to the conditions of the field of battle was not falsely attributed to the superiority of the Gauls. As, therefore, he still contemplated the abandonment of the siege, he resolved boldly to issue from his lines, and upon carefully selected ground formed for battle. This challenge Vercingetorix at once accepted, and began to move down the hill to the open ground; upon which the Roman cavalry was sent into action, and after a slight skirmish, which ended in their favor, retired upon camp with the other forces. This operation was repeated next day, and satisfied that by these measures the insolent tone of the Gauls had been sufficiently repressed, and the confidence of his own men restored, he broke up from before the city and directed his march toward the Aedui. Even this failed to draw the enemy; and unmolested by pursuit, on the third day he reached the Elaver (*Allier*), where, having repaired the bridges, he transported the army to the eastern bank.

Once on that side, he was approached by the two Aeduan leaders, Viridomarus and Eporedorix, with news that the treacherous Litaviccus, with all the cavalry in the place, had at once left Gergovia to raise a rebellion among the Aedui, and that if that people was to be saved from his baneful influence, they must themselves anticipate his arrival. Such language did not deceive the Roman governor. Many incidents had of late convinced him of Aeduan duplicity, nor could he now fail to see that the open secession of the tribe must inevitably be hastened by the departure of these two chiefs. Nevertheless, he was not disposed to detain them; for to have done so must either have placed him in a false position with regard to their government, or else have created an impression of fear. On their finally taking leave, he briefly recapitulated his own past services to their state. He had found it, he reminded them, at the lowest depth of national humiliation. Driven into the shelter of their towns, compelled to forfeit a large slice of their land, and totally bankrupt in resources, they had had to bow to the yoke of a haughty conqueror by the two-fold degradation of hostages and tribute. From this abject condition they had been raised by himself to a height of prosperity and splendor, such as not merely reinstated them in their former greatness, but conferred upon them a position and an influence that was unsurpassed in the history of their tribe. With this valedictory address, he dismissed them from camp.

Situated on the banks of the Loire in a position of conspicuous strength was the Aeduan town of Noviodunum (*Nevers*). By Caesar it had been converted into a vast depot for the general purposes of these wars. In it were detained his numerous Gallic hostages, collected from all parts of the country; here was his principal magazine, his war chest, and the greater bulk of his own and the army's baggage; here were the headquarters of his remount department for the many hundreds of animals bought up in Italy and Spain. It was at this important center that Eporedorix and Viridomarus first learned on which side the real sympathies of the country lay. Here they heard of the welcome given to Litaviccus at Bibracte,[3] the town best representative of Aeduan public opinion, and how he had been afterward joined there by the first minister of the country, Convictolitavis, together with a considerable following from the tribal council; and, most significant of all, that a public deputation was now on its way to Vercingetorix to arrange definite terms of treaty. Taking all these circumstances into account, the two chiefs came to the momentous conclusion that present opportunity more than outweighed prospective risk. Their first step was to massacre the Roman guards and mercantile residents of the place; next they divided among themselves the horses and treasure, and sent off Caesar's Gallic hostages to Bibracte, for disposal by their chief magistrate: then, feeling the defense of the town to be a military task beyond their powers, and yet determined to render it useless to the Romans, they burned it to the ground, while what corn they could not carry away at once by means of barges, they destroyed either in the river or the flames. Upon their

---

[3] See I. 23.

own initiative they then rapidly collected forces from the surrounding neighborhood, closely picketed the banks of the Loire, and in the hope of starving out their enemy on the farther side of the river, covered all the face of the country with strong patrols whose presence threatened every convoy. They were the more sanguine of success from the actual state of the river Loire; for, greatly swollen by the melting of the snows, it appeared absolutely impassable by ford.

News of so grave an import revealed to Caesar the urgent necessity of speed; for if, as in all probability would be the case, the dangerous task awaited him of constructing bridges in the face of the enemy, it was of vital importance to force an action before larger numbers could have congregated at the passage. The only alternative to this course was to abandon altogether his present plan of campaign, and to order a general retreat upon the Roman Province of the South; a step, indeed, which under existing circumstances was universally considered unavoidable. Putting aside, however, the ignominy that such a change involved, the physical difficulties in the way were insuperable. Between him and the proposed goal lay the massive barrier of the Cevennes, and the roads were likely to be impassable. But what more than all else condemned such a proposal was its certain effect upon Labienus and his legions; for the further isolation of this force was a contingency too dreadful to be contemplated. Marching, therefore, by rapid and prolonged stages, day and night alike, he suddenly appeared on the Loire to the amazement and consternation of the enemy; and finding a ford through search by the cavalry, which under existing circumstances might be considered more than adequate, where it was just possible for the men to keep their arms and shoulders clear of the water with their accoutrements resting on them, he proceeded to transport the army. To break the force of the current, the horsemen made a living dam across the stream; and as the enemy had taken fright upon the first signs of the advance, the passage proceeded in perfect safety. The country on the far side yielded abundance of corn and cattle, and thus reprovisioned, the army continued its march northward toward the Senones (*Sens*).

Section III. Labienus and the Parish

It is now necessary to revert to the fortunes of Labienus and his campaign against the Parish, which were contemporaneous with these actions of Caesar. Leaving the draft of recruits newly come from Italy to guard his heavy baggage at Agedincum (*Sens*), he set out with his four legions on his march for Lutetia (*Paris*), the capital city of the Parisii, which stands on an island in the Seine. His approach was the signal for a general muster of the local tribes, the command of which was delegated to an aged chieftain of the Aulerci, named Camulogenus, who, though heavily weighted with years, was from his profound knowledge of the art of war publicly invited to accept this role. His trained eye quickly discerned a strong position for a camp, and on the western side of the Seine, where the approach to the Parisian capital is guarded by an extensive area of marsh, which drains into the river and renders all the surrounding country unfit for military operations, he awaited the arrival of the Romans prepared to dispute the passage.

The obstacles in his way Labienus at first endeavored to overcome by building a roadway across the marsh, and under cover of movable mantlets large numbers of wattled hurdles were laid down and rubble superimposed. But the difficulties of such a course proving insurmountable, a change of plan became necessary. Shortly after

CAMPAIGN of LABIENUS against the PARISII

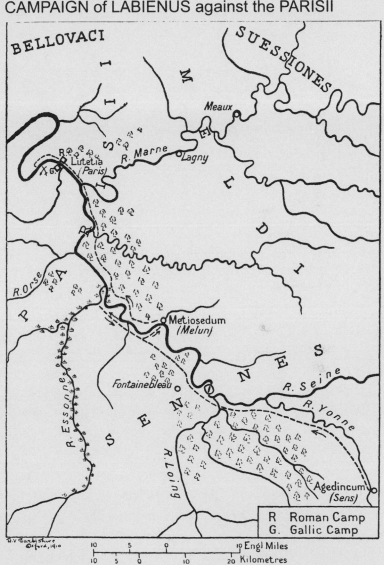

BELLOVACI

SUESSIONES

Meaux

R. Marne

Lagny

Lutetia
(Paris)

R. Orse

Metiosedum
(Melun)

Fontainebleau

R. Essonne

R. Loing

R. Seine

R. Yonne

Agedincum
(Sens)

| R | Roman Camp |
| G. | Gallic Camp |

B.V. Darbishire
Oxford, 1910

10   5   0   10 Engl Miles
10   5   0   10   20 Kilometres

midnight, therefore, he noiselessly evacuated camp, and retraced his steps as far as Metiosedum (*Melun*), a town of the Senones, situated like Lutetia on an island in the Seine. Seizing there some fifty vessels, and with these rapidly constructing pontoons, he quickly transferred to the other side a portion of his army; and as the townsfolk (or as many of them as had not been impressed for the war) were overwhelmed by the suddenness of his attack, the place was mastered without a blow. He then repaired the permanent bridge across the river, recently cut by the enemy, and having safely conveyed the whole of his forces to the right bank, continued his march northwards to the Parisian capital. Fugitives from Metiosedum carried the news of his passage to the enemy; whereupon, sending forward injunctions to break down the bridges at Lutetia and to burn the town, they abandoned their first position at the swamp, and planted themselves on the banks of the Seine right over against the capital, and immediately confronting Labienus's new camp.

By this time report was busy with Caesar's withdrawal from before Gergovia, and rumor whispered ominously that the Aedui had at last thrown off their allegiance and that the national cause was sweeping everything before it; while on the lips of many a Gaul hung the story that the great Roman commander had been successfully checked at the Loire, and was now in full career toward the Province, as the only hope of saving his army from starvation. The moment they were assured of Aeduan disaffection, the Bellovaci (*Beauvais*), whose attitude for some months had been more than equivocal, boldly threw aside the mask, and raising bands, openly prepared for war. The military situation had therefore, almost in a day, suffered a complete reversal, and the original plans formed by Labienus for the campaign had accordingly to be no less fundamentally revised. He now saw that it was no longer a question of extending his area of control, or of taking the initiative in war, but solely one of extricating himself from his predicament by a safe retreat to Agedincum (*Sens*). Seldom, indeed, has a great general been confronted with a more formidable array of obstacles. To the north the powerful race of the Bellovaci, universally acclaimed the bravest of Gallic peoples,[1] hung like a thundercloud: immediately to the south lay a well-appointed army under the veteran Camulogenus; while between the Roman expeditionary force and its base and stores rolled the mighty tide of the Seine. If ever there was need for military genius to assert itself, it was now; and in Labienus the necessary qualities were happily combined.

As the day closed he summoned his principal officers round him, and having impressed upon them the vital necessity of prompt and strict obedience to orders, proceeded to lay his plans. The vessels brought from Metiosedum (*Melun*) were placed under the separate command of Roman knights, who about 9:00 or 10:00 p.m. were ordered to drop downstream in perfect silence, and at a point some four miles distant to await his arrival. Five battalions, of whose steadiness in action he had some doubt, were left behind in garrison; while the remaining five belonging to the same legion were shortly after midnight dispatched up stream with all the baggage trains, with orders to make a considerable noise as they advanced. In company with this force went a number of small rowboats that had been impressed for service, and they also were enjoined to set up a violent splashing with their oars. Lastly, with three full legions, the commander himself a little later noiselessly left camp, making toward the point where his larger vessels had been ordered to put in.

The first thing here was to deal with the enemy's pickets, who everywhere lined the bank. Fortunately a violent storm had suddenly sprung up, under cover of which these were surprised and quickly mastered; after this, under the able management of the Roman knights appointed to the duty, the transportation of the army and its cavalry proceeded with all haste. Close upon dawn the enemy received the threefold intelligence that an unusual stir and excitement was noticeable in the Roman camp; that a large column was advancing upstream, where the sound of oars could also plainly be distinguished; and that a little lower down troops were being ferried across in boats. From these reports the natural inference was that the

[1] Belgic, cf. I. 1.

Romans were crossing at three separate places; and that the news of
the Aeduan revolt had so disconcerted their plans, that they were
now engaged in a general abandonment of their positions. Making,
therefore, a similar division of their own forces, the Parisii now proceeded, after leaving a sufficient garrison behind to watch the
movements of the camp opposite, to send a weak force in the direction of Metiosedum (*Melun*), merely to keep in touch with the small
rowboats in the river, and then with their principal strength advanced
northward to encounter Labienus.

That officer had meanwhile completed his transportation, and as
the day broke could plainly discern the enemy bearing down upon
him. Addressing his men, he urged them to be true to their great
traditions, and to keep before their minds the brilliant work so far
effected by the army of Gaul. Caesar himself, they should imagine,
under whose banner they had so often marched to victory in the
past, was that day present with them in spirit. The signal being given,
the right wing of the Roman line, held by the Seventh legion, at once
crashed through the opposing ranks and scattered the Gauls before
it: on the left, which was occupied by the Twelfth, though the leading files of the enemy went down like mown grass before the
deep-cutting Roman spears, the rest offered a very stubborn resistance, and nowhere was there any sign of flinching. The aged
Camulogenus could here be seen calling upon his men, and by pre-
cept and example doing all he could to rouse his followers to
devotion. The fortunes of the day still swayed in the balance, when
news of the critical state of the Roman left reached the officers commanding the Seventh: these at once brought their regiment round
into view of the enemy's rear, and then advanced directly upon it.
Still the Gauls refused to yield, and fighting to the last the whole
division was slowly surrounded and annihilated—their venerable
leader sharing the general fate. Not less complete was the destruction that overtook the garrison left to watch the camp of Labienus.
Upon news of the action reaching them, they at once marched out
to the support of the main body; and taking up a position on a certain height, which they failed to hold against the spirited assault of

the now triumphant legionaries, they became mingled with the stream of fugitives, and with no friendly cover near at hand either of woods or hills, were all cut to pieces by the pursuing cavalry.

This great achievement at once opened the road to Agedincum (*Sens*), and picking up there his army's heavy baggage, Labienus after three more days rejoined Caesar, with his forces intact and his stores unharmed.

Section IV. Alesia and the End

The Aeduan revolt had given a new and a more formidable turn to the war. Envoys from that people were already scouring the country, and by means of intrigues, threats, and gold, were busily engaged in spreading sedition. With waverers they had a short and ready method; for here the hostages left with them by Caesar were now at their disposal, and a hint of vengeance upon these was generally found sufficient for their purpose. One of their first measures was formally to invite Vercingetorix to a conference, in order to arrange for a joint prosecution of the war. To this proposal he acceded, but when at the interview the Aedui claimed the exclusive right of control, the Gallic leader naturally disputed its justice, and the matter was then referred to a General Council of the nation, summoned to meet at Bibracte. To the Aeduan capital there accordingly flocked in, not merely the chiefs, but crowds of other Gauls from every district of the country, and the question being left to popular decision, Vercingetorix was returned as commander in chief by an absolutely unanimous vote.

The only absentees from this council were the Remi (*Rheims*), Lingones (*Langres*), and Treveri (*Trèves*). Of these the first two were still loyal friends of Rome; and in the case of the last, viz. the Treveri, apart from their greater geographical remoteness, the continued pressure of German raids made it impossible to attend, or indeed to take any active part at all throughout this war, by sending allies to either side. Their summary ejection from the post of leadership was a crushing blow to the ambitions of the Aedui; and deeply bewailing their change of fortunes, they sadly missed the friendly hand so often extended to them by Caesar. Having put their hand to the plough, they could not, however, now turn back; and the pitiable sight was witnessed of two brilliant and promising young men, such as were Eporedorix and Viridomarus, being forced to yield obedience to the haughty dictates of Vercingetorix.

That chieftain, meanwhile, had entered on the new phase of the war with undiminished ardor. Each confederate tribe was required to give hostages for its future loyalty, which in every case were to be delivered by a fixed date; while the whole of the allied cavalry, estimated at some 15,000 men, was ordered to assemble at the new headquarters.[1] The existing numbers of infantry he declared to be sufficient: for, having no intention of provoking fortune by pitched battles, he trusted for final victory to an overwhelming force of cavalry, by which to isolate the Romans from every source of food or provender. All he asked was that his followers should patiently destroy their crops and burn their farms; seeing in such present personal sacrifices the sure prelude to permanent power and rule, which as soon as they were freed from the heel of the invader, would undoubtedly be theirs. As the first step toward the realization of these ambitious plans, he determined on the invasion of the Roman province by a series of simultaneous and concerted attacks. The Aedui and their clients the Segusiavi,[2] situated immediately beyond the Roman frontier, were ordered to raise 10,000 infantry, and strengthened by 800 mounted men, to commence hostilities against the Allobroges,[3] under the command of a brother of Eporedorix. Farther west the Gabali,[4] and the more southern districts of their

[1] Huc may indicate a proper name obliterated in *denique*. Cf. 66 init.
[2] Index. Capital Lyon.
[3] I. 6.
[4] Between Auvergne and the Cevennes.

overlords the Arverni (*Auvergne*), were launched upon the lands of the Helvii (*Viviers*);[5] and in the same way the powerful Ruteni (*Rodez*) and Cadurci were ordered to raid the Arecomican section of the Volcae (*Nimes*). Though, however, threatening war, the Gallic leader was not unmindful of any opportunity to treat; and in the case especially of the Allobroges, whom he conceived to be not quite yet settled down again after their recent rising, he made every effort to secure an alliance, plying their leaders with lavish promises of gold, and their government with the tempting prospect of future supremacy in the Province.

To meet the manifold exigencies thus created, a force amounting in all to two-and-twenty battalions[6] had been hastily assembled in the Province by L. Caesar, a staff officer of the governor's, and was now being cautiously distributed along the lines of danger. The Helvii, without waiting for reinforcements, determined to take measures for themselves, and advancing to meet their armed neighbors, suffered crushing disaster, losing in the battle one of their most prominent leaders, C. Valerius Donnotaurus, a son of the well-known chieftain Caburus, besides a host of others. After this, being no longer able to keep the field, they were driven into the shelter of their walled towns. On the other hand, the Allobroges lined the banks of the Rhone with strong military posts, and by every means in their power prepared to defend their lands. Caesar's chief anxiety lay in the enemy's marked superiority in cavalry. To redress this inequality it was now useless to look to either the Province or Italy, since all communication with both was cut: and under the circumstances he resolved to enlist as mercenaries some of the German tribes beyond the Rhine, whose pacification he had effected in previous campaigns. In reply to his summons these quickly dispatched to the seat of war one of their composite forces of cavalry and light infantry, the combination of which is so peculiarly characteristic of that race.[7] These

---

[5] VII. 7.
[6] Probably 10,000 men.
[7] I. 48.

were found on arrival to be but poorly mounted,[8] and in order to remedy the defect, the officers of the legions, the many Roman knights engaged on service, and the time-expired men of the army were ordered to change horses.

Meanwhile the enemy had left the district of the Arverni, and strengthened by the arrival of the new cavalry levy which had been called up from all the country, had effected a reconcentration of their troops. Caesar at the time was moving along the southern frontier of the Lingones (*Langres*), making for the country of the Sequani (*Besançon*), so as to be in a position more readily to aid the threatened Province (*Provence*). It was an opportunity not to be lost. Anxious to employ that branch of his army in which he so conspicuously excelled, Vercingetorix placed himself in three separate camps some ten miles distant from the Romans, and then summoned his cavalry officers around him. Explaining the whole military situation as he conceived it, he declared that at last the hour for a crowning victory had struck. The liberation of their country from the hated invader, so far at any rate as the present moment was concerned, was already accomplished: of that the flight of the Romans to the Province and their hasty evacuation of Gaul were convincing proofs. But if they wished to enjoy a future of undisturbed peace and security, much yet remained to be done; for unless prevented, the Romans would return with stronger forces, and then war would once more devastate the land. "What, therefore, we have to do," he continued, "is boldly to attack their column while hampered with its march. If the infantry of the legions attempt to go to its defense, the time so wasted will only hinder their own advance: if, on the other hand, as I confidently expect, they resolve to abandon stores and baggage and seek merely to extricate themselves, then it becomes an open question whether the loss of all the accessories of an army will be more damaging in its results than that of its prestige. I purposely omit all reference to their horse, because you will, I'm sure, agree with me that that force has not the courage

[8] IV. 2.

to show itself a yard outside the column; but to give you greater confidence in your attack, I propose to take post with the infantry of the line immediately in front of camp, where our presence will remain a constant menace to the enemy." His words were greeted with hearty acclamation by the troopers, who at once demanded that a solemn oath should be administered, that anyone who failed to ride twice through the enemy's column should henceforth be counted a homeless man, without a roof to his head, without welcome from either children, parents, or wife.

The proposal was accepted, and all present bound themselves by its terms. The next day, accordingly, Vercingetorix formed his cavalry into three separate divisions, and while two of these showed themselves in hostile line against the two flanks of the advancing Romans, the third opened an attack upon their front. The enemy's new tactics were at once reported to Caesar, who forthwith ordered a similar distribution of his mounted force, and then gave the word for a general advance against the enemy. Brisk fighting followed at each of the three points, during which the Roman column was halted and the baggage trains withdrawn within the legions. Where the progress of the action demanded it, and where the enemy's weight of numbers pressed too heavily against their weaker opponents, the infantry of the line stood ready to relieve the strain, and was at once pushed up in support. This checked the Gallic pursuit, and also by the confidence which their presence inspired stiffened the fighting spirit of the cavalry. At length the squadrons of German auxiliaries succeeded in gaining the ridge of some hills flanking the Roman right; whereupon they cleared the enemy off the heights, and then pursued them with heavy slaughter down to the neighborhood of the river, where Vercingetorix with his infantry had taken post. Seeing this, the other two divisions felt their position to become untenable, and fearful of being surrounded, broke into an abandoned flight. An indiscriminate massacre followed, during which several important prisoners were taken, among the most distinguished being three Aeduans who were brought before Caesar. These were their cavalry commander, Cotus, the recent rival of Convictolitavis in his contest for the chief magistracy; Cavarillus, who had succeeded Litaviccus, after that chieftain's treacherous revolt, as head of the Aeduan brigade of infantry; and lastly Eporedorix, a famous captain, who had led the Aeduan armies in their ancient wars with the Arverni before Caesar's arrival in the country.

His cavalry routed on all sides, Vercingetorix with his main force had withdrawn from his position before his camp, and leaving word for his convoys to get under way and to follow with all speed, set his army in motion for a city called Alesia (*Mt. Auxois*), the principal stronghold of the Mandubii (*Côte-d'Or*). Caesar merely waited to park his baggage on the nearest high ground under two out of his ten legions, and then, as long as daylight served, followed the retreating host, whose rear he further thinned by something like three thousand men. The next day he camped outside Alesia, and having reconnoitered the position, addressed his troops on the present position of the campaign. The enemy, he pointed out, were broken and dispirited by the overthrow of their mounted troops, that branch of their army on which they had chiefly relied; and bidding his men therefore accept cheerfully the task that now confronted them, he began his preparations for the siege.

The town of Alesia, at which the two rival armies had now met for the final conflict, was perched on the summit of a high plateau, so steep that its capture otherwise than by investment was practically impossible; while on two sides it was washed at its base by streams. Beneath the town, at one end,[9] stretched an open plain some three miles in diameter: on every other side the place was girt by a circle of lofty hills, which, withdrawn a little distance from the main rock, rose to an equal elevation. Immediately below the ramparts at their eastern bend, the enemy had entirely occupied the hill with their numerous camps, the approach to which was guarded by a ditch and walled enclosure, six feet high. To capture so formidable a stronghold, the siege lines as traced by the Roman commander measured eleven miles in circumference. His main camps had been entrenched on

[9] The western.

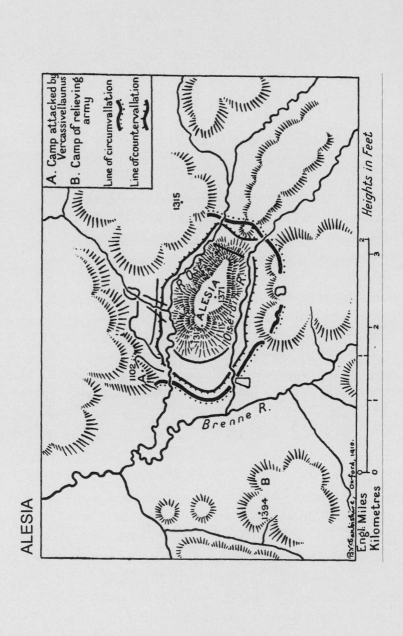

ALESIA

A. Camp attacked by Vercassivellaunus
B. Camp of relieving army
Line of circumvallation
Line of countervallation

Heights in Feet

Engl. Miles
Kilometres

By Bartholomew, Oxford, 1910.

carefully selected sites, and twenty-three smaller redoubts linked up the chain of works. In these, detachments, to meet any sudden sally from the enemy, were on duty throughout the day; while at night a line of sentinels with strong supports covered all approaches.

These works had advanced some little way toward completion, when a cavalry engagement of more than ordinary consequence occurred in the plain which, as already indicated, broke the circle of hills for a space of three miles from one terminal to the other. Fiercely contested on either side, the battle inclined against the Romans, when Caesar ordered up the German auxiliaries as reinforcements; at the same time, in view of a possible sortie by their infantry, he formed his legions in battle array on ground in front of camp. This action having restored the shaken courage of the horsemen, by enabling them to feel reserves were close at hand, the enemy was routed from the field, and in their flight being hampered by their own unwieldy numbers, were crushed together at the gates, which had been left too narrow. With eager impetuosity the Germans continued galloping on to the line of fortifications, sabering all whom they encountered: in many cases they even sprang down from off their horses, and strove to force their way across the ditch and to scale the wall. To support his daring troopers Caesar found it necessary to order the legions, in position just beyond the ramparts, to move a little farther forward. Meanwhile the panic had spread to the main body of the Gauls inside their lines, who, believing that the advancing wave of Germans would soon reach themselves, now rushed to arms: some in their terror even broke away into the town, so that Vercingetorix, to prevent a general denudation of his camps, ordered every gate to be closed. In the end, with the ground strewn with dead, and numbers of horses prizes by their side, the triumphant Germans rode back to camp.

The Gallic leader now determined to appeal to his countrymen outside, and for this purpose to send out of the beleaguered city under cover of darkness, before the lines of circumvallation were drawn quite tight, the whole of his mounted troops. Issuing his final instructions at the moment of departure, he bade them hasten home to their respective governments, and there raise every man capable of bearing arms in his country's cause. His own great services to that cause were then proudly enumerated; and the horsemen were charged to deliver his final message to his people, which was not to desert their adopted leader, nor abandon to the will of a merciless foe one who had earned some right to be called the Liberator of Gaul. The urgent need of promptitude was also strongly emphasized, and his hearers were reminded that any failure here would cost the lives, not only of himself, but of 80,000 chosen men besides. A close calculation of the food stocks then in garrison might, he concluded, give thirty days' respite; or perhaps, by practicing the strictest economy, a little longer than this. Thus enjoined, the knighthood of Gaul started on their adventurous journey, and through a gap in the lines where the Roman works were still incomplete, stole out into the night. Left to himself, their leader's first business was to direct every private store of grain to be surrendered at headquarters: disobedience to this command was to be punished by death. The livestock in the town accumulated by the Mandubii in big droves he divided up as it stood; and henceforth the distribution of corn was placed on a regular footing, and rations issued both in meager quantities and at long intervals. At the same time the fighting forces were all withdrawn from their previous position on the eastern declivity of the hill to the interior of the town; and having effected these measures he set himself to wait in patience for the expected succors from Gaul, and meanwhile made every preparation for the end.

These important movements on the part of the enemy were all reported to Caesar by prisoners and deserters; and in view of the new and critical situation which they created, the following system of defenses was now devised. A large 20-foot ditch, the sides of which were dug perpendicular, making mouth and base of equal width, was first constructed round the city; behind this the remaining fortifications, for a reason connected with the peculiar conditions of the blockade, were then withdrawn for a distance of 700 yards.[10] For

[10] The MSS. read 400 feet, but Napoleon's excavations are said to require a correction to 400 "paces," i.e. 700 English yards.

inasmuch as a very wide circuit of country had of necessity to be embraced, it was not always possible upon such extended lines to maintain an unbroken cordon of troops; and some means had therefore to be found, both of guarding against surprise by night from superior numbers of the enemy, and of protecting the troops by day when engaged upon the works from the harassment to which they would otherwise have been exposed. With this interval, then, two parallel trenches, each 15 feet wide and the same in depth, were next dug round the position; of which the interior, where it traversed the low-lying and open sections of the ground, was filled with water drawn from the neighboring streams. In rear of these came the ramparts formed of mound and palisade, 12 feet high in all, surmounted by a crenellated parapet, with large antler-like branches springing from the juncture of the mound and breastworks to break any rush by the enemy; while at regular intervals of 80 feet, the entire *enceinte* was punctuated with a series of stout wooden towers.

All this entailed a vast amount of labor, and imposed a multiplicity of duties upon the troops. Day by day, timber had to be cut and carried, provisions to be collected and transported, immense siege works to be erected; and as these undertakings frequently involved long journeys from camp, it was inevitable that the Roman forces available for the purpose should become greatly reduced. In addition, as was only natural, the Gauls made periodic attempts to test the strength of the fortifications, and, debouching from several gates at once, would deliver a spirited attack upon the lines. It was soon plain to Caesar that, in order to husband his troops, and the better to economize the defense, artificial obstructions of a still more extensive and complex description were required. These he proceeded, therefore, to construct as follows. Trunks of trees, or boughs of exceptional strength, were cut down and their heads lopped and sharpened to a point. Ditches, 5 feet deep, were then everywhere dug about the ground, into which the timbers so formed were dropped, and after being firmly fastened at the base, to prevent their being wrenched aside, were left to stand with their lateral branches just resting above the soil. These being arranged in rows of five, and tied and lashed together into a single set, anyone who was then unfortunate enough to trespass upon what the troops facetiously termed their "boundary stones," found himself impaled upon spikes of the most deadly nature. In front of these, set zigzag fashion in the form of a quincunx, a number of pits were next dug out, each 3 feet deep, with sides slightly converging inward. Into these, after their upper ends had been sharply pointed and hardened off in the fire, smooth stout logs, of about the diameter of a man's thigh, were lowered, with 4 inches or less left standing above the ground; and a foot or so of each hole having been filled in and stamped down to secure firmness at the base, the rest was overlaid with brushwood and brambles, so as the more perfectly to disguise the trap. The rows of this form of entanglement were placed eight deep, 3 feet separating each; and the nickname given them by the troops, from a fancied resemblance to the flower, was that of "lilies." As a last obstacle, the ground in front of these was planted thick with small wooden pegs, dug down to their full depth of 1 foot, but bearing on their heads a highly formidable iron barb, which once more, in the rough language of the soldiery, were to serve as "spurs" to their opponents.

Such then was the system of defenses that formed the Roman lines of contravallation against the Gauls under Vercingetorix in the town; and as soon as it was completed a similar system in all respects was at once constructed as lines of circumvallation against the anticipated succors from without. These last were drawn in accordance with the natural features of the ground, and embraced a circuit of nearly fourteen miles. In this manner Caesar confidently believed that his rear was sufficiently fortified against any attack that might be made upon it; yet in spite of this, in view of the possibility of having to abandon the blockade under circumstances fraught with danger to himself, a standing order was maintained that all sections of the army should keep constantly by them thirty days' rations both of food and fodder.

While the Romans were thus toiling at Alesia, the Gallic nation was preparing for its great counterstroke. A national assembly of all the more distinguished chiefs was summoned, at which it was decided to modify the original proposals of Vercingetorix; and in lieu of a mobilization of the adult population of the country, to make each of the allies responsible for a definite number of combatants. The reason for this was that in a mixed multitude of the sort proposed it would be impossible either to enforce discipline, maintain a tribal organization, or find sufficient food. Upon the Aedui, therefore, and their allies, 35,000 men were jointly levied: they included the Segusiavi, Ambivareti, Brannovican Aulerci, and Blannovii. The same number was demanded of the powerful Arvernian confederacy, viz. the Eleuteti, Cadurci, Gabali, and Vellavii. Twelve thousand each formed the quota of the Sequani, Senones, Bituriges, Santoni, Ruteni, and Carnutes; 10,000 that of the Bellovaci; 8,000 that of the Pictones, Turoni, Parish, and Helvetii; and 5,000 from each of the Ambiani, Mediomatrici, Petrocorii, Nervii, Morini, and Nitiobriges. The Aulerci Cenomani contributed a similar number, the Atrebates 4,000, the Veliocasses, Lexovii, and Eburovican Aulerci 3,000 apiece, the Raurici and Boii 2,000 each; and lastly, the maritime states of the West usually known as Armorican, a title embracing the Curiosolites, Redones, Ambibarii, Caletes, Osismi, Veneti, Lemovices, and Venelli, sent a combined contingent 30,000 strong. Out of this list, the Bellovaci (*Beauvais*) failed to make good their engagement, on the ground that they preferred to make war independently on the Romans, and were not disposed to recognize authority; afterward, however, in deference to an earnest appeal from Commius the Atrebatian, a trusted friend of the tribe, they consented to furnish 2,000 warriors.

The name of this last chieftain will doubtless have come as familiar to the reader, who will have recalled that in previous summers he had been loyally and usefully employed in Caesar's service across in Britain. In recognition of this conduct the Roman governor had exempted his state from the ordinary charges of subject countries, restored to it a local independence both of public and private rights, and incorporated under its sway the neighboring people of the Morini. But the chance of winning back their freedom, and recovering their ancient military renown, had so powerfully united all ranks, that, indifferent alike to the claims of gratitude and the recollection of past friendship, men now flung themselves into this war with a passion and abandonment that nothing could surpass. The result was shortly seen when 8,000 cavalry and some 240,000 infantry stood ready to march, for the seat of operations. In a grand review held in the country of the Aedui the official numbers were checked and the officers appointed. The supreme command was divided between four great chieftains, Commius the Atrebatian, the two Aeduan leaders Viridomarus and Eporedorix, and an Arvernian named Vercassivellaunus, a cousin of Vercingetorix. These in turn were supported by elected representatives of each tribe, who formed a central and consultative body for the general supervision of the war. In buoyant spirits and lighthearted gaiety the vast assemblage now started for Alesia; nor was there in its ranks a single man who questioned the result. Arguing that the Romans would now be caught between two fires, they were satisfied that these could never face a desperate sally from the town on the interior lines of circumvallation, and at the same time endure the sight of squadron after squadron and regiment after regiment deploying from outside.

Meanwhile at Alesia itself the covenanted day for the appearance of the relieving force had come and gone: supplies were exhausted, and no ray of light as to what was passing among the Aedui had as yet penetrated to the city: a council of war was summoned, and a discussion opened on the final chapter of the siege. Amid a multitude of counselors, some urging surrender, others a bold and vigorous sortie while strength remained, there stood forth one whose speech, owing to the very brutality of its sentiments, deserves recording. This was a certain Arvernian named Critognatus, a man of noble extraction and wide influence, who now rose to address his fellow chiefs as follows:

"I am not concerned, gentlemen, to discuss the opinion of those among us, who, by a gross abuse of language, gloss over, under the specious title, of capitulation, what is nothing less than slavery of the most degraded kind. Such men, in my poor judgment, are little better than renegades, and should find no seat in the council chamber of their nation. Rather let me deal with those who favor an immediate sally; for in their advice, so eagerly welcomed by yourselves, I gladly recognize the note of ancient greatness.

"To be unable to endure a little hunger shows surely a pusillanimous, not a heroic spirit; and men to lead a forlorn hope can always more readily be found than those who will suffer and not complain. Were it merely a question of sacrificing our own lives, the proposal under consideration would have my approval—so much self-esteem you may safely grant me—but, as it is, any measures that we form at the present juncture must inevitably involve the rest of Gaul, which, in obedience to our appeal, has risen to our aid. Suppose we now decide to make of our 80,000 men a single hecatomb; what stomach for a fight, think you, will our friends and relatives possess, when they see the battlefield already become a shambles? I appeal to you not to rob deliberately of your assistance those who, for your sakes, have boldly hazarded their all; nor, by an act of thoughtless impulse, or from inability to face hardship, sacrifice the future interests of your country, and thereby rivet chains of bondage upon her people such as time will never break. What is the motive that prompts to such a counsel? Is it that you question either the sincerity or the courage of our supporters, simply because they are overdue? Then, pray, turn your eyes in the direction of those Romans yonder, toiling so desperately upon those outer works, and ask yourselves whether they can be doing that for fun. Granted that where communication is cut, and no message can reach us from outside, absolute proof of the truth of what I say is not attainable; yet, that the relieving force is on its way is surely evident from the feverish haste of those who, night or day, never lay aside their tools. What, then, you say, is my advice? Why, simply to do what our great ancestors did, in a war that for importance cannot for a moment be compared with this,—I mean that with the Cimbri and the Teutones. There, when they were no longer able to keep the field, but cooped within their walls were haunted by the same grim specter of starvation, they kept themselves alive by devouring the bodies of all whose age unfitted them for war, and by so doing staved off surrender. Such a policy, even did it lack a precedent, it would in my opinion be an honor to initiate, and to hand down for imitation to posterity. For what parallel can be drawn between that old invasion and today's? The German hordes, after devastating the land of Gaul and working incalculable mischief, at length passed on in search of other victims; our laws, our constitution, our lands, our liberties, they left intact. The Roman invader, on the other hand, has no such object. That which brought him here was petty jealousy of another nation's greatness, a nation of whose strength and chivalry in war he had heard the praises; and he will never rest till he has firmly entrenched himself upon its towns and villages, and fixed his accursed yoke, that nothing can shake off, upon its freeborn sons and daughters. Such indeed is the policy that has inspired every war that they have waged; and if its fruits today in distant lands are unfamiliar to you, you have merely to cast a glance upon the present state of Southern Gaul, where, in the Roman Province that has been established, ancestral laws and systems have been rudely overturned, and under the iron heel of a Roman governor all liberty has been trampled in the dust for ages."

A vote being taken after this speech, it was resolved that all whose age or bodily infirmities incapacitated them from active service should immediately quit the city, and that Critognatus's proposal should be kept only as a last resort. Should circumstances, however, compel it, and should the Gallic reinforcements still delay, then, rather than submit to terms of peace and capitulation, his plan was to be adopted. Feeling, moreover, that the Mandubii were responsible for the presence of the noncombatants in the fortress, they forced that people to share the fate of their wives and children; and these, on arriving outside the Roman lines, addressed the most piteous appeals to the troops to take them as their slaves, provided only they gave them food.

Strongly picketing all the ramparts, however, Caesar gave the order that none were to be admitted.

Meanwhile the Gallic army under Commius and his compatriots, destined for the relief of Alesia, had reached the environs of that city, and seizing an outlying hill, not more than a mile from the Roman works, had entrenched itself upon it. On the morrow after their arrival, their cavalry descended to the open plain, which, as will be remembered, intervenes for a space of three miles between

the two converging lines of heights, and filled it from end to end:
their infantry also at the same time moved out in force, taking cover
among the adjacent hills. As all the low-lying ground was in full
view of Alesia, the garrison no sooner beheld their friends swarming
in the valley below, than rushing to get a sight of the auspicious
event, they abandoned themselves to an ecstasy of joy. The gates
were flung open, and once more the fighting forces moved out to a
position before the town; where filling the first of the Roman
trenches with fascines and rubbish, they made every preparation for
a sally or other similar effort.

On the Roman side Caesar had long perfected his arrangements,
and every section of the army having had its proper quarters assigned
it along both the outer and the inner lines, each man was able, at a
moment's notice, to go straight to his individual station on the walls.
The hour for action, therefore, having come, the Roman commander ordered his cavalry to advance from camp, and at once to
engage the enemy. From their respective points in the huge amphi-
theater of hills the various Roman camps looked down upon the
field of battle, and thousands of legionaries now took up their stand
to watch with straining eyes the fortunes of the fight. Interspersed at
intervals among the Gallic horse were archers and other light-armed
skirmishers, valuable alike for the assistance they could give their
own men at a critical moment, as also for breaking a charge from the
opposing cavalry. The Roman troopers suffered heavily from these
sharpshooters, and large numbers had to leave the field. In a little
while the Gauls became assured that in sheer fighting qualities they
were the superior of their opponents, while numerically of course, as
they could see, they far outdistanced them. From both sides, therefore, of the combatants, both from those who were so closely
immured within the iron ring of the Roman siege lines, and from
those whose work it was to pierce this ring, fierce war cries now rent
the air, each answering each, as all parties strove to nerve their cham-
pions to the fray. On an arena which was commanded by every eye,
and on which, therefore, no act of special gallantry or its reverse
could escape detection, the eagerness to win applause, and the dread

of being branded as a coward, were powerful incentives to either army. All through the afternoon the battle raged blindly, victory inclining now this way and now that, when, toward sunset, the Germans in a certain quarter of the field closed up their squadrons, and charging home with fury upon the enemy, drove them back at the sword's point. Their overthrow at once exposed the archers who had been acting in support, and who were now quickly surrounded and cut down. The whole line thereupon gave way, and following up their advantage, without once permitting any chance of rally, the Roman horsemen pushed their pursuit almost as far as the enemy's entrenchments. Thus the first round of the great contest was over, and its result was a cruel blow to the new hopes of the besieged; they had moved out to witness a victory, and it was with heavy hearts and premonitions of ultimate defeat that they now regained the town.

After a day's interval had elapsed for the adequate preparation of fascines and scaling ladders, the Gauls once more issued from camp, and about midnight noiselessly made their way toward that portion of the Roman works that spanned the low-lying flats. There, startling the night with a shout that echoed up to the besieged and was meant to apprise them of their advance, they suddenly opened upon the Roman guards a tremendous fire of slingbolts, arrows, and stones, intended to sweep them from, the ramparts; and then, covered by this, proceeded to throw down their fascines and to make ready for escalade. At the same instant Vercingetorix's bugle call was heard answering from the town and the besieged commenced to move down the hill. The alarm found the Romans in no wise unprepared; for, since every man from previous practice knew instinctively his position on the walls, they at once advanced to the lines, where, by means of the various kinds of ammunition that been accumulated for the purpose, they endeavored to keep down the assailants' fire. The darkness being all but impenetrable, the number of wounded men on either side rapidly increased, the greatest damage being caused by the artillery. The part of the lines chosen for the assault by the enemy was under command of M. Antonius and C. Trebonius; and these officers, to relieve the great pressure upon the defenders now from time to time withdrew battalions from the nearest forts and dispatched them to the point of danger.

Generally speaking, it was only while at a distance from the works that the fire of the Gauls, owing to their weight of numbers, proved so destructive: at closer range it rapidly died down before the manifold obstructions that barred their way. As they advanced, many, to their dismay, tripped upon the "spurs" that everywhere studded the ground; others tumbled into the pits, and were forthwith spitted upon the "lily" heads; others, again, who survived these perils, were thrust through with the great siege pikes wielded from the rampart and towers, and fell back into the ditch. So it continued till dawn, the enemy's wounded steadily mounting up, and the defenses still unbreached. With daylight, however, they became anxious lest their unshielded flank should be turned by a descent in force from the camps above, and hastily retreated to their lines. As to the concerted attack from within, the assailants here wasted so much time in filling up the outer trenches, and in getting into position the various instruments of breach which they had so carefully prepared beforehand, that before they could come within effective range of the Romans the report arrived that the others had departed. Their cooperation thus proved abortive, and they returned to the town without result.

Thus the Gauls had twice essayed the task before them, and twice they had conspicuously failed. Before entering on a third attempt, they resolved to summon to their assistance the advice of those acquainted with the neighborhood, and to make a careful study of the position and fortification of those Roman camps that lay upon the heights. On the north side there rose a hill, the formidable dimensions of which had prevented the Roman engineers from completely embracing it within their lines; and the camp here formed had perforce to be left in a somewhat critical position, on a gently falling slope. This camp was occupied by two legions, under command of C. Antistius Reginus and C. Canninius Rebilus, two of Caesar's generals of division. Having therefore acquainted themselves through their scouts with the character of the surrounding country, the enemy's leaders proceeded to form a picked body of

60,000 Gallic infantry, drawn from such tribes as were generally considered the hardest fighters; and a plan of action and the method of carrying it out having been secretly agreed upon, it was arranged to make their approach as nearly as possible at the hour of noon. The leadership of this force was entrusted to the Arvernian chieftain Vercassivellaunus, one of their four supreme generals and a near kinsman of Vercingetorix. Leaving camp shortly after sundown, and marching uninterruptedly throughout the night, this division reached its destination with the earliest streak of dawn, and ensconcing itself behind the shoulder of the hill that has been already mentioned, lay down to rest after its long fatigue. As soon as their commander judged it close to midday, he once more set his men in motion for the particular camp that has been described; while simultaneously the Gallic cavalry advanced from its main position toward that section of the works that crossed the plain, and their other forces showed themselves outside the lines.

Each of these movements was plainly discernible by Vercingetorix from his watchtower in Alesia, and accordingly he at once moved out to support the main attack: fascines, poles, battery sheds, hooks for breaching the rampart, and the various other requisites for a successful sortie, previously prepared for the purpose, were now brought up. Thus at a single moment from end to end of the Roman lines the roar of battle broke upon the ear. The enemy, made desperate by past failure, were resolved to leave no stone unturned, and with sure judgment swooped upon every weak spot in the defenses. With such extended lines to guard, the Roman strength was necessarily much divided, nor was it easy to meet adequately the manifold demands that were made upon it. Not the least of the many disconcerting circumstances to which the legionaries were now exposed, was the hoarse shout of battle in their rear; they were continually conscious that their own position was dependent upon the steadfast perseverance of others; and of all tests by which human nature can be tried, the most severe is that of some peril that obstinately remains unseen.

Selecting some central point from which to survey the field of battle, Caesar stood ready to reinforce all threatened points. A common instinct told all combatants, friend and foe alike, that the hour for a superhuman effort had arrived. The Gauls knew well that, unless they could pierce and break that fortified ring, their cause was lost: the Romans saw before their eyes, with every stroke they dealt, the longed-for consummation of all their hopes. The most critical fighting occurred along the upper line of works, against which Vercassivellaumis, it will be remembered, had been dispatched. The additional strain here imposed upon the defense by the inclined position of the camp was tremendous. The enemy dividing their forces, while some threatened the battlements with their fire, others advanced to the breach under the usual formation on such occasions—the "tortoise" roof of shields; and for both operations a steady stream of reserves stood always ready. Every available man brought up his load of earth and rubbish to make a causeway, and soon not only had the Gauls a clear ascent before them to the ramparts, but by the same methods the Roman obstructions hidden in the ground were also neutralized. Strength and ammunition were both fast failing the hard-pressed troops.

On receiving information of the critical state of things in this quarter of the field, Caesar detached Labienus with six battalions to relieve the pressure. Should that fail to check the advance, then that officer had instructions to withdraw contingents from the surrounding forts, and issuing from the lines to fight an action in the open. This last measure, however, was only to be adopted in case all others failed. The Roman commander elsewhere strove to animate the defense by a personal visit to the trenches; where, appealing to his sorely harassed men not to succumb beneath the trial, he showed how on that day and on that hour hung the fruit of all their victories. On the town side, the attacking party had decided to abstain from any attempt against the lower works where they crossed the plain, as being too formidable for assault; and directing their energies against the rugged ground above, they proceeded to bring up into position the various engines of offence that they had prepared beforehand. With a murderous fire of spears and other missiles, they drove back the outposts from their place upon the turrets, and then hastening to fill the trenches with earth and fascines, strove to wrench aside the rampart and parapet with the powerful hooks they had made for the purpose.

A relieving force was at once dispatched by Caesar under the younger Brutus, quickly followed by a second under C. Fabius; and, the battle still continuing to increase in fury, he himself led up to their support a third body of reserves. This turned the scale in favor of the Romans, and the enemy being here definitely repulsed, he was able to proceed with all haste to that part of the field to which Labienus had previously been sent. For this purpose he detached four battalions from the neighboring redoubt, adding also a force of cavalry, part of which was to go with the infantry, and part to make a detour of the outer lines and to take the Gauls in rear. Meanwhile Labienus himself had found it more and more difficult to cope with the severity of the attack, and ditch and earthwork each failing to stop the advance, he rapidly concentrated some forty[11] separate battalions, taking as occasion offered from all the nearest forts, and then informed Caesar of what he conceived the situation now demanded. Caesar thereupon strained every nerve to reach the scene of action.

From their position on the heights above the enemy had a wide prospect of all the rolling country at their feet, and recognizing the approach of the Roman commander in chief from the conspicuous color of his uniform, usually worn by him in action, and the infantry battalions and cavalry squadrons following at his back, they lost no time in opening the engagement. As the two hostile lines advanced upon each other, both raised the shout of battle, a shout that was immediately taken up and echoed all down the line of ramparts even to the most distant point of the works. Discarding the use of the heavy javelin, the Romans trusted solely to their swords. The enemy maintained a stubborn fight till suddenly in their rear appeared the Roman cavalry; and fresh battalions coming up at that moment to swell the attack, the Gauls then turned and fled. The wave of fugitives broke itself upon the serried lines of horsemen

[11] So the MSS., but generally suspected.

waiting to receive them, and a fearful carnage ensued. Among the killed was Sedulius, the warrior chieftain of the Lemovices, while among those taken in the rout was the famous Arvernian leader Vercassivellaunus. Eighty-four regimental colors were brought as trophies to Caesar; and of the once majestic host that had marched to the relief of Alesia, only a tiny fraction struggled back to camp. The sight of this unresisting slaughter of their comrades crushed the last spark of hope from the spirits of the garrison, and a general retreat from the inner face of the lines now took place. This in turn reacted on those without, since immediately upon its news the entire Gallic encampment broke up in confusion and fled; and, but for the exhaustion of the troops caused by the repeated calls made upon their strength throughout an exceptionally trying day, the annihilation of the enemy must have followed. As it was, the cavalry a little after midnight was sent in pursuit, and catching up the rear guard, took heavy toll in killed and prisoners; the rest of the fugitives then scattered, and melted away to their homes.

On the morrow of this disastrous day Vercingetorix convened a meeting of his captains, and addressing them for the last time as their commander, told them that, as he had not entered on this war from motives of self-aggrandizement or pride, but solely as the champion of a downtrodden people, now that Fortune had proved ungracious, to her decision he meant to bow. But since such was to be the end, he was ready on his side, he continued, to submit himself absolutely to their decree; and they could either kill him, and so satisfy the just demands of the Romans, or they could deliver him alive into their hands. A message to this effect was sent out by the garrison to Caesar, who returned the answer that all arms must be surrendered, and every chief appear personally before him. Taking his seat at a point well within the fortified lines, a little distance from his own camp, the Roman governor then formally received their submission; the Gallic chiefs were brought out under escort, Vercingetorix was handed over as a prisoner, and all arms were thrown to the ground. The remaining Gauls, with the exception of the Aedui and Arverni, who were retained in the hope of bringing pressure to bear upon their governments, were then distributed as booty, one to every Roman soldier.

These measures satisfactorily disposed of, the Roman forces entered Aeduan territory, and at once brought that people to its submission. A little afterward envoys arrived from the Arvernian authorities to announce on their behalf an unconditional surrender; and from them a large number of hostages was demanded. The legions then went into winter quarters. The Arvernian and Aeduan prisoners, some 20,000 in all, were restored to their own people. The actual distribution of troops for the winter months was as follows. Two legions and a force of cavalry were sent under T. Labienus to the Sequani (*Besançon* and district), having M. Sempronius Rutilius attached: two under C. Fabius and L. Minucius Basilus were stationed among the Remi (*Rheims*) to watch the powerful Bellovaci (*Beauvais*); one marched with C. Antistius Reginus to the Ambibareti (*Upper Loire*), another with T. Sextius to the Bituriges (*Bourges*), and a third with C. Caninius Rebilus to the Ruteni (*Rodez*). Two more were quartered on the Aedui along the Arar (*Saône*), with the special duty of safeguarding and accelerating the supply of grain, the first at Cabillonum (*Chalons-sur-Saône*) under Quintus Tullius Cicero, the second under Publius Sulpicius at Matisco (*Mâcon*); while lastly, the governor himself decided to make his headquarters at the Aeduan capital of Bibracte.[12] In recognition of the year's campaign, a general thanksgiving of twenty days was, on receipt of dispatches reporting the events, accorded by the government in Rome.

[12] Cf. I. 23.

INDEX TO PROPER NAMES

Garumni 86
Gates 86
Geidumni 137
Geneva 5, 6
Gergovia 186, 205–14, 226
Germans 1, 20–42; 44–47; 72, 75;
    89–92, 93–100; 114, 130–33, 149;
    153–59, 167–80; 230–34, 246
German cavalry 39; 174; 230, 232,
    243
Germany 90; 121; 158, 167, 169,
    172; 230
Gobannitio 186
Gorgobina 190
Graioceli 7
Greek character, use of 21; 143;
    164
Grudii 137

Harudes I 24, 41
Helvetii 1–22, 31; 94; 170; 241
Helvii 188, 232
Hercynian Forest 169, 170
Hibernia 121

Iccius 45, 48
Illyricum 65; 72; 113
Indutiomarus 114, 115, 129,
    147–51; 153, 158
Italy 7, 26, 30; 63, 65; 67; 112; 132,
    152, 175; 183, 184, 187, 188,
    222, 224, 232
Itius port 113, 116

Jupiter 166
Jura 2, 4, 6

Labienus, T. Atius 7, 16, 43, 44; 51,
    11, 61; 75; 111; V 117, 119, 126,
    127, 131, 137, 142–51; 156, 158,
    175, 207; 224–30, 249, 250, 252
Latovici 4, 20
Leman Lake 2, 6; 67
Lemovices 186, 241, 251
Lepontii 94
Leuci 31
Levaci 137
Lexovii 74, 75, 80, 88; 241
Liger 73; 187, 191, 221, 223
Lingones 19, 31; 94; 183; 189, 230,
    233
Liscus 12–13
Litaviccus 210–15, 221, 222, 235
Lucanius, Q. 135
Lucterius 187, 188
Lugotorix 125
Lutetia 154; 224, 226

Mallius 82
Mandubii 235, 238, 244
Mandubracius 124, 126
Marcomani 41
Marius, C. 30
Mars 166
Matisco 252
Matrona 1
Mediomatrici 94; 241
Meldi 115
Menapii 47; 74, 87; 92, 103, 111;
    153, 155, 156, 158, 175
Mercury 165
Messalla, M. Valerius 2, 27